Fight for the Air

Fight for the Air

John Frayn Turner

Pen & Sword
AVIATION

First published in Great Britain in 2000 by Airlife Publishing Ltd

Reprinted in this format in 2014 by
Pen & Sword Aviation
An imprint of
Pen & Sword Books Ltd
47 Church Street
Barnsley
South Yorkshire
S70 2AS

ISBN 978 1 78346 303 9

A CIP catalogue record for this book is
available from the British Library

Printed and bound in England
By CPI Group (UK) Ltd, Croydon, CR0 4YY

Pen & Sword Books Ltd incorporates the Imprints of Pen & Sword Aviation,
Pen & Sword Family History, Pen & Sword Maritime, Pen & Sword Military,
Pen & Sword Discovery, Pen & Sword Politics, Pen & Sword Atlas, Pen &
Sword Archaeology, Wharncliffe Local History, Wharncliffe True Crime,
Wharncliffe Transport, Pen & Sword Select, Pen & Sword Military Classics,
Leo Cooper, The Praetorian Press, Claymore Press, Remember When,
Seaforth Publishing and Frontline Publishing

For a complete list of Pen & Sword titles please contact
PEN & SWORD BOOKS LIMITED
47 Church Street, Barnsley, South Yorkshire, S70 2AS, England
E-mail: enquiries@pen-and-sword.co.uk
Website: www.pen-and-sword.co.uk

Acknowledgements

I am grateful and glad to acknowledge various British official sources published by HMSO. I would also like to offer my thanks to the United States Department of the Army for permission to refer to the files of *Yank Magazine.* The Reference and Photographic Libraries of the Imperial War Museum, London, have always been helpful and courteous.

In addition, I have drawn on certain material from the following of my other books: *The Battle of Britain* (Airlife); *VCs of the Air* (Airlife); *British Aircraft of World War 2* (Sidgwick and Jackson); *Battle Stations* (Putnam, USA); *Famous Air Battles* (Arthur Barker); *The Yanks Are Coming,* with Edwin R.W. Hale (Midas UK and Hippocrene USA); and *Fight for the Sky,* with Douglas Bader (Sidgwick and Jackson).

Finally, I would like to pay sincere tribute to everyone mentioned in this book, and respectfully dedicate it to all of them.

John Frayn Turner

Contents

1 *The* Blitzkrieg *Begins*

The storm broke on 10 May 1940. The *Blitzkrieg* began. The German juggernaut thundered through the Low Countries. Enemy *Panzers* trampled the defences of Holland and Belgium, while *Luftwaffe* bombs hailed down on seventy airfields in France and elsewhere. Royal Air Force bombers and fighters went into action at once.

So sudden was the Allied withdrawal from their prepared positions along the River Meuse that they did not have time to blow up the Maastricht bridge, as they had done all the others on this reach of the river. Now the bridge was to become a threat to the retreating armies as the Germans built up a powerful force in the immediate area. Once across the bridge, the Germans would be in a strong position to cut the Allied front in two.

The order went out to RAF bomber squadrons stationed in France to destroy the bridge. But the Germans had defended their gain powerfully and ground guns kept up a barrage of fire against the attacking aircraft, while enemy fighters maintained constant patrols. Yet in spite of these defences, the RAF made eight separate attacks. Pinpoint bombing at that stage of the war and in those conditions was out of the question, however, and none of the eight sorties succeeded.

To some extent, the whole operation in Europe might depend on that one bridge, yet the umbrella of fighter cover, coupled with the ground guns, made any further attacks almost impossible. Such was the situation on 12 May, only two days after the start of the *Blitzkrieg* attack.

On that day, two separate attacks were made by two separate squadrons. First, a squadron of Blenheims delivered an attack from 3,000 feet in the face of fierce anti-aircraft fire (*flak*). Their leader described it as the heaviest he could have imagined. On approaching the target, the squadron broke formation in order to run in from several directions. But as they were bombing, the leader spotted enemy fighters and immediately called on his squadron to regain formation. They did so at once and faced the fighters, which were driven off by concerted fire. Out of the twelve Blenheims, eight returned to their base, and every one of these had been hit at least once.

That same day, the commanding officer of 12 Squadron stationed at Amifontaine assembled his pilots and called for volunteers to attack Maastricht. Every pilot stepped forward, but as only five Battle bombers were wanted, the pilots scribbled their names on slips of paper and the five crews were chosen by ballot.

The five bombers were escorted by a fighter force of Hurricanes, and leading the five was the Battle piloted by Flying Officer Donald Garland.

Flight of Battle bombers on reconnaissance. Only one man came back from a formation of five Battles that attacked the vital bridge at Maastricht over the River Meuse on 12 May 1940

Still a few weeks off his twenty-second birthday, Garland had been promoted from pilot officer only three months earlier. With him in the single-engine Fairey Battle flew Sergeant Thomas Gray, an observer with more than ten years' service since his enlistment in 1929 as an apprentice.

While the Battles flew straight for Maastricht, the Hurricanes swept the sky to ward off any opposition from enemy fighters. But as the bombers could not hope to effect any surprise, they were bound to meet heavy fire from the ground, against which the Hurricanes would be powerless. The way back – if there were one – would have to be through fast fighter formations of the *Luftwaffe*.

The bridge spanned a section of the Meuse known as the Albert Canal. As it moved into their sight through a haze of early *flak* bursts, enemy fighters put in their first appearance. The Hurricanes kept these clear of the five Battles, but the ground guns got an accurate range on the bombers, which had to fly through a blizzard of shrapnel. Even German machine-gun posts, too, joined the heavier fire.

Lashed by *flak*, the leading Battle flew on into the firing, with machine-gun bullets embedding themselves in the fuselage and the whole bomber rocking from the blast of a near-miss. Through the smoke, Garland glimpsed German lorries on the bridge as he pushed his stick down directly towards it. He dived straight through twin bursts of fire and loosed his bomb-load. In spite of the opposition, he delivered his dive-bombing attack from the lowest possible altitude and the other four Battles followed his lead.

A plume of water beside one of the supports signalled a very close drop. A lorry belched oil fumes about a third of the way across the bridge, halting the following traffic. Not that it could have continued anyway, for one of the bombs scored a direct hit, right in the centre of the bridge's roadway. The surface crumbled away and some struts collapsed. The whole bridge area became a mass of flames obscuring the vision of the Hurricane pilots high above the scene. Yet as it cleared a little they could be sure of one thing: the bridge was blown. The bridge busters had done their job. Later reconnaissance confirmed that one end of the bridge had been demolished and the structure put out of action, at least temporarily.

After 'Bombs Gone', Garland and the other pilots concentrated on their escape from Maastricht. Garland had flown them there; Gray had navigated. But on the way out, the inevitable happened. Enemy fighters broke through the screen of Hurricanes to attack the already scarred Battles. Exactly what happened will never be fully known but, as a result of either ground or air attack, four of the five bombers crashed. Garland and Gray, as leaders, attracted most enemy attention, so it was inevitable that they would be hit and killed – as they were. One Battle plunged into the river itself; another ploughed furrows in surrounding fields. Only one much damaged bomber returned to its base.

Heroic as the action had been, though, it did not stop the enemy advance for long. Two days later, the Germans crossed the Meuse at two places, one near Sedan – famous from the First World War.

At first it seemed possible to destroy the bridges they were using. Six Battles made the first attack at about 5 a.m. All returned, the pilot of one being wounded. Shortly after 0730 hours, four more Battles renewed attacks and hits were claimed on a pontoon bridge near Sedan. All four returned safely. However, the situation deteriorated, and by 1400 hours a much larger force of bombers was standing by to attack this and four other bridges between Mouzon and Sedan. Sixty-seven Battles took off soon after 1500 hours; only thirty-two returned, less than half the force. The rest had fallen to intense *flak* and German fighters. Two pontoon bridges were destroyed and another damaged, and two permanent bridges received direct hits.

During the days that followed, six crews of the Battles filtered back to their base, among them a pilot, wounded in two places, who succeeded in swimming the Meuse. Elsewhere, an observer and an air gunner had tended their wounded pilot for more than twenty-four hours, only leaving him when he died. They also crossed the Meuse to safety. But the bravery of the bomber crews was rendered of little account. The bridges were broken; so too were the French. The Germans had found other avenues for their advance.

2 *The Air Battle of Dunkirk*

Six squadrons of Hurricanes were on the Continent as Germany invaded the Low Countries. Augmented by three further squadrons, they went into action at once. On 13 May, Dowding, in charge of the RAF Fighter Command, sent out thirty-two more Hurricanes plus pilots before he decided to stop. By then the proportion of aircraft and pilots overseas was over one-third of the total strength.

The losses in the first week of that mid-May offensive amounted to twenty-two Hurricanes in combat and fifteen damaged on airfields. They destroyed nearly double that figure of German aircraft. By 17 May, exactly a week after the first attack, only three squadrons could be said to be near operational level. On 21 May, the order was issued for all the pilots and Hurricanes to fly back to bases in England, although actual events were to defer their return.

Meanwhile in Britain, Spitfires had been increasingly active. Two Spitfire squadrons had tasks outside the normal range of their duties. Number 74 Squadron had provided air cover for a destroyer bringing the Dutch Royal Family from Holland to England. And 92 Squadron detailed four of its Spitfires as fighter escort to a Flamingo aircraft carrying Mr Churchill to France on 16 May – with his message to the French that they could expect no further air fighter forces to be spared from Britain.

From 23 May, Spitfires found themselves ranged against the *Luftwaffe* in mass encounters. Flying from Hornchurch, 92 Squadron ran into half a dozen Messerschmitt 109s in the Dunkirk/Calais region, eliminating all six for the destruction of one Spitfire. Later the same day in the same area, the squadron met a large force of Messerschmitt 110s with the score-line of 17 to 3 in favour of the RAF.

Pilot Officer Alan Deere of 54 Squadron typified the pilots who flew and fought during the ensuing fortnight that culminated in the evacuation of Dunkirk. Flying from England on 23 May, he began by shooting down two Messerschmitts over Calais. Within two hours he was back over Calais climbing with his squadron to attack fifteen Heinkel 111s and nine Messerschmitt 110s. Just as they were about to sail into attack, a yell came over the radio telephone: 'Watch out – 109s!'

Convoys of Messerschmitt 109s dropped out of the skies at immense speed. The mix-up became general. But the British pilots did amazing things with their Spitfires. They destroyed eleven and damaged two without loss to themselves: not a bad beginning for 54 Squadron.

During the fight, Deere found himself on the tail of a 109 which flicked and rolled away. It dived madly for the cover of a cumulus cloud at

Lockheed Hudson over the historic armada evacuating British Expeditionary Force troops from Dunkirk

10,000 feet, with the Spitfire hard after him just beyond range. Deere, a New Zealander, dropped into the cloud, too, his flight instruments gyrating crazily having toppled as a result of his violent manoeuvres. Flashing out of the cover at 400 miles an hour, he saw the enemy 1,000 feet below him and dropped on its tail. Before he could get within range, the Messerschmitt opened all out and fled, climbing at full speed.

Unfortunately for the German, the Spitfire was the faster. At 13,000 feet Deere got him right in his sights and held him there while squeezing the firing button on his control column for ten seconds. With flames flickering around the cockpit, the enemy went down, followed by Deere, who saw him hit the ground and explode.

With three victories that day to his credit, Deere went out again at dusk to help cover the evacuation from Boulogne. Fires were raging below. A British cruiser plastered German batteries somewhere inland. But not an enemy appeared in the skies, so at 2200 hours his flight of Spitfires turned for home. On that first day, Deere had flown for seven hours and twenty minutes.

Two days later, he was flying at 20,000 feet over Dunkirk again, when the squadron attacked Junkers 88 bombers and twenty Me 110s making for two British destroyers on escort or evacuation duty. The Spitfires dived in to the attack. Deere set an enemy aircraft alight and followed it down to see it crash on a beach near Dunkirk itself. During that dive, he experienced for the first time what it was like to be attacked. For an instant he was spellbound by the sight of the tracer bullets streaming past his wings. There was a terrific bang. He was flung upside down, diving straight at the sea only 1,000 feet below, and he managed to pull out of his descent just above the surface. As he headed for home, he saw a hole in his port wing nearly big enough to crawl through, but he managed to fly the fighter to England and land safely on a flat tyre. He found that it had been a cannon shell exploding in the tyre that had upset him and all but sent him crashing into the sea. That was his first escape, but he did not really count that one. In the near future he experienced at least six more escapes . . .

Next day the evacuation of the British forces from Dunkirk had already begun and 54 Squadron went over to protect the troops from German bombers. Deere dived after a Junkers 88 at 400 miles an hour and sent it down in flames. On the following morning, he was given command of a flight and sent to patrol the beaches again. They were crowded with troops. A dense cloud of smoke from burning oil tanks blotted out the sky over the actual port. It was a few minutes after 0400 hours when he arrived with his Spitfire over the beaches. At once he began to chase and close on a Dornier 17.

Burning oil tank destroyed by the RAF at Dunkirk. Other bombs damaged railway marshalling yards

The tail-gunner of the bomber opened fire at extreme range to try to drive off the Spitfire. Unluckily for Deere, some shots hit his fighter, causing the glycol to start leaking and then pouring from it. Despite this, Deere continued to return the fire of the Dornier for as long as he could see ahead. But the Spitfire had been so completely disabled that Deere had no alternative but to make a crash-landing somewhere along the beach. He managed this, quite an achievement in the desperate circumstances, but the impact between aircraft and shoreline knocked him out. Coming round a minute or two later, Deere immediately became aware of the engine smoking furiously. Not wishing to risk being burned, he ripped off his straps, got clear of the cockpit, and sat down on the beach. At that moment, he could only curse his bad luck rather than appreciate how fortunate he was just to be alive. Deere had commanded his flight for barely one hour before being shot down for the second time in a few days.

He had actually crashed several miles from Dunkirk. The rest of that day became one long struggle for him, as he found himself one small part of the mass British retreat. He had never seen anything so terrible as the ruins of Dunkirk. He got to the evacuation beach at last and actually fell asleep. Awakened by crowds of tired soldiers milling on the beach, he took his place in the queue to get away and eventually boarded one of the rescue destroyers. After five hours of dodging bombs from aircraft, they sighted the white cliffs of Dover.

On 28 May, 213 Hurricane Squadron had their first taste of Dunkirk as they flew straight into a scene of Junkers and Heinkels on the verge of bombing British troops far below on and off the beaches. Messerschmitts were acting as escorts. From that moment on, both 213 and 242 (Canadian) Squadrons became airborne four, five, even six times a day. In these hectic hours, the two squadrons totalled twenty-six Dunkirk victories at a cost of nine Hurricanes and five pilots.

The whole of 242 Squadron successes in this phase could be epitomised by the young Canadian from Calgary, Willie McKnight. He shot down an Me 109 over Dunkirk on that very first day, followed by a couple more plus a Dornier 17 on 29 May. Two days later, he got two more Me 110s and on 1 June a pair of Junkers 87s. He was killed in January 1941 . . .

The Hurricane squadrons still in France fought furiously. Number 501 Squadron was one of the last remaining in France. It was based at Anglure, fifty miles east of Paris, and operating from a forward strip at Boos, five miles south of Rouen. Thirteen Hurricanes led by Flying Officer E. Holden intercepted twenty-four Heinkel 111Ks, escorted by twenty Me 110s. Eleven Heinkels were definitely destroyed and others damaged. The Hurricanes suffered hardly any damage and all pilots returned safely.

About one-third of the 229 RAF aircraft lost throughout the whole Dunkirk period were Spitfires. The statistics of losses made grim reading. Out of 261 Hurricanes, seventy-five had been shot down or destroyed on the ground as a result of enemy activity; 120 were unserviceable or lacked the fuel to fly home and so were burnt on French airfields; sixty-six were flown back to Britain to fly and fight again. The RAF had lost Hurricanes equivalent to a quarter of its overall fighter strength.

A postscript to Dunkirk: Douglas Bader was a flight commander of 222 Squadron under the leadership of Squadron Leader 'Tubby' Mermagen. They had orders to patrol over Dunkirk.

'Take-off at 0430, sir' Douglas's batman said in his ear. Soon they were flying out over the sea. Below they suddenly saw some of the immortal 'little ships': spreadeagled across from the coast of south-east England to the Continental coast. This marked the squadron's first real introduction to the war at close quarters. The Spitfires were there to try to protect the Allied Expeditionary Force in its desperate evacuation from the beaches.

Ju 87 *Stuka* dive bombers caused a lot of trouble to the troops at Dunkirk

'Aircraft ahead.'

A squadron of Messerschmitt 110s. But they banked away from a fight and aimed for cloud cover, which they found. Douglas Bader had now at least seen the *Luftwaffe*; they existed.

The 0330-call routine continued for another couple of days or so. Take-off at 0430 hours. The black smoke spread ever wider, ever denser. Now they flew much lower than the original 12,000 feet; more like 3,000. But too soon their lack of fuel forced them to leave the skies over Dunkirk, and enemy aircraft were free to return to attack the Allied ground force still there.

One more morning. Over the beaches, Bader and the others spotted Me 110 fighter-bombers, but again the *Luftwaffe* pilots turned away. Douglas and his whole flight went after them and suddenly saw Me 109s. The enemy fired at the Spitfires. The 109s were close enough for their black crosses to be clearly seen even at over 300 mph. One enemy fighter was on fire, and perhaps destroyed. On landing, Douglas discovered that two of the squadron's pilots and aeroplanes were missing. That was all they knew at that stage. They might be safe, they might not.

June now and the patrols went on from Hornchurch. From less than a mile overhead, they watched the ever-changing epic of Dunkirk. Most of the ground forces had got away. Only the valiant rear troops remained. By 4 June Dunkirk was over. Douglas Bader flew on the very last patrol over the beaches on 4 June. The remnants of material and craters and wrecks could not fully convey what had happened there. Then he headed for home and a brief rest. They had all been on duty non-stop for over a week. Bader slept the clock around almost twice. Soon afterwards he was given command of a squadron – the Canadian 242 Squadron which had suffered such a mauling in France. The Battle of Britain lay ahead of them . . .

3 *The Battle of Britain*

The Battle of Britain was one of the crucial conflicts of the twentieth century. If Britain had lost it, the war would have been lost. Fortunately it was won – just. It lasted officially from 10 July 1940 to 31 October – 114 days. This classic battle was fought both in the air and on the ground. It comprised a balance between the longshots of the large-scale combats and the individual close-ups of the pilot's-eye-view.

Direction of the battle was vested in HQ Fighter Command at Bentley Priory. Number 11 Group in the south-east of England bore the brunt of the air fighting, but 12 and 10 Groups also played pivotal parts. 12 Group

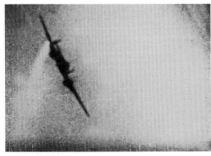

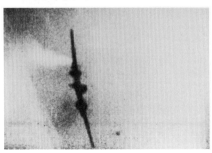

RAF pilot's-eye-view of an Me 110 at the moment of attack and immediately afterwards. Smoke from hits clearly visible

Operations Room at HQ Fighter Command. The officers on the dais look down on the plotters around the map table. The battle scene changes almost from second to second

were based some forty miles north of the Thames, while 10 Group operated from further west of England. But no matter whether the participating pilots were in 10, 11 or 12 Groups, they all contributed to the eventual victory.

The Battle of Britain created many famous fighter names: Peter Townsend, Johnnie Johnson, Bob Stanford-Tuck, Richard Hillary, Cocky Dundas, Sailor Malan, Alan Deere, Douglas Bader, Ginger Lacey, James Nicolson, John Cunningham – and many more.

But the battle could not have been fought at all without those two matchless immortals – the Spitfire and Hurricane. R.J. Mitchell has gone down in history as the designer of the Spitfire – the first of The Few. But equal credit is due to the man behind the Hurricane – Sydney Camm.

At the time of the Munich Crisis in September 1938, when war could easily have broken out, only five RAF squadrons had Hurricanes and none had Spitfires. At the outbreak of war a year later, there were nearly 500 Hurricanes in service and some 400 Spitfires. But Britain was still short of these fighters, and worse still, of qualified pilots to fly them.

It was estimated that fifty-two fighter squadrons were the minimum required to defend Britain from air attack. By the fall of France, the count was thirty-six squadrons, the majority of which were equipped with Hurricanes. What would happen?

Bob Stanford-Tuck: fighter ace par excellence

After the Fall of France and the evacuation from Dunkirk, came early probings and raids by the *Luftwaffe* during June. Bader was given command of 242 Squadron, whose pilots had had such a rough time in France and were very demoralised. By early July, the *Luftwaffe* had regrouped on French and Belgian airfields, and were ready for the fight.

The battle began on 10 July. A week or so later came the outmoded two-man-crew Defiant fighter's baptism of fire and swansong – all in one day. Nine Defiants took off from Hawkinge with orders to help protect our convoys. They were pounced on by marauding Messerschmitts, which shot down six in mere minutes. That was virtually the end of this fighter for front-line combat.

The first really large-scale phase of the battle was from 8–18 August. Hundreds of enemy bombers, escorted by fighters, attacked shipping and ports on the south-east and south coasts – from Dover to Portsmouth and beyond. Dogfights over the Isle of Wight involved 160 enemy aircraft, while 130 went for a convoy off Bournemouth. Multiply the following hundreds of times and you have an idea of just one raid on one single day: On 11 August, Pilot Officer Stevenson was flying off Dover:

'There were about twelve Me 109s diving at me from the sun and at least half of them must have been firing. Suddenly there was a popping noise and my control column became useless. I found myself doing a vertical dive, getting faster and faster.

I pulled the hood back. I got my head out of the cockpit, and the slip-stream tore the rest of me clean out of the machine. My trouser leg and

Aftermath of the attack on oil storage tanks at Shellhaven on the Thames, 7 August 1940

both shoes were torn off. I saw my machine crash into the sea a mile off Deal. It took me twenty minutes to come down. I had been drifting eleven miles out to sea. One string of my parachute did not come undone and I was dragged along by my left leg at about ten miles an hour with my head under the water.

After two or three minutes, I was almost unconscious. Then the string came undone. I got my breath back and started swimming. There was a heavy sea running. After an hour and a half, an MTB came to look for me. I kicked up a foam of water and it saw me. It picked me up and took me to Dover.'

12 August: presaging the imminent launch of enemy onslaughts on airfields, the three most forward of all were hit on this day – Manston, Lympne, and Hawkinge. Junkers 88s hit Hawkinge at teatime. This was the airfield overlooking Folkestone. Its surrounding terrain had historic connections, with Caesar's Camp within a mile or so. Now other invaders were in the vicinity. Several RAF squadrons seemed ready. But despite their numbers, the fast-flying Junkers released their loads on target, leaving hangars and other perimeter structures either destroyed or afire. Craters pitted runways, but Hurricanes somehow managed to land there – an obstacle course in piloting skill. Despite damage and the occasional unexploded bomb, Hawkinge stayed open for business – the job of servicing and refuelling fighters from further north.

Despite large losses by the enemy, they renewed attacks on Portsmouth on both 13 and 15 August. In some of the raids at this time, the Germans used between 300 and 400 aircraft. The 13th of August was

Classic shot of Spitfires in flight banking steeply in a fast turn

Eagle Day for the enemy, when the air assault would really begin in earnest and the sky begin to be cleared for the intended invasion by sea. Alan Deere was, as we have said, shot down seven times – and survived. This is what happened to him on Eagle Day, as he found himself nearly as far out as Calais:

'Bullets seemed to be coming from everywhere and pieces were flying off my aircraft. My instrument panel was shattered; my eye was bleeding from a splinter; my watch had been shot off my wrist; and it seemed only a matter of moments before the end.

Never did it take so long to get across thirty miles of sea, and never had my aircraft gone so slowly – or so it seemed. My good old Merlin engine carried me safely, however, and I had just reached Folkestone when my pursuers broke off the engagement. Two minutes later, my machine burst into flames. I was now at 800 feet. Desperately I tore off my straps, pulled back the hood, and prepared to bale out. I was still doing 300 miles an hour, so I pulled the stick back to get more height.

At about 1500 feet, I turned on my back and pushed the stick hard forward. I shot out a few feet and somehow became caught up by the

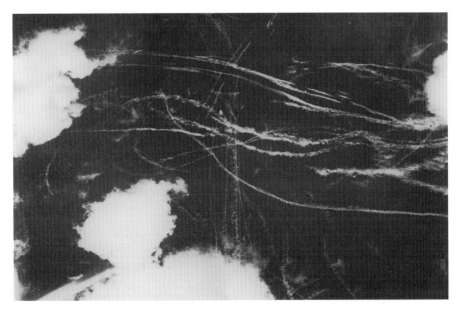

Typical trails in the skies over southern England

bottom of my parachute. I twisted and turned, but wasn't able to get either in or out. The nose had now dropped below the horizontal and was pointing at the ground, which appeared to be rushing up at a terrific speed.

Suddenly I was blown along the side of the fuselage, hitting my wrist a nasty smack against the tail. Then I was clear. I made a desperate grasp at the ripcord and with a jolt the parachute opened. None too soon. I hadn't time to breathe a sigh of relief before I landed with a mighty thud in a plantation of thick shrubs.'

On 15 August, phalanxes of bombers – hundreds of them – attacked not only south coast towns, but fighter stations, too: Hawkinge; Martlesham; Lympne; Middle Wallop; Kenley and Biggin Hill. This day marked the largest air battles so far. Five major actions were fought, on a front of 500 miles. Twenty-two squadrons were engaged and the losses were seventy-six enemy aircraft to thirty-four British. A recognisable disaster for the *Luftwaffe*. On the same day, too, Ian Gleed led five Hurricanes to meet 120 of the enemy. Flying right at this force, Gleed called to his Hurricanes on the radio: 'Come on, chaps, let's surround them'!

Next day, Flying Officer Marrs survived this:

'Petrol was gushing into my cockpit at the rate of gallons, all over my feet, and there was a sort of lake of petrol in the bottom of the cockpit. My knee and leg were tingling all over, as if I had pushed them into a bed of nettles. There was a bullet-hole in my windscreen. Another bullet spattered my leg with little splinters. About five miles from the aerodrome, smoke

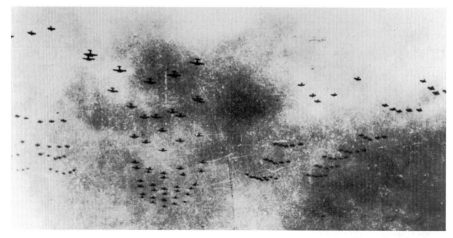

They came in their hundreds – and hundreds

began to come from under the dashboard, and I thought the whole thing might blow up at any minute. I glided towards the aerodrome. One wheel came down, but the other one wouldn't. There was nothing for it but to make a one-wheel landing. I felt jolly glad to be down on the ground without having caught fire. I hopped out and went off to the MO to get a lot of metal splinters picked out of my leg and wrist.'

And on the same day, the one Victoria Cross awarded to a fighter pilot in the Battle of Britain went to Flight Lieutenant James Nicolson. Flying his Hurricane with his squadron, Nicolson and the rest made contact with the enemy four miles over Southampton Water.

Four cannon shells hit his aircraft. One pierced the cockpit, injuring one

Hurrying to their Hurricanes: Pilots of 601 Squadron

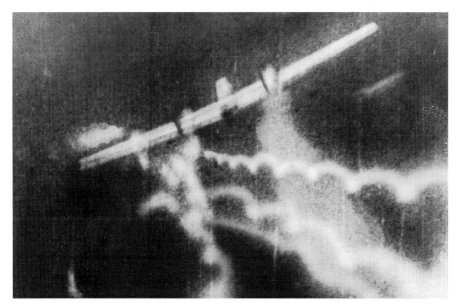

Aerial combat photograph taken by camera guns as fitted to both Hurricanes and Spitfires. It shows concentrated fire into port engine of an Me 110

of his eyes; another hurt his foot; the other two damaged the engine and set fire to the gravity tank. Petrol poured out of the tank. Flames started to spread and scorch the whole aircraft. Nicolson could scarcely see, and burns began to effect him, too. The cockpit floor was burning. He reached for the hood-release and struggled out of his seat, his limbs already severely scorched. Then he saw a Messerschmitt in front of him.

He slid back into the flaming cockpit and took hold of the stick again, while his feet groped for the rudder bar. Somehow he kept the engine going and sighted himself on the enemy. His wounded eye was getting worse. Up to his waist in flames, his hands blistering on the controls, he battled on and pressed the firing button. The Messerschmitt reeled away and hit the ground. But Nicolson was still in a blazing furnace of a fighter. Somehow he summoned up the strength to bale out. He pulled his ripcord and then passed out. He landed unconscious just outside Southampton, with bad burns on his hands, face, neck and legs. But before that, as he was still drifting down – one of the Local Defence Volunteers fired on him and hit him in his buttocks. Then they rushed him to hospital, where he hung between life and death for two days and nights: a charred, charcoal colour. Then followed recovery, recuperation, and the VC.

Next day the targets were Biggin Hill and Kenley – followed by a lull due to weather. On 24 August, phase two opened. The *Luftwaffe* unleashed the first of some thirty-five major raids on inland fighter stations and aircraft factories. Prominent among the aces at this stage was Flight Lieutenant Ginger Lacey. A chemist's assistant before the war, his

'Ginger' Lacey and his Hurricane: one of the highest scoring aces

fame rests on two things: a formidable number of successes in shooting down enemy aircraft – plus his survival after baling out of blazing or otherwise damaged fighters nine times altogether. Once he dropped two miles before his parachute opened. Nine Lives Lacey, they called him. The *Luftwaffe* lost large numbers in this fortnight of phase two – but they could afford to do so more than the RAF.

Just flying in a fighter is bad enough. But being shot at as well is far worse. Geoffrey Page returned to North Weald after a hard day's combat, while the battle was still in the balance. A message told him that his mother had phoned. He returned her call. 'I'm very worried about you, darling,' she said maternally. As he had had several thousand rounds of bullets fired at him during the day, he too had been a bit worried about himself! He listened while she went on: 'I don't think your batman is drying your socks out properly and you might catch a nasty cold . . .'

Civilians still did not know what was going on in the skies above them – despite the mass raids on airfields and towns all over the country. From the south right up to Merseyside, people were being slaughtered.

30 August: 800 enemy aircraft aimed for inland airfields. Biggin Hill took the biggest punch of a 48-hour air armada. The RAF pilots were

already battle-weary. But it was life or death. Donald Stones' Hurricane collided with a Heinkel and he somehow got out and landed safely. Others 'took to the silk' – parachuted – to survive fanatical fighting. And still others force-landed, crash-landed, or simply crashed. A direct hit on a Biggin Hill shelter trench killed officers and men – and women.

All through August, 12 Group north of the Thames had been growing more and more impatient at only being called on for defensive patrols over 11 Group airfields. Air Vice-Marshal Leigh-Mallory and Squadron Leader Douglas Bader thought the whole concept of our air strategy was wrong in many basic ways. Manston, Hawkinge and Lympne were all too vulnerable to enemy bombing on the Kent coast. Often the RAF had to climb *away* from the enemy to gain height before meeting them. Dowding left too much control to AVM Park of 11 Group, they thought. Squadrons from 12 Group were being called, but also often too late. Bader thought 12 Group should have scrambled them early – so that they could be flying south and at vital altitude to meet the oncoming enemy. He hated the idea of flying over an airfield to try to defend it. His idea was to find the enemy and hit them hard – leaving 11 Group to tackle them as they were on the retreat. This was the opposite of 11 Group thinking, which was that there was not enough time for 12 Group to do this. Was Bader's view coloured by a wish to get glory by leading a squadron – or even a wing – hell for leather? Some said so. But there was a lot in what he advocated.

Legless legend Douglas Bader and his Hurricane of 242 Squadron. Bader led the Duxford wing of five squadrons

So to 30 August. At last Bader was scrambled in time. Ten aircraft of his 242 Squadron routed 100 of the enemy. Bader dived straight into the middle of them and the rest followed. Later he said:

> 'Now, there's one curious thing about this air fighting. One minute you see hundreds of aeroplanes in the sky, and the next minute there's nothing. All you can do is to look through your sights at your particular target – and look in your mirror, too, if you are sensible, for any Messerschmitts which might be trying to get on your tail.'

Air Vice-Marshal Leigh-Mallory phoned Bader that evening to congratulate him on the squadron's success. Douglas replied: 'If I'd had more fighters, we would have shot down more of the enemy.' The losses for the day were German thirty-six, British twenty-six. The RAF were holding their own, but lacked pilots and aircraft – and their airfields were being blasted and plastered by the bombers that got through. Enemy losses were high, but they could still afford them.

On the same day that Bader began his actions in earnest, Alan Deere survived his fifth escape – this time landing right in the middle of a heavily-laden plum tree. You could say, plum in the middle . . . Then on 31 August he was nearly killed on the ground. Heinkels bombed his airfield and as he was taking off one bomb burst right in front of him. His fighter was flung upside down and Deere himself careered along the

Three gallant WAAF girls all awarded the Military Medal for remaining at their posts under heavy aerial bombardment: Sergeant Joan Mortimer, Corporal Elspeth Henderson and Sergeant Helen Turner

ground with his head scraping the soil. Flames crept in on him, too, but a colleague, Pilot Officer Edsall, managed to get the door off the plane when it stopped and haul him out headfirst.

Tom Gleave took off from Kenley on 31 August, but his Hurricane caught fire and he got badly burned. He baled out, landed safely, but thought that the services of a doctor were needed. In fact, the celebrated plastic surgery unit at East Grinstead had to create almost a fresh face for him . . .

Peter Townsend now. Climbing in his Hurricane from Croydon, he felt a blast of shot splattering his plane. The windscreen was starred, scarred with bullets and he had to bale out, too. He landed in a wood, lit a cigarette from his case, and then a policeman ran up to him and asked: 'Your name and address, please,' as if it were a minor speeding offence! The day's losses: German forty-one, British thirty-nine.

At the start of September, the airfields were really under siege daily – especially the beleaguered pair of Biggin Hill and Kenley. The Biggin buildings still standing were unsafe for occupation. The rest were rubble. So the ground staff were in the thick of it, too. Men of the RAF and women of the WAAF. Women like Flight Sergeant Gartside, hit in a raid. She said: 'Don't worry about me, I'm all right.' She had, in fact, broken her back but recovered to be invalided out of the service.

The WAAF were having to take it, all over Biggin Hill. Elspeth Henderson and Helen Turner served at a special switchboard as bombs fell very near them. Then came a direct hit, but they carried on. The building caught fire and flames spurted and spat around them. At last they left. It was the same story at each station raided: North Weald; Debden; and others. Section Officer Petters at Debden said:

> 'Fifteen seconds after the warning, we were just entering my trench – when I was hurled down four steps into pitch blackness. Pieces of the trench fell on us and my tin hat was knocked off. After the all-clear, there was a solid ring of craters around us – fifty within fifty yards of our two trenches. And an enormous one just outside our shelter.'

Some WAAF drivers had been caught in the MT yards, so dived under their vehicles. When they emerged, they found three large craters in the centre of the yard. One off-duty WAAF was washing her hair when the alarm went, and ceiling plaster fell about her. She dived under a table. Those in the Ops Room carried on coolly although the lights went out and the phones failed. There were unexploded bombs all around the WAAF quarters.

Finally, Corporal Joan Hearn was the telephone operator of her unit as bombs began to fall. She was alone at the phones when heavy bombs burst near. All the windows of the block were blown in. Glass splintered all over the floors. The walls cracked and looked like collapsing. Joan continued to report the course of enemy bombers over the phones. She went on reporting the results of plots coolly. And in one of the most dramatic messages ever sent by a woman at war, she said: 'The course of

Half-a-dozen He 111s en route for England

the enemy bombers is only too apparent to me, because the bombs are almost dropping on my head.'

The raids on airfields went on until 6 September. Next day, the enemy changed tactics and opened the third phase of the battle. They switched from their main goals of RAF airfields to try and kill London. Some say this was their fatal mistake, because the airfields were being badly battered and were vital to survival. All this time, too, the threat was imminent of invasion by the enemy. But this could not materialise without air superiority. And the *Luftwaffe* had so far failed to achieve it. Throughout the battle, as well, a running disagreement existed between the German Navy which wanted naval targets hit, the Air Force which favoured airfields, and their High Command which went eventually for the capital and other cities.

The attacks on London came in wave after wave of bombers, twenty to forty at a time. But sprays of enemy parachutes blossoming in the blue sky symbolised the price being paid. The daylight assault on London lasted at this stage for four weeks with virtually no break. From the Docks and the East End, raids spread to Greater London. On 12 September, an enemy plane penetrated the defences to bomb Buckingham Palace. It was shot down by 'Nine Lives' Ginger Lacey. One famous German photo showed a Heinkel overhead what is now Canary Wharf.

Two Do 17s flying above fires started by bombs in the London Docks area on 7 September 1940. This was the day that marked the start of the air onslaught on London

Typical Battle of Britain sky

Dowding and Park finally needed 12 Group as Leigh-Mallory and Bader conceived the idea of the Big Wing. Early in September, Douglas was first given command of three squadrons, and then five. Day and night raids on London continued. These attacks by as many as 200 bombers plus as many fighters resulted in lethal actions killing many aircrew on both sides. Several men in the case of each enemy bomber shot down. The 12 Group Duxford Wing augmented 11 Group and achieved some spectacular successes behind Bader's leadership. 'Will you patrol between North Weald and Hornchurch, Angels twenty?' the 12 Group controller asked him. Never one for blind obedience, Bader climbed hard to the south, high over Staines. This was thirty miles from Hornchurch and within 11 Group airspace. He got his Wing between the sun and two big shoals of bombers with the usual pack of escorting Me 109s. The rest of this typical Wing action is, as they say, history. Johnnie Johnson told me: 'Fortunately for Bader, neither North Weald nor Hornchurch was attacked.' Then he referred to the results of the Duxford Wing: 'Twenty enemy aeroplanes destroyed before bombing, for the loss of four Hurricanes and two pilots.' That was with three

Spitfire on patrol over the coast

squadrons. Leigh-Mallory gave Douglas Bader two more to make a Wing of five. Some sixty fighters in all.

The battle went on – and on. But the climax was approaching. Germany had to win before the autumn and winter for any possibility of invasion. The RAF pilots were feeling the ceaseless strain. And Dowding knew he was still short of them – and getting shorter.

So dawned 15 September. This is recognised as the day that the battle was won. Not over, but won. Mass raids were launched in the morning and afternoon. Combat reports of RAF pilots might read: 'Place attack was delivered – Hammersmith to Dungeness.' The RAF shot them out of the sky. Not without loss. A Polish pilot, Flight Lieutenant Shlopik typified too many. The report of his action on this day ended with the poignant words: 'This pilot could not sign, as he was killed . . .'

After midday there was a slight lull for Sunday lunch. Then the mass air armada continued. The time was 3 p.m. The battle was not yet done. Churchill was still in front of the map in the 11 Group operations room. Twenty-odd squadrons of both 11 and 12 Groups had been scrambled during the day, including Bader's five. Churchill turned to AVM Park and asked: 'What other fighter reserves have we available?' Park replied: 'There are none, sir.'

The stakes had been high. The margin incredibly narrow. By tea-time the all-clear had sounded and the tide had been turned. The enemy losses were too high. Hitler postponed the invasion indefinitely. Even so, that was far from the end of the story. Losses for October were German 318, British 144. And then the Blitz went on against London and all the other major cities for a further six months: 40,000 civilians were killed, 46,000 injured, and a million homes damaged or destroyed. But by 31 October, it was officially reckoned that the Battle of Britain was won.

4   *Attack on the* Gneisenau

Twenty-four men comprised the crews of six Beaufort torpedo bombers of 22 Squadron. The date was 6 April 1941. The time was 0420 hours. The place was St Eval airfield, Cornwall. The destination: Brest. And the target: the 32,000-ton German battle-cruiser *Gneisenau*. In one seven-week cruise in the North Atlantic *Gneisenau* with her sister ship, *Scharnhorst*, had sunk or captured twenty-two Allied ships.

Hitler dreamed of joining these two battle-cruisers with *Bismarck* in the North Atlantic, and causing such havoc that Britain would be starved into submission within sixty days. *Gneisenau* had a vital role to play in that plan. The briefing officer told the Beaufort crews: 'The result of your mission will vitally affect the war at sea.'

Nothing went right on that black, rainy morning at St Eval. The plan was that three of the aircraft carrying bombs should go in first and bomb the torpedo-nets believed to be protecting the ship, and that the other

Beaufort torpedo bombers of the type flown against the Gneisenau

three should make the torpedo strike. The torpedoes were not to be launched until after the bombing attack. But two of the aircraft carrying bombs got bogged down. In revving up to pull out they only embedded themselves more firmly. So only four planes took off – one with bombs, three with torpedoes. But the pilots of the torpedo planes did not know of the failure of two of the bomb planes to get away.

On any normal mission, that appalling start would have resulted in the four planes being recalled. But this was no normal mission. Less than a fortnight previously, a directive from Winston Churchill had laid down: 'If the presence of the enemy battle-cruisers in a Biscayian port is confirmed, every effort by the Navy and the Air Force should be made to destroy them there. And for this purpose serious risks and sacrifices must be faced'.

It was on 28 March that RAF reconnaissance planes confirmed reports from the French Resistance that *Scharnhorst* and *Gneisenau* were at Brest. At once the main weight of the RAF bomber offensive was switched to Brest. The RAF was smarting under the Prime Minister's comment that its inability to damage targets of this type constituted a 'very definite failure'.

Churchill had done the RAF less than justice; but he had appreciated the situation correctly. Serious risks and sacrifices must be faced in an endeavour to destroy or cripple these ships; the sacrifice, for instance, of a number of torpedo bombers and their crews.

But the ship-busters were not called in at once. For a week, although hampered by bad weather, Bomber Command pounded away. Two hundred aircraft took part in the attacks. But not one hit was scored. One bomb did fall near the ships but failed to explode. And it was that freak that brought the torpedo bombers into action. It became the first link in a chain of events which saved Britain from starvation.

Because of the nearness of the unexploded bomb, *Gneisenau* had to be moved out of dry-dock into the harbour while a bomb-disposal team dealt with the bomb. *Scharnhorst*, already out of dry-dock and in the harbour, was tied up to the north quay, protected by a torpedo boom. There was no room for *Gneisenau*, and as it would only be a matter of hours before the bomb was moved or made harmless, it was decided to run *Gneisenau* straight back into dry-dock when the bomb was cleared.

This was on 5 April. On the same day, a Photographic Reconnaissance Unit Spitfire photographed the harbour. This was one of the two or three decisive photographs of the war, comparable with the photographs of Peenemunde and the prototype flying-bomb V weapon.

Gneisenau had left the security of dry-dock, and lay exposed in the inner harbour of Brest. It might be possible to attack her with torpedoes. It was now or never. For beyond doubt, *Gneisenau* would be back in the safety of the dry-dock within twenty-four hours. A Beaufort strike was therefore planned for the next day.

The task was given to 22 Squadron. At first the idea was strongly opposed by the commanding officer, Wing Commander F.J. St G. Braithwaite. He was then thirty-four, a tall, impressive man, much admired by the crews under his command. He argued, correctly enough, that such an operation had not more than one chance in a thousand of success. Braithwaite, like any good squadron commander, looked at things first from the point of view of his squadron. Normally one was inclined to resist with all one's power any operational conception which meant sending one's crew on a sortie from which they had not even a sporting chance of returning. There might naturally be exceptions, but even these should offer, except in the most desperate circumstances, something like an even chance of success. A torpedo attack on a capital ship in harbour could have only one ending. Braithwaite and the crews of his squadron knew this well enough. The question was, would there be any real chance of damaging the ship?

What was the prospect facing a torpedo-carrying aircraft? The inner harbour of Brest was protected by a mole bending round it from the west. Even at the farthest point, the mole was less than a mile from the quayside. *Gneisenau* was anchored at right angles to the quay, some 500 yards from the eastern boundary of the harbour, about equidistant from the mole and the quay.

To aim a torpedo, an aircraft would have to fly across the outer harbour and approach the mole at an angle to the anchored ship. This meant exposing itself to crossfire from the protective batteries of guns clustered thickly round the two arms of land that encircled the outer harbour. And in this outer harbour, just outside the mole, were moored three heavily armed flak-ships, guarding the approach to the battle-cruiser. On rising ground behind the quay, and in dominating positions all around the inner harbour, stood further batteries of guns. As an aircraft approached the mole, over 1,000 guns would be trained on it, 250 of them of heavy calibre. In addition, it would have to face the guns of *Gneisenau* and *Scharnhorst.*

Nothing, it seemed, could possibly penetrate these defences. The density of flak that could be put down by these guns represented an impossible barrier. But suppose an aircraft did get through? As it approached the mole, under withering fire, the pilot would have to line up his aircraft and aim and drop his torpedo before he crossed the mole, so that the torpedo splashed into the water immediately beyond the mole and had the longest possible distance to run to the target.

The distance from the mole to the *Gneisenau* was not more than 500 yards. If the torpedo were dropped inside this range it would be too close; it would not have time to arm itself and settle down to its running-depth. It would thus pass harmlessly under the target and fail to explode.

Everything depended on the pilot's approach to the mole being at roughly the right dropping angle. He would have only a few seconds from the moment of sighting *Gneisenau* to the dropping of the torpedo, and there would be no room for more than tiny adjustments of course. In those few seconds, every gun in the harbour would be firing at him

Flying Officer Kenneth Campbell led the six Beaufort Torpedo bombers in their attack on the *Gneisenau*

from behind, from a beam, from dead ahead. The chances of living through those few seconds to take effective aim seemed infinitesimal. And if the drop were made, what afterwards? The pilot would be forced to climb at once to avoid the rising ground ahead. His aircraft would be silhouetted above the massed guns like a clay pigeon.

But the forces backing the operation were too strong for a squadron commander, and Braithwaite set about putting a plan into operation and making it work. The first problem was to deal with the torpedo-nets. It would be much too bitter an ending for an aircraft to succeed in its mission, and then for the torpedo to be caught in a protective net. The nets must be ruptured first. Hence Braithwaite's decision to put bombs instead of torpedoes in three of his available six planes.

Although the bombers were to go in first, he ordered the torpedo planes away from St Eval before the bombers, so that they would be in position to make their strike after the intended bombing attack on the nets.

All three torpedo planes got away safely with the one bomb plane that was not bogged down. The captains of the three torpedo planes were: Flying Officer Kenneth Campbell, Flying Officer Jimmy Hyde, and Sergeant Pilot Camp. Campbell came from Saltcoats, Ayrshire and was the youngest of a family of six. He was tall, fair-haired and good-looking, a complex character, high-spirited in play and aggressive in action. Hyde was an Australian, an experienced pilot who had completed more than fifty operations. Camp was a red-headed Irishman, wild and unpredictable. These were the men who set out on the million-to-one chance on that stormy morning.

The four aircraft took off at various times between 0430 and 0515 hours. But the weather had now upset the navigation. The only pilot carrying bombs lost his way, and eventually dropped his bombs on a ship in convoy near the Ile de Batz.

Camp also got a long way off course, and did not arrive at Brest until 0700 hours. He approached the harbour from the south-west, as briefed, crossing the Ile de Longue at 800 feet. It had been daylight for over half an hour, and he knew he had missed his rendezvous, but he was still prepared to go in.

The weather was atrocious, thick with early-morning haze and mist. He came right down to sea-level, and almost before he realised it, he found he was flying between the two arms of land encircling the outer harbour. But he could not get a definite pinpoint. Suddenly his aircraft was boxed in by flak, as he came under heavy fire from the flak-ships and shore batteries. He had little idea of his precise direction, and it was pointless to go on. He pulled up in a climbing turn to the east, and almost immediately found himself in cloud.

Camp was unaware that every gun in the harbour had been alerted half an hour earlier by the arrival of Campbell and Hyde. These two pilots had reached Brest independently soon after dawn. Both had loitered outside the harbour, waiting for the bomb explosions, unaware that two of the bomb-carrying Beauforts had failed to take off, and that the third had lost its way.

Campbell, a few minutes ahead of Hyde, began a wide circuit, watching for some sign of the other aircraft. The light was seeping in under the horizon, like a chink in a curtain. It was going to be virtually a daylight attack, and that would surely multiply the already mammoth odds tenfold. Campbell had seen no explosions, but perhaps he was the last to arrive. He had better go straight in.

As Campbell set his compass to steer for the inner harbour, as yet invisible in the mist ahead, Hyde was making his landfall. Suddenly Hyde saw an aircraft flash by beneath him. He just had time to pick out an 'X' on the fuselage – the aircraft letter. He called his navigator:

'Who's in X?'

'Campbell.'

'It looks as though he's going in. Has anyone seen anything? Any explosions, I mean?'

'Not a thing.'

'He's going in all right. I can't think why.'

Hyde continued to circle outside the harbour, waiting for Campbell to come out. He had been a long time on 22 Squadron – longer than anyone. Throughout, he had been that rarity – a pilot who coupled dash with steadiness and a strict regard for orders. There had been no explosions, so there could have been no bombs. The orders were to wait for the explosions.

Meanwhile, Campbell had brought his aircraft down to 300 feet and was aiming for the right-hand end of the mole. In the outer harbour, the cloud-base was low and he streaked along beneath it, intermittently in cloud. Ahead of him out of the mist he picked out the flak-ships. There was the mole – a thin line on the water. If *Gneisenau* was still anchored to the same buoy he was perfectly placed for a stern attack.

Campbell began his dive down towards the east end of the mole. He could see the flak-ships clearly now. Beyond the mole, a massive shadow was resolving itself into the stern of *Gneisenau*. He swung away to starboard, and then back to port, making an angle of 45 degrees with *Gneisenau*. He flattened out his dive, fifty feet above the water. The flak-ships were upon him.

He raced between them at mast height, unchallenged, squinting down the barrels of their guns. The mole was only 200 yards away. He looked steadfastly ahead, every nerve alert, steadied the aircraft, and aimed the nose deliberately. When the mole disappeared under the windscreen he released the torpedo. Aircraft and torpedo crossed the mole independently, the nose of the torpedo tilted downward towards the water. The defences of Brest were taken by surprise. Still the Beaufort was unchallenged by anti-aircraft fire.

Gneisenau towered above them like a mammoth warehouse, and there was no sign of any protective net. Campbell began to pull away to port to clear the hills behind the harbour, making for the sanctuary of cloud. In perhaps another fifteen seconds they would be safe. But the peaceful harbour of Brest had been aroused from its lethargy. The Beaufort now had to fly through the fiercest, heaviest, and most concentrated barrage that any single aircraft had ever faced or would ever face again. Nothing could live in such a wall of steel.

There was the blinding, withering fire which they had awaited and which they knew must come. Their last sight was of the flashing guns of *Gneisenau*, lighting the hills behind the harbour, the hills over which they had watched the last dawn they would ever see. The Beaufort, out of control, crashed into the harbour. What happened in those last moments will never be known. Stabbed by a hundred points of steel, the Beaufort kept flying when almost any other type of aircraft must have been brought down.

Campbell may have been killed some seconds before the crash came. Sergeant Scott, the Canadian navigator, may have tried to drag Campbell off the stick and take over. When they lifted the aircraft out of the harbour, it was said by the French Resistance that a blond Canadian was found in the pilot's seat. Campbell and his gallant crew took the secrets of those last despairing seconds with them.

What did the strike achieve? The damage was such that had the battle-cruiser been at sea it would have sunk rapidly. The Germans had to put nearly every ship in the harbour alongside to support it and pump out the water, and it was only with the greatest difficulty that they were able towards the end of the day to get *Gneisenau* back into dry-dock. Eight months later, the starboard propeller shaft was still under repair. Hitler's dream of joining the two battle-cruisers up with *Bismarck*, in the North Atlantic, and ending the war was shattered. When *Bismarck* came out, it had to face the Royal Navy and Fleet Air Arm alone.

Although photographic reconnaissance suggested that *Gneisenau* had been hit, Britain did not know for many months how serious the damage actually was. Nothing could be taken for granted and Britain had to go on hitting at this ship for the next ten months. No-one, anyway, could easily believe that the million-to-one chance had come off. The news of the strike eventually filtered through to London in March 1942.

Campbell and his crew were buried by the Germans in the grove of honour, in the cemetery at Brest. Campbell's complete crew consisted of Sergeant Scott, Sergeant Mullins, and Sergeant Hillman.

5 *Beating the Blitz*

After fighting with distinction in the Battle of Britain, John Cunningham turned to night flying as the need for night fighters rose urgently – when the Battle merged into the Blitz on London and other cities. Just how the Blitz was beaten can be illustrated through the experiences of 'Cat's Eyes' Cunningham.

His night-fighting career began in the early winter months of 1940 and his first success was on 19 November, when he destroyed a Junkers 88 over the East Midlands. By the beginning of 1941, Britain's winter weather, coupled with better defences in anti-aircraft guns, barrage balloons and night fighters, resulted in a change of enemy plans. Instead of concentrating a large number of bombers in space and time over a target, they switched to smaller groups which were scheduled to reach their targets at successive periods, in order to prolong the raids. The barrage balloons and the guns kept the bombers high, while the night fighters tackled them eagerly.

Firemen tackle the result of an incendiary raid

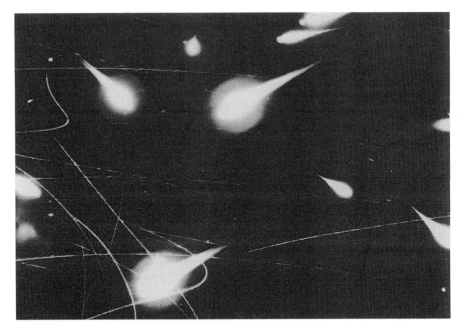

Patterns made by bursting anti-aircraft shells

By spring 1941, Cunningham had become both busy and successful. Night flying was a different, alien world where impressions were muted. The stars and moon provided his only light from above, and below the cities were blacked out completely, unless an occasional fire from enemy bombs or incendiaries broke the darkness. Yet Cunningham had to know exactly where he was all the time. A 24-year-old pilot with less than two years' experience behind him, he adapted himself and grew accustomed to this unlit universe.

When an enemy raid was on, of course, he could see the stabs of search-lights hunting out the bombers, and the curving tracer-sprays or shell-bursts far below. Or perhaps a pattern of coloured lights would dot the earth, denoting an airfield. Cunningham learned to absorb all these distant images instinctively and to react to them rationally yet rapidly.

He flew in a dim mixture of darkness and stellar sheen, at a speed approaching twice that of the enemy bombers, and he learned to recog-nise the ghostly glow of an aircraft on a bombing mission. His main job was to keep it in range long enough to make an attack. It hardly needs stressing how very difficult the art of night fighting was, but Cunningham mastered all its hazards to become the greatest night-fighter ace of all. He hated being referred to by his nickname of 'Cat's Eyes' though.

He was airborne in a Bristol Beaufighter on the night 11/12 April 1941, when base radio notified him of the approximate details of enemy bombers. Working within the network of the coastal ground control inter-

The battle by moonlight. Hurricane night fighter pilot about to take off to intercept enemy raiders in the 'Blitz'

ception stations, he continued to be guided by base radio towards the enemy until the aircraft's own radar (AI) picked them up on the small screen. With him as usual on this flight was Sergeant C.F. 'Jimmy' Rawnsley as AI operator.

This was what happened on that particular patrol, as told in the tense, technical style of the report:

'Put on to north-bound raid 13,000 feet. Final vector 360 degrees and buster (full speed).

'Told to flash (to operate A.I.) but no contact received. G.C.I. station then told us to alter course to 350 degrees and height 11,000 feet. While going from 13,000 to 11,000 a blip (flash of light in the A.I. set) was picked up at max. range ahead. On operator's instructions I closed in and obtained a visual at 2,500 feet range (checked on A.I. set) and about 30 degrees up.

'Identified E/A (enemy aircraft) as Heinkel 111 which was flying just beneath cloud layer and occasionally going through wisps which allowed me to get within 80 yards of the E/A and about 20 to 30 feet beneath before opening fire. Immediately there was a big white flash in the fuselage centre section and black pieces flew off the fuselage. E/A went into a vertical dive to the right, and about half a minute later the sky all around was lit up by an enormous orange flash and glow. Bits of E/A were seen to be burning on the ground.

'I estimated my position to be about Shaftesbury but called Harlequin and asked for a fix so that my exact position could be calculated.

'One Me 111 destroyed. Rounds fired 64.'

Cunningham made it sound easy. Flying by day in cloud was hard enough. Doing this at night was immeasurably more so. As well as good eyesight, the pilot had to possess other vital qualities for success or survival. The night-fighter pilots used to spend a short time before operations in dimly-lit rooms, wearing dark glasses.

Here is how Cunningham described one of his many operations.

'Try to imagine the moonlit sky, with a white background of snow nearly six miles below. Somewhere near the centre of a toy town, a tiny place is burning. Several enemy bombers have come over, but only one fire has gained hold. After all the excitement of my combats, I can still see that amazing picture of London clearly in my mind.

'It was indeed the kind of night that we fly-by-nights pray for. I had been up about three-quarters of an hour before I found an enemy aircraft, having searched all around the sky when I suddenly saw him ahead of me. I pulled the boost control to get the highest possible speed and catch him up. I felt my Hurricane vibrate all over as she responded and gave maximum power.

'I manoeuvred into position where I could see the enemy clearly with the least chance of his seeing me. As I caught him up I recognised him – a Dornier 'Flying Pencil'. Before I spotted him I had been almost petrified with the cold. I was beginning to wonder if I should ever be able to feel my hands, feet or limbs again. But the excitement warmed me up.

'He was now nearly within range and was climbing to 30,000 feet. I knew the big moment had come. I daren't take my eyes off him, but just to make sure that everything was all right, I took a frantic glance round the 'office' – that's what we call the cockpit – and checked everything. Then I began to close in on the Dornier and found I was travelling much too fast. I throttled back and slowed up just in time. We were frightfully close. Then I swung up, took aim, and fired my eight guns. Almost at once I saw little flashes of fire dancing along the fuselage and centre section. My bullets had found their mark.

'I closed in again, when suddenly the bomber reared up in front of me. It was all I could do to avoid crashing into him. I heaved at the controls to prevent a collision, and in doing so I lost sight of him. I wondered if he was playing pussy and intending to jink away, come up on the other side, and take a crack at me – or whether he was hard hit. The next moment I saw him going down below me with a smoke trail pouring out.

'I felt a bit disappointed, because it looked as if my first shots had not been as effective as they appeared. Again I pulled the boost control and went down after him as fast as I knew how. I dived from 30,000 feet at such a speed that the bottom panel on the aircraft cracked, and as my ears were not used to such sudden change of pressure, I nearly lost the use of one of my drums, But there was no time to think of these things. I had to get that bomber. Then as I came nearer I saw he was on fire. Little flames were flickering around his fuselage and wings. Just as I closed in again, he jinked away in a steep climbing turn.

'I was going too fast again, so I pulled the stick back and went up after him in a screaming left-hand climbing turn. When he got to the top of his climb, I was almost on top of him. I took sight very carefully and gave the button a quick squeeze. Once more I saw little dancing lights on his fuselage, but almost simultaneously they were swallowed in a burst of flames. I saw him twist gently earthwards and there was a spurt of fire as he touched the earth. He blew up and set a copse blazing.

'I circled down to see if any of the crew had got out, and then I suddenly remembered the London balloon barrage, so I climbed and set course for home.

'I had time now to think about the action. My windscreen was covered with oil, which made flying uncomfortable and I had a nasty feeling that I might have lost bits of my aircraft. I remembered seeing bits of Jerry flying past me. There were several good-sized holes in the fabric, which could have been caused only by hefty lumps of Dornier. Also the engine seemed to be running a bit roughly, but that turned out to be my imagination. Anyway, I soon landed, reported what had happened, had some refreshment, and then up in the air once more, southward ho for London.

'Soon after, I was at 17,000 feet. It's a bit warmer there than 30,000. I slowed down and searched the sky. The next thing I knew a Heinkel was sitting right on my tail. I was certain he had seen me, and I wondered how long he had been trailing me. I opened my throttle, got round on his tail and crept up. When I was about 400 yards away, he opened fire – and missed. I checked my gadgets, then I closed up and snaked about so as to give him as difficult a target as possible. I got into a firing position, gave a quick burst of my guns and broke away.

'I came up again, and it looked as if my shots had had no effect. Before I could fire a second time, I saw his tracer bullet whizzing past me. I fired back and I knew at once that I had struck home. I saw a parachute open up on the port wing. One of the crew was baling out. He was quickly followed by another. The round white domes of the parachutes looked lovely in the moonlight.

'It was obvious now that the pilot would never get his aircraft home and I, for my part, wanted this second machine to be a 'certainty' and not a probable. So I gave another quick burst of my guns. Then to fool him I attacked from different angles. There was no doubt now that he was going down. White smoke was coming from one engine, but he was not yet on fire. I delivered seven more attacks, spending all my ammunition. Both his engines smoked as he got lower and lower. I followed him down a long way and as he flew over a dark patch of water I lost sight of him.

'But I knew he had come down, and where he had come down – it was all confirmed later – and I returned to my base ready to tackle another one. But they told me all the Jerries had gone home.

"Not all," I said. "Two of them are here for keeps."'

One of Cunningham's closest escapes came in August 1941. Shortly after joining a new aquadron he took off in a Beaufighter on a night interception over East Anglia. It was, in fact, his first operational flight with his new squadron, and he marked it by shooting down a Heinkel. But an hour or so later, on the same patrol, he spotted another aircraft. After one long-range burst he found that his aircraft was overshooting his quarry and turned away for another attack. As he did so the enemy opened fire on him, piercing the petrol pipe to the port engine. Not surprisingly, the engine gave out, but Cunningham managed to get back to base and land with just his starboard engine.

So it went on. Cunningham and Rawnsley gathered decorations regularly, and became well established as the leading night-fighter team. The pilot described his sixteenth victory like this.

'There was nothing left but a hole in the ground after I went to inspect the wreckage. The combat was over in a matter of minutes. I got on his tail, gave him less than a half-second burst and he caught fire. He crashed not far from my airfield.

'The German pilot who is in hospital was thrown out as the FW began to break up. He had the presence of mind to pull his ripcord. When I landed they told me he had been taken to hospital suffering from burns.'

Cunningham disposed of one adversary without using a single bullet.

After a hard tussle, in which he had used up all his ammunition, he decided to dive on the enemy aircraft, a move that so staggered the enemy that he dived to try to evade Cunningham. The enemy, however, left it too late to straighten up again and crashed.

Gradually, ground and air radar advanced, and by New Year's Day 1944 Cunningham's successes had a certain inevitability about them. The only change was that he now flew a Mosquito. At one minute past midnight on 2 January, Cunningham shot down a fast enemy bomber attempting to raid Britain, bringing his score to nineteen. Later he said:

'We had a bit of a chase after this one – in fact we went right across the Channel to the French coast. My observer spotted it as an Me 410. It sped off homewards, taking evasive action all the time. However our Mosquito was faster, and when I came within 250 yards, right behind it, I gave it a short burst. There was an explosion and considerable flame. The bomber dived away sharply and for a moment I lost sight of it. I looked down and realised that I was over the French coast, somewhere near Le Touquet. Next moment I saw the Hun again, this time exploding in a great flash on the ground, and a big orange glow was my last sight of it.'

Needless to say, the observer referred to was still Jimmy Rawnsley. The glow was later reported to have been seen by a Royal Observer post on the English side of the Channel.

Gradually the night-bomber Blitz was beaten. The fighter pilots grew more and more experienced, and with the aid of radar to detect enemy bombers before they crossed the coast, the night fighters could be ready and waiting. Eventually the enemy turned to the V1s and V2s but these too were mastered.

6 *Hunting the* Bismarck

This is how *Bismarck* was hunted and sunk. It is a bird's-eye-view seen by RAF Coastal Command and the Fleet Air Arm. Without their help, the battleship might never have been found at all.

'I give you the hunter's toast: good hunting and a good bag.' With these words Admiral Lutjens ended his speech to the ship's company of *Bismarck*. They were heard throughout the vessel; those who could not be on deck listened to them through the loudspeakers situated in various parts of the battleship.

The time was a few minutes past noon on Monday 19 May 1941. That evening *Bismarck* weighed anchor and put to sea, taking a northerly course from Kiel Bay. It was the intention of Admiral Lutjens to raid commerce in the Atlantic, just as he had done earlier in the year, flying his flag in *Gneisenau*. Together with *Scharnhorst*, they had sunk twenty-two British and Allied ships, including *Jervis Bay*. *Gneisenau* and *Scharnhorst* were now in Brest and had already suffered damage from the attacks made on them by aircraft of Bomber and Coastal Commands. If Germany was to obtain a decision in the Battle of the Atlantic, other units of her navy had to be sent to sea, and *Bismarck* and *Prinz Eugen* were chosen. For *Bismarck*, it was to be her first and final voyage . . .

She formed the main unit of a squadron made up of the 8-inch cruiser *Prinz Eugen*, two destroyers and two mine-bumpers. After passing through the Great Belt, they moved up the coast of occupied Norway and on the morning of 21 May entered a fjord near Bergen, where they anchored. There had been little sleep on board that night, for an air raid alarm had kept crews at action stations until 0830 hours. And in the early afternoon, another alarm lasted a quarter of an hour. A little before dusk, the squadron put to sea again.

That day, an aircraft of Coastal Command, in the course of a reconnaissance of the Norwegian coast, had flown as far north as Bergen, where reconnoitring the approaches to the port, the pilot had discovered two warships, one of large size, at anchor in a small fjord. On his return he made a cautious report of what he had seen to one of the station intelligence officers. While they were talking, the prints of the photographs the pilot had taken were brought in; the intelligence officer saw that what the pilot surmised was indeed the truth. He spoke immediately with Coastal Command headquarters, who ordered the prints be sent direct.

A slight difficulty arose. The only aircraft available to take them to headquarters was that of the pilot who had just finished the patrol. Moreover, it was now evening. Nevertheless, he took off and flew south until with night fallen, he found himself short of petrol on the outskirts of

Nottingham, his home town. Here he landed and roused a friend of his, the owner of a garage and a car. They continued the journey together, driving through the night and the blackout at an average speed of 52 m.p.h. The prints were delivered at Coastal Command's headquarters in the early hours of the morning, and the Admiralty and the photographic experts confirmed the opinion of the intelligence officer in Scotland. *Bismarck* and *Prinz Eugen* were at large.

Early that same morning, the German warships were attacked by six Whitleys and six Lockheed Hudsons of Coastal Command, but the attack was unsuccessful, for the weather was very thick. Only two of the aircraft reached the fjord, where they dropped their load of armour-piercing bombs with no observed effect. Throughout that day, 22 May, the weather remained atrocious. Nevertheless, reconnaissance of the Norwegian coast was maintained from first light until dark. Every available aircraft of Coastal Command on the east coast of Scotland and the coast of Yorkshire was pressed into service.

They flew at times through a full gale, at times through dense haze and cloud extending downwards to sea level. Hour after hour they plunged into the mist shrouding Bergen harbour and the nearby fjords. It was in vain. No ships were seen, and one pilot expressed the opinion that the enemy was no longer there because 'I collided with nothing though I flew over the harbour at sea level'.

His conjecture was proved accurate at about 1830 hours that evening when the clouds above Bergen lifted for a moment. This proved long enough for a shore-based naval aircraft, a Maryland, to get a clear view that showed there were no warships there.

Sunderlands were vital as long-range maritime reconnaissance and patrol aircraft in the hunt for the *Bismarck*

Throughout that long day, *Bismarck* and *Prinz Eugen* had in fact been steaming steadily northwards, having parted company with their destroyers in the small hours. At 0100 hours on 23 May they altered course to pass through the Denmark Strait between Iceland and Greenland. By this time they were fully aware that they had been seen, but they judged that their route offered the best chance of eluding the British fleet now steaming to intercept them.

The weather on 23 May was still very bad – too adverse to patrol the Norwegian coast. Sunderland flying boats and Hudson aircraft, however, were able to cover the passages between Iceland and the Faroes and between the Faroes and the Shetlands. The Sunderlands maintained their patrol in relays from 0615 to 2115 hours and the Hudsons from 0400 to 1715 hours. The Sunderlands covered more than 2,000 miles in a single sortie; but now the weather turned against them as they encountered strong headwinds, fog, rain squalls and heavy cloud, in which severe icing developed. In addition to the Sunderlands, two Catalina flying boats covered the Iceland channel, beginning their patrol at 1300 hours, but they had to abandon the task when unbroken cloud down to 300 feet, accompanied by unceasing rain, reduced visibility to less than 1,000 yards.

That evening, HMS *Suffolk* sighted the German warships in the Denmark Strait, and soon afterwards a Sunderland and a Hudson from Iceland set off in the long twilight of those far northern latitudes to search for the enemy. The Hudson was unable to find them and returned, but the Sunderland carried on. In the meantime, the two warships had also been seen by HMS *Norfolk*. The two cruisers shadowed the enemy throughout the night.

Next morning, 24 May, another Hudson took off, and at 0554 hours sighted *Bismarck* and *Prinz Eugen* engaged in combat with HMS *Hood* and HMS *The Prince of Wales*. Low cloud made it impossible to identify the opposing forces with certainty, but it was seen that one of the ships had suffered two direct hits, the second of which had been followed by an explosion.

Meanwhile the Sunderland from Iceland had arrived in the neighbourhood of HMS *Suffolk*, and on sighting this ship saw at the same time the flash of gunfire well ahead.

'As we closed'. In his report, the captain said: 'two columns, each of two ships in line ahead, were seen to be steaming on parallel courses at an estimated range of twelve miles between the columns. Heavy gunfire was being exchanged and the leading ship of the port column was on fire in two places, one fire being at the base of the bridge superstructure and the other farther aft. In spite of these large conflagrations she appeared to be firing at least one turret forward and one aft.'

At first the captain of the Sunderland could not identify the burning ships. He turned towards the starboard column and noticed that the second of its two ships was making a considerable amount of smoke and that oil escaping from her was leaving a broad track on the surface. He went closer, and as he did so the ship on fire in the column blew up.

A few seconds later, the Sunderland came under heavy anti-aircraft fire, just at the moment when its captain was identifying the ships in the starboard column as *Bismarck* and *Prinz Eugen.* He was forced to take immediate cloud cover. When he emerged into an open patch five minutes later, the damaged ship had almost completely disappeared. He now realised she was British, though he did not learn till later that she was HMS *Hood,* as only part of the bows was showing. She sank almost at once, and when the Sunderland flew over the spot all that could be seen was an empty raft, painted red, surrounded by wreckage in the midst of a large patch of oil.

Watching the remainder of the action, the captain of the Sunderland saw *The Prince of Wales* turn away under cover of a light smokescreen and open the range to about fifteen miles. The Sunderland closed on *Bismarck* to make quite certain of her identity and then, returning to the area of *Suffolk,* exchanged visual signals with her and learned that the ship sunk was in fact *Hood.* It was then about 0715 hours.

Throughout that day, the Royal Navy continued shadowing the German ships. A Catalina of Coastal Command saw them at 1232 hours and remained in contact for two hours, signalling their course and speed to the pursuers at intervals. Coming under anti-aircraft fire, though, the flying-boat developed engine trouble which forced it to return to base. This was the last contact with the enemy made by Coastal Command that day. Both *Norfolk* and *Suffolk* with *The Prince of Wales* held on. HMS *King George V* and the aircraft carrier *Victorious* were now rapidly approaching. The Commander-in-Chief of the Home Fleet was flying his flag in *King George V.*

On board *Bismarck,* there was much rejoicing, not without good reason. She had damaged *The Prince of Wales.* She had sunk *Hood.* That evening there was a large extra issue of sausage, chocolate and cigarettes. Hitler conferred the Knight Insignia of the Iron Cross on the First Gunnery Officer of *Bismarck.* True, the speed of the ship had been reduced, for a shell from *Hood* had partially flooded some of her compartments and had also made it impossible to use the oil fuel in the forward bunkers. It was this leaking oil which had left the broad stain on the sea seen by the Sunderland crew. But despite this, a formidable unit of the British Fleet had been disposed of, while another still more formidable had been damaged.

Captain Lindemann, in command of *Bismarck,* was overruled in the next decision as to their movements by his Admiral. The senior officer ordered *Prinz Eugen* to part company, while *Bismarck* held on her course for a French port. Night fell without further incident, but soon after midnight, torpedo-carrying Swordfish from *Victorious,* supported by Fulmars, delivered an attack in which a hit was scored on the starboard side.

Survivors from *Bismarck* spoke subsequently with surprise and admiration of the courage displayed by the British pilots. One Swordfish, they said, after being hit, still tried to get into a position from which to release its torpedo – before plunging into the sea. The anti-aircraft fire of *Bismarck* was tremendous, many of the guns becoming red hot with use. Our losses in this attack were two Swordfish and two Fulmars, the crews of the Fulmars being saved. It was put about on board *Bismarck* that forty-seven British aircraft had been destroyed – a slight exaggeration.

Soon after 0300 hours on 25 May, visibility became very bad and contact with *Bismarck* was at last lost by *Norfolk* and *Suffolk*, which had shadowed her so tenaciously since sunset on 23 May. When last seen, her speed had been reduced to twenty knots. It now seemed to the Admiralty that, in view of the damage she had sustained and her heavy consumption of fuel, she would either double back on her track and return to Norway or make for one of the French ports in order to refuel and refit. Coastal Command did its best to cover both contingencies.

All that afternoon and throughout the night, three Catalinas searched the area. They remained airborne for 19 hours 36 minutes, 20 hours 54 minutes, and 22 hours 21 minutes respectively. They saw nothing of the enemy, though one of them passed over a warship in the dead of night and was not able to identify it, low cloud making the use of parachute flares impossible.

During 26 May, Hudsons patrolled the Denmark Strait all day in very adverse weather. Sunderlands, with the help of a Catalina and a Hudson, covered the passage between Iceland and the Faroes. None of these aircraft sighted the enemy. Units of the Royal Navy were taking up fresh dispositions. The main body of the Home Fleet was steaming at high speed on a south-westerly direction from northern waters. Another force, headed by HMS *Renown*, was steaming north-westwards at speed from Gibraltar, while HMS *Rodney* and *Ramillies*, on escort duty in the North Atlantic, proceeded to move in the direction of the enemy.

On board *Bismarck*, the mood of exaltation began to give way to one of anxiety. This increased to alarm when, shortly before midday, Admiral Lutjens informed the crew that it had proved impossible to shake off the pursuit and that, though aircraft and U boats would be forthcoming as soon as the ship came within their range, an action would almost certainly have to be fought – in which case the best they could hope for would be that *Bismarck* would take some of the British Navy to the bottom with her. Yet as the day wore on, an no aircraft appeared over them and no hostile ships were sighted, their spirits rose again, especially when at evening they entered a U boat area.

Dawn on 26 May broke over a heavy-swelling sea, above which scudded broken clouds. During the morning, the weather became somewhat hazy. At 1030 hours, a Catalina flying-boat appeared above *Bismarck*. It had taken off from a base in Northern Ireland seven hours earlier and was one of the two sent to patrol some 500 miles out into the

Atlantic almost due west of Land's End. Contact with *Bismarck* had been regained after a lapse of thirty-one-and-a-half hours. A crucial achievement.

This had been brought off by brilliant calculation on the part of the Air and Naval staff, whose plotting of *Bismarck*'s probable course was accurate enough to enable the Commander-in-Chief, Coastal Command, to design the pattern of his patrols so as to place them exactly where the enemy was most likely to be found. The sighting of *Bismarck* at this stage was, in fact, the second principal factor which ensured her destruction. The first was the reconnaissance which had found her originally near Bergen and then discovered that she had sailed.

The pilot of the Catalina said:

> 'George (the nickname given to the automatic pilot) was flying the aircraft at 500 feet when we saw a warship. I was in the second pilot's seat when the occupant of the seat beside me, an American, said "What the devil's that?" I stared ahead and saw a dull black shape through the mist which curled above a very rough sea. "Looks like a battleship" he said. I said "Better get closer. Go round its stern."
>
> 'I thought it might be the *Bismarck*, because I could see no destroyers round the ship and I should have seen them had she been a British warship. I left my seat, went to the wireless operator's table, grabbed a piece of paper and began to write out a signal. The second pilot had taken over from George and gone up to 1,500 feet into broken cloud.
>
> 'As we came round he must have slightly misjudged his position, for instead of coming up astern we found ourselves right over the ship in an open space between the clouds. The first thing I knew about this was when two black puffs appeared outside the starboard wingtip. In a moment we were surrounded by black puffs. Stuff began to rattle against the hull. Some of it went through and a lot more made dents in it.
>
> 'I scribbled "end of message" and handed it to the wireless operator. In between the smudges of the bursting shells, I looked down on the ship, which seemed to me to be one big winking flame. She was taking violent avoiding actions by turning hard to starboard, heeling well over.'

The Catalina took similar action to dodge the anti-aircraft fire. None of the crew was hit, though a piece of shell passed upwards through the floor between the two pilots as they were changing places. The only casualties occurred in the galley, where one of the crew, who was washing up the breakfast things, dropped two china RAF plates and broke them.

Touch with the *Bismarck* was lost again temporarily, for the evasive action taken by the Catalina had removed her some miles from the ship. At 1115 hours, however, aircraft from the *Ark Royal*, now about seventy miles away, found her again. Another Catalina in the area was diverted from its patrol zone and reported sighting the enemy at 1328 hours. It kept the *Bismarck* more or less in view during the afternoon, though it lost her at intervals owing to the bad visibility. It had to return to base at 1800 hours.

Some three hours later, an event occurred which was the final factor in settling the fate of the *Bismarck*. She had been shadowed on and off by aircraft of Coastal Command or by naval aircraft throughout the day on 26 May. Three powerful forces of the Royal Navy were closing in on her. Then at 2055 hours, fifteen torpedo-carrying Swordfish from the *Ark Royal* launched an attack.

It lasted half an hour, and when it was over, the *Bismarck*'s steering gear was wrecked and her rudders jammed at an angle of between ten and fifteen degrees, thus causing her to turn in circles. Throughout that fierce half-hour, she put up a tremendous A.A. barrage, firing off practically all her A.A. ammunition. The Swordfish darted through it like flashes of lightning to score two and possibly three hits. No aircraft was lost, the only casualties being a pilot and an air-gunner who were wounded.

The position of the *Bismarck* was now desperate. Despite all her efforts, her divers could only free one rudder. The other remained jammed and immovable. That night, destroyers including the *Cossack* went in close and delivered six torpedo attacks, scoring three more hits.

Dawn on 27 May found the *Bismarck* striving to make about ten knots. By now the main British force had come up, and at 0845 hours the great ships opened fire. In less than an hour, *Bismarck* was a blazing wreck, but she did not surrender. The *coup de grâce* was given by the torpedoes of HMS *Dorsetshire*. *Bismarck* went down shortly afterwards with her colours flying. She could never have been sunk without the crucial co-operation between the Royal Navy, Fleet Air Arm and Coastal Command.

7 *The Struggle for Malta*

Malta was the key to the Mediterranean – and the air battles of Malta reflected British fortunes from the Dunkirk days to the desert victory. From June 1940 to November 1942, the island had 3,215 air raid warnings: an average of one every seven hours for two and a half years. Axis aircraft dropped 14,000 tons of bombs; killed 1,468 civilians; destroyed or damaged 24,000 buildings; and lost 1,129 aircraft.

When Italy declared war on 10 June 1940, the island's aerial defence comprised just three Sea Gladiators, which became known as *Faith, Hope* and *Charity*. At first, the Axis bombers flew in tight groups, usually despising fighter escort over a target they regarded as defenceless. But one formation of five Macchi 200 fighters also came in on the first day. Flying Officer W.J. Woods filed the first combat report on Malta:

'We sighted a formation of five S.79 enemy aircraft approaching Valetta at a height of approximately 15,000 feet. We climbed until we were slightly above them, and then Red Two delivered an attack from astern. The enemy had turned to sea. I delivered an attack from astern and got in a good burst at a range of approximately 200 yards. My fire was returned. I then broke away and returned over the island at approximately 11,000 feet, south of Grand Harbour.

'While still climbing to gain height, I observed another formation of five enemy aircraft approaching. They were at about the same height as myself. I attacked from a beam at about 150 yards and got in one good burst. The enemy started firing at me long before I opened up. This formation broke slightly but left me well behind when I tried to get in an attack from astern.

'Just after that, when again climbing to gain more height, I suddenly heard machine-gun fire from behind me. I immediately went into a steep

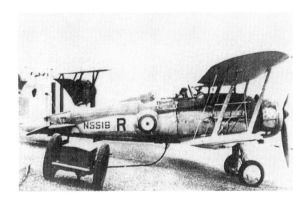

Faith of *Faith, Hope* and *Charity* – the three antiquated Gloster Gladiators defending Malta in the earliest days

left-hand turn and saw a single-engine fighter diving and firing at me. For quite three minutes, I circled as tightly as possible and got the enemy in my sight. I got in a good burst, full deflection shot, and he went down in a steep dive with black smoke pouring from his tail. I could not follow him down, but he appeared to go into the sea.'

By 16 June, *Faith, Hope,* and *Charity* had forced the Italians into the luxury of fighter escort. The *Regia Aeronautica* on that day flew in three formations, all of which the Gladiators managed to disperse. At the end of the second week of war on Malta, Berlin radio claimed that the Italian air force had 'completely destroyed the British naval base at Malta.'

Late on 22 June, after a rare raid-free day, the Italians sent an S.79 bomber to take photographs of the Grand Harbour so as to leave no doubts about the claim. Flight Lieutenant Burges reported:

'Ordered to intercept enemy aircraft reported approaching Malta. Enemy sighted at 13,000 feet when we were at 12,000 feet. Altered course to intercept and climbed to 15,000 feet and carried out stern attack from above enemy. Port engine and then starboard engine of enemy caught fire and attack was discontinued.'

The Italians did not get their photographs. The bomber fell into the sea and two of the crew followed it down by parachute. These were the first Axis airmen to be brought captive to the island.

Before the end of the month, four Hurricanes landed at Malta on transit passage from Britain to Egypt. The Air Commodore commanding Malta obtained permission to keep them there. This was fortunate for the island, as two of the Gladiators had met with accidents on their airfield and were temporarily out of service. The Gladiators survived for many more months on active service, but the main fighter defence now passed to the Hurricane. During the darkest period of the battle, Hurricanes were to be the mainstay of Malta, the single obstacle between the island and its conquest.

From then on, the service and civilian population of Malta were determined to hold on at all costs. Convoys could still get through to Malta. And on 1 July, Malta-based aircraft of the Fleet Air Arm actually struck at oil storage tanks in Sicily.

The Italians seemed surprised that they should meet any difficulty in overwhelming Malta, and decided to make an extra effort during July. A handful of fighters always met them, two or three engaging up to a score of the enemy. On 13 July, a dozen CR42s were engaged by a lone Hurricane and a lone Gladiator – probably the only one serviceable at the time. The Hurricane was damaged. The enemy were trying to reduce the island's fighter strength by sending over more of their own fighters. The total force of fighters operational at that particular moment amounted to one Hurricane and two Gladiators, which hung on like the grimmest death hoping for more Hurricanes. They had little else but faith and hope.

On 16 July, after five weeks of the Battle of Malta, the RAF lost its first fighter. This crashed 100 yards away from a CR42 brought down during the scrap. Both pilots were killed. The Italians lost a total of ten aircraft.

On 2 August 1940, HMS *Argus* steamed to within 200 miles of Malta to fly off twelve Hurricanes and two Skuas. This consignment arrived safely and formed the basis for a proper fighter flight. During August, the enemy turned from the shipyards to the airfields and tried to wear down the fighter reinforcements. Then came the dive-bombers, Junkers 87s piloted by Italians. Twenty of these attacked the Hal Far airfield on 15 September, dropping delayed-action bombs. Then the arrival of the *Luftwaffe* on Sicilian airfields marked a more serious stage in the long battle. But at least by then they had lost the Battle of Britain.

On 17 November, twelve more Hurricanes and two Skuas were embarked in *Argus*. The Italian fleet forced the aircraft carrier to put about at the Hurricanes' extreme range from Malta. Out of twelve Hurricanes and the two Skuas, only four Hurricanes and one Skua reached Luqa, Malta. The rest ran out of fuel *en route.*

Soon afterwards, the aircraft carrier HMS *Illustrious* arrived in the Grand Harbour with a convoy. She was listing badly and down at the stern – having been dive-bombed by the Germans for seven hours off the island. During the next few hours, the sirens sounded for enemy reconnaissance planes several times. People and aeroplanes waited for the attack.

The plan to defend the ships was to mount a barrage over the harbour, thus confronting the enemy with a screen of fire. The dive-bombers would have to contend with this to reach their targets. Over seventy aircraft came in, between 1300 and 1445 hours. To meet them there was only the fighter force of three Fulmars and four Hurricanes. The enemy's main target was *Illustrious* in French Creek.

From the guns rose a box barrage of more ferocity than Malta had yet heard, amplified by the guns of the ships in the harbour. The fighters waited to catch the enemy as they came in and as they banked away from the Grand Harbour. Sometimes the fighters followed the enemy through the blanket of barrage. An officer of the Royal Artillery saw this happen:

'I was on a light anti-aircraft gun position in the harbour area for one of these attacks, and I can still see clearly a German bomber diving through that terrific curtain of steel, followed by a Fulmar. The bomber dropped his bomb and proceeded to sneak his way out through the harbour entrance a few inches above the water. He was so low that he had to rise to clear the breakwater, which is only some 15 feet high. He was obviously wobbling badly, and as he rose the Fulmar pilot shot him down into the sea on the far side of the breakwater. The Fulmar pilot then landed at his airfield and later I received a message from him to say that he didn't think much of our barrage. However, he never flew that particular plane again, so badly was it damaged.'

Opposite *Illustrious*, a merchant vessel, *Essex*, lay loaded with high-explosive torpedoes and ammunition. An enemy bomb fell straight down a funnel and burst in the engine room, the ensuing explosion being contained by the bulkheads. That was the end of one ship. Two hundred houses were wiped out by this raid and 500 damaged. The church clock of Our Lady of Victories pointed to twenty past two for the rest of the war, a continued reminder of the air battle fought that day. On 23 January, *Illustrious* sailed east under her own power and two days later anchored in Alexandria.

February 1941 marked the start of the second assault from the air. The enemy made large-scale minelaying raids on the harbours and creeks. On 17 February, the islands were raided for the eleventh night in succession, yet the harbour remained effective.

In the middle of this month, the Germans began to step up their quest for air superiority. The pilots of the small Hurricane force were losing a lot of sleep, while still having to face the sweeps of the Me 109s. On 16 February, two formations of Me 109s were sighted over Malta. They split up at the approach of the Hurricanes, one formation climbing above the oncoming aircraft, while the other dropped below them.

Flight Lieutenant J.A.F. MacLauchlan led a Hurricane flight. He said:

'While on patrol over Luqa at 20,000 feet, we were attacked by six Me 109s. As previously arranged, the flight broke away to the right and formed a defensive circle. I saw four more Me 109s coming out of the sun. Just as they came within range, I turned back towards them and they all overshot without firing. I looked very carefully but could see no more enemy aircraft above me, so I turned back to the tail of the nearest 109. I was turning well inside him and was just about to open fire when I was hit in the left arm by a cannon shell. My dashboard was completely smashed, so I baled out and landed safely by parachute.'

MacLachlan's left arm had to be amputated. When he came out of hospital, he went out in a Magister flown by a colleague. After this he flew the plane himself and landed perfectly. A few days later, having flown a Hurricane again, he asked to rejoin his squadron. This was made possible by the fitting of an artificial arm back in Britain. After this he was to fly on many more successful operations.

The assault on Malta went on. Although since the outbreak of war the few fighters there had claimed as many as ninety-six enemy aircraft destroyed for the loss of sixteen fighters and eleven pilots, the opposition were slowly gaining an upper hand and flying lower and lower. They were neutralising the striking power of the air forces on Malta, and in the course of ten days nearly all the RAF flight leaders were lost. Then March opened with a further blow, reported in this signal:

Malta under siege and suffering several air raids daily

'Blitz raid of several formations totalling certainly no less than 100 aircraft, of which at least sixty bombers attacked Hal Far. A few of these aircraft dropped bombs and machine-gunned Kalafrana. Damage at Kalafrana was slight both to buildings and aircraft. One Sunderland unserviceable for few days. Damage Hal Far still being assessed

'Preliminary report as follows: "three Swordfish and one Gladiator burnt out. All other aircraft temporarily unserviceable. All barrack blocks unserviceable and one demolished. Water and power cut off. Hangars considerably damaged. Airfield temporarily unserviceable. Eleven fighters up. Enemy casualties by our fighters two Ju 88s, two Ju 87s, one Do 215, two Me 109s, confirmed. One Ju 88 and three Ju 87s damaged. By A.A., one Me 110 and eight other aircraft, confirmed, also four damaged. There are probably others which did not reach their base but cannot be checked. One Hurricane and one pilot lost after first shooting down one Ju 87 included above.

'For this blitz every serviceable Hurricane and every available pilot was put up and they achieved results against extremely heavy odds. The only answer to this kind of thing is obviously more fighters and these must somehow be provided if the air defence of Malta is to be maintained.'

The raids did not decrease, but towards the end of April another twenty-three Hurricanes arrived. The original three Gladiators had been found in a group of packing-cases. From this pitiful beginning, the air defences of Malta at last looked more realistic. A month later, more Hurricanes flew in – and about June the *Luftwaffe* left Sicily for the Russian front. There was even a Malta night-fighter unit, and Blenheim bombers attacked Syracuse. But the battle for Malta was not yet over . . .

8 *Pearl Harbor and After*

Sunday, 7 December 1941: Pearl Harbor Day. Day of Infamy. At 0755 hours on that Pacific Sabbath morning, Japanese dive bombers swarmed over the United States Army air base of Hickam Field and the naval air station on Ford Island. A few minutes earlier, the Japanese had dealt with the naval air station at Kaneoke Bay. These were the Americans' main airfields in the whole Hawaiian area. Although caught completely unaware, the ground crews dashed into the flames enveloping their precious planes, set ablaze by showers of incendiaries. Ignoring the pain of burns and the continuous threat of fuel explosions, the crews stripped off any free machine guns they could, loaded them hastily, and pointed the muzzles skyward at the retreating second and third waves. Amazing as it seems, one enemy aircraft was actually shot down by a fluke hit from one of these machine guns.

The first few minutes of the raid put temporarily or permanently out of action 150 of the 202 naval aircraft of all types on the island of Oahu. Of the remaining fifty-two planes, fourteen were ready too late for any action in the Pearl Harbor attack, and so only thirty-eight took to the air at all on that dramatic day. Among these planes were eighteen scout bombers from an aircraft carrier which reached the area actually during

US Naval Air Station – with aircraft caught on the ground

the raid. It is all too clear, therefore, that the United States Navy had to rely on anti-aircraft fire for its primary – and almost its only – weapon. This disastrous condition exposed the fleet to continuous air attack.

It was bare seconds after the perfectly timed assault on the air stations that Japanese torpedo planes and dive bombers swung in to pinpoint their attack on the heavy ships in Pearl Harbor itself. This first phase of the historic morning lasted from 0755 till 0825 hours. The moment the alarm was received, the machinery went into action and by 0759 hours – less than four minutes later – heavy guns of the fleet opened fire on the second wave of dive bombers as they swooped down. The first Japanese plane screeched into the water at exactly 0800 hours. On an aircraft tender moored at the naval air station, drama became crowded into a matter of moments. Fire from repeated high-altitude attacks swept the ship, as one of her anti-aircraft guns hit yet another plane – which tore its way into the deck. At this precise second, the tender's captain chanced to look over the side of the vessel and saw the shadow of an enemy two-man suicide submarine not a dozen yards away. He called to the gunners, and an immediate hit forced the midget sub to expose her conning tower. But even so, the tender could not claim the submarine, for at that instant, too, a destroyer passed directly over it and sank it with one blast of depth charges. All that was compressed into a mere thirty seconds.

Still the first half-hour, and already several ships were going down from the sheer weight of bombs. Men from ships put out of action were managing at any cost to return to the fight. As one vessel capsized crazily, her survivors swam through scalding oil to clamber up the ladders of other, unhit, ships and join their gun crews. The crew of another disabled vessel swam away from the comparative safety of the shore, which lay only a few yards off, and struck towards mid-channel, where they were hoisted aboard outward-bound destroyers – the fastest-moving ships in this deathtrap of a harbour.

Quick thinking saved lives – and ships. An aviation machinist's mate aboard one ship saw that flames from the huge vessel threatened a repair ship alongside. He did not wait for orders. He ran through the blaze and slashed the lines holding the two ships together. Freed, the smaller craft drifted clear.

Only in the final moments, when remaining aboard appeared hope-less, would men leave their ships. The crew of one followed her around on her outside as it capsized, firing their guns first from her side and then by the keel, until they were literally under water themselves and had to jump clear. Back on the dock, those same men stood and cheered a more fortunate ship as she cleared the fateful harbour and steamed out after the Japanese. Then with portable guns, they went on with the fight again as more waves of bombers buzzed overhead.

By now, rescue had become a paramount need. One ship picked up hundreds of men hurled into the water by the fury and force of explo-sions from torpedoes or bombs. Burning oil turned the water into lethal

Pearl Harbor: 7 December 1941. Despite being damaged by torpedoes, the light cruiser USS *Helena* (left) brought down six enemy aircraft during the infamous attack

liquid. One man's voice screamed above the din as he jumped and fell into a molten pool. And all the while, smoke, dust, destruction – and death. The plop and the plume of near-misses; the tracery of torpedoes as they skimmed under the surface towards their sitting targets. The whole harbour seemed shrouded in smoke, punctuated by the regular relentless explosions on deck or hull. Ships sank at every angle imaginable. Often at their moorings.

Meanwhile, what was happening to the attackers? The gunners did all they could to try to disperse the bombers, but with American aircraft virtually grounded, it remained a one-sided struggle. Machine-guns sent two of the first wave of torpedo planes spinning in a short spiral to the harbour, where they exploded in a mixture of flame and foam.

Then suddenly at 0825 hours a comparative lull fell over the scene, though air activity continued with one or two sporadic attacks by both dive and horizontal bombers. The respite lasted a quarter of an hour. At 0840 hours it was shattered by more horizontal bombers droning in from the Pacific, crossing and recrossing their targets from various directions in a devastating raid. Then as the sticks of bombs straddled decks mercilessly, the dive bombers reappeared on cue. Enemy pilots put their planes into almost vertical dives and watched the flaming fleet get nearer and nearer. Then just as it seemed they must crash, they pulled the bombers out of the dive at the last possible second and roared flat over the ships, strafing indiscriminately. On and on this went for another hour, until by 0945 hours the last of the enemy aircraft had exhausted its bombs and bullets, and turned for home. That is, those still surviving. American gunfire destroyed twenty-eight out of 105 planes – over a quarter. Three Japanese submarines went to the bottom, too.

The time had come for the Americans to count the cost at Pearl Harbor. The battleship *Arizona* was totally lost. First its boiler had exploded, then a bomb had passed literally through the smokestack, where it set off the whole forward magazines. The battleship *Oklahoma* had capsized, but would be righted and repaired in time. Also either sunk or put out of action for a long time were the battleships *California, Nevada* and *West Virginia*; three destroyers, the *Shaw, Cassin* and *Downes*; the minelayer *Oglala*; and the target ship *Utah* and a large floating dock. Three other battleships and three cruisers received less damage, while other minor vessels were also struck.

That comparatively small force of Japanese aircraft managed to destroy eighty Naval aircraft and ninety-seven Army planes. The most murderous losses of all, of course, were in men themselves. At 0750 hours, Pearl Harbor was barely stirring from slumber. Two hours later, 2,117 officers and enlisted men of the Navy and Marine Corps were killed; 960 were still reported as missing a year later; and 876 were wounded. The army sustained far fewer losses – 226 men killed, 396 wounded.

How had it happened? Many answers have been given. But the facts remain that the Japanese fleet carrying the aircraft left Hitokappu Bay at the northern extremity of the empire a week earlier; refuelled on 3 December; crossed the International Date Line far northwest of Pearl Harbor; then altered course to arrive at a point due north of the Hawaiian Islands by 2130 hours on 6 December. From there it was a mere step to Pearl Harbor.

So the United States was in World War 2 with a vengeance. Stunned for a moment by the horror of Pearl Harbor, and then stirred to anger, the nation began slowly to recover.

The Japanese, meanwhile, gave the Navy no chance for rest. The Navy and Marines began to feel further rapid effects of Japanese aggression when air raids were directed next on the advance marine garrison at Wake Island. Then Midway and Luzon received heavy attacks, and the situation on Guam seemed worse still. By 13 December, less than a week after Pearl Harbor, the Navy Department could not communicate with Guam, most southerly of the Marianas Islands. Some 400 Naval men and 155 Marines were stationed there and the last reports indicated that the bombing raids had been followed up by enemy landings.

December 8–22: by land, sea and air the attacks came against Wake during these fearful two weeks. One man managed to convey as well as anyone else ever could the events on that remote mid-Pacific island.

Major W Bayler was on temporary duty in Wake to help establish a base of operations for the Marine Corps aviation unit. This unit of a dozen planes arrived shortly before the Japs attacked. Bayler kept pencilled notes of each dramatic day:

'8 December, 0700–1158: Received word bombing Oahu. "General Quarters" station. 24 Jap bombers on a northern course hit airdrome in close column of division Vs from 3,000 feet. 100-pound fragmentation bombs and simultaneous strafing. Casualties 25 dead, 7 wounded, 7 airplanes burned, destroyed.

9 December, 1145: 27 Japs. Bombed hospital, Camp No 2. Killed several patients, 3 dead. Got one Jap plane.

10 December, 1045: 27 Jap bombers. No casualties.

11 December, 0500: Landing attempt by 12 Jap ships, including light cruisers, destroyers, gunboats, 2 troop or supply ships. Jap casualties: 1 light cruiser, 2 destroyers, 1 gunboat, 2 bombers.

Note – That Japs closed in to 4,700 yards before 5- and 3-inch guns opened up at pointblank range.

12 December: 27 Jap planes bombed Peale and Wake from 22,000 feet. No casualties.

13 December: All quiet.

14 December: 32 Jap planes hit airdrome. Two killed, 1 plane shot down.

15 December, 1100: Dawn raid by 3 four-engine seaplanes. 27 Jap bombers. Shot down 2 Japs.

16 December, 1745: 41 Jap bombers hit Camp 2 and airdrome. Jap four-motor plane raid. One Jap shot down.

17 December: 32 Jap bombers at 1317 hit Camp 1, Peale Island, Diesel oil supply, mess hall, and pumps of evaporators, Camp 1.

18 December, 1140: One Jap high rec. plane (2 engine).

19 December, 1030: Jap bombers hit airport and camp.

20 December: All quiet – first day of bad weather.

Total casualties: 28 dead, 6 wounded as of 20 December.

The revelation that the Japanese were allowed to close to 4,700 yards in the attempted landing before the defenders' guns opened up showed real courage on the part of the commander. After these enemy raids, only three US planes at Wake were in serviceable condition. Then the enemy scored a direct hit on one of these before it got off the ground, and a second one crashed trying to take off too quickly. So then there was one. A lone aircraft against the whole Japanese force being hurled on Wake. Their troops landed on the island on 23 December, and by Christmas Eve the Navy had to admit its capture.

Christmas 1941: So Wake fell, with more losses on both sides. The battle continued not only on the islands, but in the waters surrounding that large chain. The enemy discovered the USS *Heron*, a small seaplane tender, off the Philippines, and attacked her for seven horrific hours. Ten four-engined flying boats and five twin-engine landplanes delivered the onslaught, yet the captain and ship's crew were determined she should not go down. The captain handled her with uncanny skill and although fighting against the heaviest possible odds, he managed to take evasive action so successfully that only one bomb registered a direct hit on USS *Heron*, while three very near misses fell uncomfortably close. The crew counted forty-six 100-pound bombs dropped by the enemy planes plus three torpedoes launched against her. The ship's guns shot down a flying boat, damaged at least one other, and acquitted themselves well. The *Heron* made port and lived to fight another day in the brand-new year of 1942.

9 *The Channel Attack*

Lieutenant-Commander Eugene Esmonde was serving on the aircraft carrier HMS *Victorious* when it took part in the destruction of *Bismarck*. After *Victorious*, Esmonde joined HMS *Ark Royal* in August 1941. He had been aboard HMS *Courageous* when she went down in 1939, and now, on 13 November 1941, another carrier was to be sunk before his eyes. Mortally hit a few miles from Gibraltar, the famous carrier limped along for nearly twelve hours, during which time her Swordfish squadron flew several sorties carrying members of the crew to the comparative safety of Gibraltar. A destroyer took off the rest of the 1,600 ship's company, and before *Ark Royal* tilted too severely the last Swordfish ever to take off from the flight deck headed for Gibraltar, too.

Esmonde later reformed the squadron at Lee-on-Solent with seven of the officers who had been in *Ark Royal*, and what the squadron lacked in experience they made up for in enthusiasm.

So to 1942. Early in February, the Admiralty suspected that *Scharnhorst*, *Gneisenau* and *Prinz Eugen* might break out from their French port of Brest and try to force a passage through the English Channel to their home ports in Germany. The Fleet Air Arm had a long account to settle with *Scharnhorst* and *Gneisenau*, for eight of *Ark Royal*'s Skua crews had perished in an attack on the enemy battleships at Trondheim, as well as two Swordfish in an attack off the Norwegian coast in the same campaign. Although naval aircraft had sighted the two ships more than once in the Atlantic, no striking force had ever caught them. Esmonde had already asked to be allowed to lead his squadron against them if the need for such an attack ever arose.

One evening Esmonde called his squadron officers to his cabin and told them to be ready for a strike at any moment; the aircraft were prepared and armed with torpedoes. There was a 'flap' at 0300 hours next morning and the officers were briefed, but it proved to be a false alarm – a strange coincidence in view of what was soon to happen.

Next morning the squadron flew to an RAF station in Kent, arriving in a blizzard, and were put on five minutes' readiness. Esmonde was in fact expecting to make a night attack on the German ships, and arrangements had been made for RAF fighters to accompany the Swordfish as flare-droppers. The maintenance ratings had to dig the dispersed aircraft out of the snow in the morning and run the engines three times during the day to keep them warm.

On 11 February, Esmonde went to Buckingham Palace to receive the DSO he had been awarded for the *Bismarck* action. Next morning, Thursday 12 February, Sub-Lieutenant (Air) B.W. Rose, RNVR, was returning to the mess with his observer after a practice flight when a lorry with some of the squadron officers came tearing past. One of them shouted: 'The balloon's gone up.'

It was then a few minutes after noon. The RAF Headquarters had reported that the three ships had at last broken cover and appeared in the Channel, with an escort of destroyers, torpedo boats, E-boats and mine-sweepers, and a fighter escort described as the biggest ever seen over a naval force.

Rose and his observer ran back to the crew room to put on their flying kit again, and just as they were ready Esmonde came rushing in to give them orders: 'Fly at 50 feet, close line astern, individual attacks, and find your own way home. We shall have fighter protection.'

The Fleet Air Arm did not waste time. Already the enemy ships would be well along the French coast and nearing the Straits of Dover. The aim was to try to intercept this massive force of more than two dozen surface craft, and attack them before they could reach the sandbanks north-east of Calais.

The six Swordfish crews climbed into their slow, torpedo-carrying biplanes, taxied out and took off at about 1230 hours. They were grouped

Lieutenant Commander Eugene Esmonde, Fleet Air Arm. Esmonde led the valiant attack on the German battleships in February 1942

into two sub-flights of three each, flying in echelon. Only a few Motor Torpedo Boats, the Dover shore batteries, and ten Spitfires were able to support them, the fighters zigzagging across the course keep their speed of advance down to that of the Swordfish. Already by 1942 the biplanes, with their Pegasus engines and single gun turrets, were rightly regarded as out-of-date.

By now, the German warships had passed through the Straits of Dover and were some ten miles north of Calais. According to the subsequent German account, they had left Brest with their escort of destroyers immediately after an RAF raid at 2030 hours the previous night. The E-boats and minesweepers had joined them up-Channel hugging the French coast. Their covering umbrella of shore-based fighters could be relieved and reinforced from the French coastal airfields at short notice. As the squadron passed through the Straits, the long-range batteries on the Kent coast opened fire, but the ships took evasive action. They were also able to avoid the torpedoes fired by the MTBs and destroyers that tried to intercept them.

The Swordfish sighted the enemy after twenty minutes' flying time. The vessels were a mile and a half away, steaming in line ahead, with *Prinz Eugen* leading, followed by *Scharnhorst* and *Gneisenau*; they were almost through the Straits. Visibility had been patchy during the flight, sometimes right down, and at other times up to a couple of miles.

The force went into the attack over the destroyer screen, meeting the anticipated intense anti-aircraft fire as they closed towards the capital ships. Esmonde in aircraft No W.5984/825 was still flying at only fifty feet when a shell ricocheted off the water and hit the belly of his Swordfish, causing him to steer an erratic course from then on. Johnson, the air gunner of Rose's aircraft next astern, was hit.

Then the ships' guns quietened and the fighter attacks began. About fifteen Me 109s and FW 190s dived out of the clouds onto the tails of the Swordfish, and the Spitfire escort became involved in a general dogfight. An FW 190 ripped off the top of the mainplane of Esmonde's aircraft and he went straight down into the sea.

Rose was attacked both from ahead and astern, at a range of some 200 yards. He dodged as well as he could while his observer, Sub-Lieutenant (Air) E. Lee, RNVR, stood up in the after-cockpit and shouted 'Port' or 'Starboard' as the attacks came in. They could see the tracer bullets streaming past, and the Swordfish was being hit continually. Moreover, the constant evasive action slowed down its advance, while to make matters worse there was no-one to work the rear gun. Johnson had been either knocked unconscious or killed instantaneously, and Lee could not move his body.

In spite of Lee's watchfulness, Rose was hit by splinters from a cannon shell that struck the bulkhead behind his seat. Now leading the formation, and with his engine faltering, he decided they must attack without delay. He selected the leading ship and, getting as good a position as he could, dropped his torpedo at a range of about 1,200 yards and saw it running well. It was difficult to observe results, but directly he had made his attack the fighters ceased to pay any further attention to him, concentrating instead on the others. One Swordfish had two Focke-Wulfs on its tail, their flaps and undercarriages down to retard their speed, attacking whichever way the pilot turned.

The third aircraft, piloted by Sub-Lieutenant (Air) C.M. Kingsmill, RNVR, had the two top cylinders of its engines shot away. The engine and the upper port wing caught fire, yet the air gunner, Leading Airman D.A. Bunce, continued to engage the enemy fighters and saw one crash into the sea. Although all the crew of this Swordfish were wounded, Kingsmill kept control long enough to aim his torpedo in the direction of the second enemy ship, then turned with difficulty and tried to land near some vessels – which turned out to be E-boats. They opened fire on him but he kept flying until his engine finally cut out. The Swordfish crashed on the water a few hundred yards from some British MTBs and eventual rescue; although the crew had first to take to the icy wintry water because their dinghy had been destroyed by fire.

The three Swordfish aircraft in the second sub-flight were piloted by Lieutenant (Air) J.C. Thompson, RN, Sub-Lieutenant (Air) C.R. Wood, RN, and Sub-Lieutenant (Air) P. Bligh, RNVR. They were seen crossing the destroyer screen to attack, taking violent evasive action, but proceeding steadily towards the enemy capital ships. Nothing further was seen of them after that.

As soon as Rose had dropped his torpedo, he tried to make as much height as possible and went out on the port wing of the destroyer screen. He had climbed to 1,200 feet when Lee told him that petrol was pouring out of their starboard side. It was obvious that he could not reach the English coast and he decided to make for some MTBs. He was within four miles of them when his engine cut out but, undeterred, he glided down towards the sea, pulled his stick well back and pancaked down. As he said later, 'The Swordfish sat down very nicely'.

Rose climbed out of his cockpit into the sea, while Lee tried, unsuccessfully, to remove Johnson, the air gunner, from the after-cockpit. Rose could not help him because his left arm was useless. Despite this incapacity, when the dinghy was washed out into the sea Rose recovered it and got it upright. Lee held it while Rose climbed into it, then he went back to the aircraft to make another attempt to remove Johnson. He could not do so and had to leave him. There was no doubt that Johnson was already dead.

Lee then joined Rose in the dinghy, but the sea was choppy and the little craft soon filled with water. They tried baling it out with their flying helmets, though without much success. Then from their emergency gear they took out the marine distress signals and the aluminium dust-markers. The dust formed a silver pool around the dinghy and could be seen at a distance. But they flung the dust to windward and it blew back on them, so that they looked like a couple of shining tin soldiers. However, they could use the empty tins for baling out the dinghy, and when it was dry they fired the distress signals. Two MTBs then closed in on the dinghy. By that time they had been in the water for an hour and a half. Rose was suffering severely from his wounds, and both he and Lee were numb with the cold.

Only five aircrew survived from the Swordfish striking force, Lee being the only one unwounded. Having made his report to the naval authorities, he apologised for having to hurry away, but as he explained, he was now acting senior officer of the little squadron.

10 *Can One Man Save a Carrier?*

The carrier USS *Lexington* was with a force of four heavy cruisers and ten destroyers, planning to attack Rabaul in New Britain, when they were spotted by enemy flying boats which wheeled off for some stronger support. Soon they were back and the first heavy bomber approached *Lexington* and her escorts. Two of the six US fighters keeping constant watch overhead peeled off to attack it – and the plane quickly went down in flames. The second enemy plane went the same way. The next one copied the course of the original flying boats and went home for reinforcements.

When they came, the stage was ready for one of those fights to a finish when the lives of all the men witnessing it might hang on the outcome. Another half dozen American navy fighters flew off *Lexington*'s deck to join the first six.

Nine Japanese bombers in a V formation pointed straight at the carrier. The original fighter force was getting short of fuel before the battle began, but throttled forward to engage. In a spluttering few minutes, five of the enemy bombers left searing trails of flame in the sky as they plunged into the Pacific. This rattled the Japanese, who found the next phase too much for them. The US ships loosed all they had at these last four bombers, frightening the pilots so badly that their bombs sank harmlessly into the sea. The planes tried to turn and flee back to Rabaul, but the American fighters were still airborne and shot down all but one of them.

But something serious was taking shape as the fighters flew in pursuit of these last four planes. *Lexington* had managed to get fifteen more fighters up to help in the chase, exchanging these for five of the original ones which needed more fuel and ammunition. At the exact moment that all the airborne fighters except two were well away from the carrier dealing with the enemy planes, another nine bombers droned down toward *Lexington.* And at the second the two US fighters took on this next wave, the machine guns of one of them jammed – so he could do nothing but fly clear to safety. This left one lone fighter flying between the enemy and the ship. Its pilot: Lieutenant Edward H. 'Butch' O'Hare.

O'Hare took on all nine. He raced down on the V formation from the rear and their right. Down on *Lexington* everyone who had a second to spare watched what happened next. O'Hare pressed his gun button just before his fighter reached the enemy right flank. The two end planes collapsed and crashed. Weaving underneath the rest, he then gave another bomber a burst. It limped out of the V, which was already a ragged arrow. Two more of the group lost bits of wings and fuselage as they struggled to save the formation. So five of the nine never reached the target to drop their bombs.

Although the *Lexington* was saved at least once, she finally succumbed in the Battle of the Coral Sea. But not a single man was lost in abandoning the carrier

The quartet who got through did drop them, but hurriedly and inaccurately. They were anxious to get away from this daredevil. Then as the scattered group struggled to find some order, O'Hare went into them again. One, two, three. All went spiralling into the sea before his guns. In just four minutes, he had shot down five of the nine bombers and hit three more.

But the brief battle was not yet through. For as these three sputtered homeward, each short of one or more engines, they ran right into *Lexington*'s main force of fighters as it was flying jubilantly back from wiping out the first bombers. All three Japanese bombers received mortal machine-gun fire. The last plane ran for it as fast as a bomber could, pursued by Lieutenant Edward H. Allen in a navy scout bomber. Both planes flew at about the same speed, but whenever the Yanks managed to come within range, the recoil from their guns retarded the scout bomber just long enough to allow the enemy to gain ground again. Although the enemy escaped, both Allen and Lieutenant Commander John S. Thack won the Navy Cross.

But to O'Hare went the coveted Medal of Honor. Admiral Brown said that *Lexington* owed her life to him alone, so the answer to the question: 'Can one man save an aircraft carrier?' is 'Yes, O'Hare did it'.

The sequel to the story must be told.

Off the Marshall Islands on 27 November of the following year, O'Hare was flying from the carrier *Enterprise* at night. After a scrap with enemy planes, a lagging Japanese pilot became mixed up with three American Hellcats about to return to their carrier. O'Hare flew in one of these Hellcats, and in the firing that broke out when the Japanese was discovered, O'Hare's plane was hit. It lurched over. The flaming fighter took O'Hare with it into the sea. A tragic end.

11 *Early Strikes at Japan*

Sgt Edward J. Saylor wa one of General Doolittle's men on a raid against an aircraft plant at Kobe, Japan, in April of '42. He was a native of Brussett, Montana. He called it just a little crossroads post office. Saylor finished high school at Jordan, Montana, in 1937 and spent the next two years working in western states as a logger, farm hand and cow puncher. He enlisted in the Air Corps in 1939. Eglin Field, Florida, was his last American base before he was engaged in active duty over Japan. Here is his account of how he shared in Brigadier General Jimmy Doolittle's bombing raid on Kobe and Tokyo on 18 April. Exactly as he wrote it soon afterwards:

'Hirohito, the Yanks are coming, pal! They're coming with a rush and a roar and some hell to be splattered over this little island empire. I can hardly wait, bub. We're over Japan now.

'It's 1.40 pm, and a clear day. Below me the country is rugged, but through the valleys the land is streaked with green, with trees and terraces.

Mitchell B25s twin-fin medium bomber and ground-attack aircraft were used in early strikes at the enemy. Mitchells could carry a cannon, 14 machine guns and 5,000 lb of weapons

'Maybe I got a little bit of a catch in my throat, but I don't notice it much. We're just fifteen minutes away from our target, and we're sailing along at four thousand feet. We're flying B-25s, and they're very new and fast.

'The skies are empty and clear. We've left the other planes in our squadron, and here we are all alone sitting over several million Japs.

'Yes, I have got a catch in my throat, because thinking of all those Japs down there somehow makes me think of Bataan peninsula, and to think of Bataan peninsula makes me sore.

'That gives you a strange feeling to be sore when the ground below looks so peaceful and when you see the farmland down below and it looks so damned impersonal.

'I used to live out west, and I've never been to Japan before, thank God, but I've heard stories about how they plant stuff on these terraced hillsides in the Far East, and I keep wondering how they work it, having been a farmer once myself.

'I am also keeping a sharp watch out for cherry trees. I have been meaning to go to Washington for years to see them, but I have never seen them and I understand they are out of fashion right now.

'These are just random thoughts, and all these thoughts probably come and go in a fraction of a second, because I am looking for enemy planes eight to the dozen every second, and there are no more enemy planes than there are cherry trees.

'The skies are empty.

'I have been sitting here just feeling the throb and roar of the big B-25. They're beautiful ships, wonderful ships. I think of the other boys off over Tokyo and Yokohama, Osaka and Nagoya now. We're headed for Kobe, to hit the big wharves there, and then over to an aircraft factory where they make Yakashimas. I promise I will get a few of those babies which I understand are being used to strafe our troops.

'After I pan some lead into those babies, those planes will look like St Valentine's Day in Chicago has come to the aircraft industry of Japan.

'The skies are still empty and vacant, and very clear. It's 1.43 now, and we're all at battle stations.

'Our pilot is Lt Donald G. Smith of San Antonio, Texas, and he knows his business. He can throw this little old ship around like I once saw a guy throw an old Jenny around at a fair back in Montana, and he could do more things with that Jenny than a monkey can do with a coconut. Smith is sure good, all right. When we started coming into Japan, he skimmed the waves so close that I could almost taste the salt water from the spray in my mouth, no kidding.

'Our navigator-bomber is a guy named Lieut Howard A. Sessler. He's from Boston, and he's ready to go to work with his bombsight.

'Hirohito, you better watch out for guys named Sessler and guys from Boston.

'Now this will give you birds a laugh. Here we are sitting up over Japan

B25 similar to those used on the Doolittle raid, here seen overflying US Marines assaulting Cape Gloucester on New Britain on Boxing Day 1943

in a few hundred-thousand-bucks'-worth of airplanes, and what kind of bombsight you think we got? That damned thing cost twenty cents, no kidding. Doolittle – General Doolittle – he was afraid that in case any one of us got shot down, we didn't want the Japs to get hold of those Norden bombsights. So we rigged up a sight that cost twenty cents.

'But, brother, that sight is going to cost Emperor Hirohito and what they call the Elder Statesmen several million bucks' worth of stuff in a few minutes.

'Few minutes! Right now, I mean. We just sighted the outskirts of Kobe. The skies are still vacant, and that scares you a little. 1.52 and we're over the edge of the city. We're coming in at 2,000 feet. Lieut Sessler is talking over the interphone in his Boston accent which always gives me a hell of a boot, it sounds so English:

'"That's our baby," the looie is saying. "I see the target."

'We roar across the city, raising such an almighty racket the noise kind of bounces back, it seems like, and the Japs down there are running back and forth, but the Japs don't seem to catch on to the fact that the Stars-and-Stripes Forever are right up there over their heads, equipped with plenty of horsepower and plenty of bombs and that darned old 20-cent bombsight.

'There's our target.

'He's an aircraft factory, a mess of buildings down there, scattered over a block or better. There are the docks.

'All we got to do now is let go.

'Hirohito, the Yanks are coming, sprinkling it along the course.

'"Let 'em go, Sess," Smith yells to the bombardier.

'I felt her go when she went. The bombs, I mean. Sweet as you please, that B-25 takes sudden uplift, a little bit of a lurch, and the minute I felt it I knew.

'Hirohito, the Yanks have arrived.

'I can't see where the bombs land, but I know that we're square on the target with the whole works. We're rolling along at 240 mph now and that ain't any cadence-count either. We're well away from that factory before the hell starts breaking loose and the fires start.

'The Japs are waking up, though. They start a mild epidemic – that's what the Lieutenant called it – a mild epidemic of anti-aircraft fire.

'The stuff comes up like powder-puffs, but we're high-tailing it away from the barrage. The Japs can't estimate our speed, and they never catch up with us. We don't give them a chance, either. We drop right down almost to water level and haul out of there in a hurry and there I get salt spray, it seems like, in my mouth again.

'I wish I could have stuck around to see the look on Hirohito's face when they brought him the messages that night.'

Sgt Edward J. Saylor

12 *Malta Victory*

After the comparative calm of the latter half of 1941, the New Year opened as a shocking contrast. On one of the most desperate days, 7 March 1942, the first Spitfires appeared. The armed Spitfires flew in from the aircraft carrier HMS *Eagle*. They numbered fifteen. They were to be used against the enemy fighter escorts in sections of four or six, while the Hurricanes dealt with the bombers.

An RAF Sergeant manning a fire-tender on one of the airfields that day wrote:

> 'The Spitfires came waggling their wings as if to say OK boys we're here. But that very same evening the gen went round that a big plot was building up over Sicily and within half an hour or so we were to see that Jerry really meant business. Standing at a vantage point in the village of Zurrieq, I saw the first waves of 88s coming all the way over the island. They dived down on Takali where the whole batch of Spits had landed. We tried to count them as they came in, but it was an utter impossibility. Straight down they went, and one could see the stuff leave the kites before it really got dark.
>
> 'The guns were belting rounds up like nothing on earth; tracers filled the sky, and if things weren't so serious one could have called it a lovely sight. The din was terrific and Takali seemed to be ablaze from end to end. The lads would shout that some gun or other had stopped firing, and the crew had been knocked out. But no; they've started again pushing up rounds harder than ever. The Jerry seemed to be under orders to finish the place and, by hell, he tried his best.'

Although the raids continued throughout the week, the Spitfires went into action and destroyed their first aircraft within three days of the raid. Detailed to intercept Me 109s, they shot down one, with two other probables. But their presence produced enemy attacks on the dispersal points, with much resultant damage to the Spitfires. By 2 April, no single section of Spitfires was operational.

Meanwhile another struggle was taking place in the seas around Malta and in its harbours and docks. By April the Germans knew that they could not advance in the North African desert without cargoes from Europe. Malta threatened these. Air power was thus tied down in Sicily to try to neutralise Malta, which might otherwise have been diverted elsewhere.

During April, 6,728 tons of bombs fell on Malta. Nearly half fell on the dockyards, and most of the rest on the three airfields of Luqa, Takali and Hal Far. In April alone, 300 people were killed and over 10,000 buildings destroyed or damaged, so the civilians suffered as much as service

After the war, Gladiator 'Faith' being presented to the people of Malta. This was the sole survivor of Faith, Hope and Charity, the three aircraft with which the RAF first faced Italian bombers

personnel. An average 170 enemy aircraft flew over every day: waves of twelve to fifteen Junkers 88s and 87s came in at intervals of a few minutes. Three raids a day became typical. During this month, a total of almost twelve-and-a-half days was spent under alert.

Although one Hurricane squadron had been re-equipped with Spitfires and a second in April, the Hurricane once more came to bear the brunt of the battle after many Spitfires had been lost on the ground. Sometimes a raiding party of a hundred Axis aircraft would be met by only a dozen Hurricanes. Sometimes the odds were even greater than that.

On 15 April 1942, Malta was awarded the George Cross. Five days later, fifty-four Spitfires set out for Malta from the aircraft carrier USS *Wasp*, though only forty-seven actually arrived. They were virtually chased in all the way. No sooner had they touched down than they were attacked on the ground, and many of them were 'spitchered' while they were still being refuelled, rearmed and serviced.

Over 300 bombers were sent over in one day to try to destroy them and by the end of the next day only eighteen Spitfires were serviceable.

Within three days of landing, all the Spitfires had been grounded. The Germans lost nearly 200 aircraft in April, but RAF losses were proportionately still worse: twenty-three Spitfires lost and fifty-seven damaged, with eighteen Hurricanes lost and thirty damaged. The air raids continued unceasingly, with ever fewer fighters to counter them. Fortunately for the Maltese defences, the Germans made the great mistake of easing up for a few days at the end of the month, when something else had happened to sway events.

Spitfires to the rescue!

Sixty-four Spitfires were scheduled to land on the airfields from 0100 hours onwards on Saturday 9 May. These flew off *Wasp* and *Eagle*. But the RAF had to be careful not to lose them before they could be brought to bear on the epic struggle.

One of the new Spitfire pilots described his day like this:

'Took off from the *Wasp* at 0645. Landed at Takali at 1030. The formation leader flew too fast and got his navigation all to hell, so I left them 40 miles west of Bizerta, five miles off the North African coast, and set course for Malta – avoiding Pentellaria and Bizerta owing to fighters and flak being present there. Jettisoned the long-range tank 20 miles west of Bizerta and reached Malta with twenty gallons to spare in main tank. Of the 47 machines that flew off the *Wasp*, one crashed into the sea on take-off, one force-landed back on to the deck as he had jettisoned his auxiliary tank in error, one landed in Algeria, one ran out of petrol between Pantellaria and Malta, one crashed on landing at Hal Far, and one crashed off Grand Harbour.

'On landing at Takali I immediately removed my kit, and the machine was rearmed and refuelled. I landed during a raid and four Me 109s tried to shoot me up. Soon after landing the airfield was bombed but without much damage being done. I was scrambled in a section of four soon after the raid, but we failed to intercept the next one, though we chased several 109s down on the deck. Ate lunch in the aircraft, as I was at the ready till dusk. After lunch we were heavily bombed again by eight Ju 88s.

'Scrambled again in the same section after tea – no luck again. One Spit was shot down coming in to land and another one at the edge of the airfield. Score for the day, 7 confirmed, 7 probables and 14 damaged for the loss of 3 Spits.

'The tempo of life here is just indescribable. The morale of all is magnificent – pilots, ground crews and army, but life is certainly tough. The bombing is continuous on and off all day. One lives here only to destroy the Hun and hold him at bay; everything else, living conditions, sleep, food, and all the ordinary standards of life have gone by the board. It all makes the Battle of Britain and fighter sweeps seem like child's play in comparison, but it is certainly history in the making and nowhere is there aerial warfare to compare with this.'

On the next day, the minelaying cruiser HMS *Welshman* was due at

Malta soon after dawn. And throughout that day the RAF protected the vessel against enemy raids. Morning, afternoon and evening they came. The same pilot describing his first day on Malta had this to say about the second:

'We climbed up to 4,000 feet, and then the barrage was put up by the harbour defences and the cruiser. The C.O. dived down into it and I followed close on him. We flew three times to and fro in the barrage, trusting to luck to avoid the flak. Then I spotted a Ju 87 climbing out of the fringe of the barrage and I turned and chased him. I gave him a one-second burst of cannon and he broke off sharply to the left. At that moment, another Ju 87 came up in front of my nose and I turned into him and I let him have it. His engine started to pour out black smoke and he started weaving. I kept the button pushed hard, and after a further two or three-second burst with the one cannon I had left, the other having jammed, he keeled over at 1,500 feet and went into the drink.

'I then spotted a 109 firing at me from behind and pulled the kite round to port, and after one and a half turns got on his tail. Before I could fire, another 109 cut across my bows from the port side and I turned straight on his tail and fired till my cannon stopped through lack of ammo. He was hit and his engine poured out black smoke, but I had to beat it as I was now defenceless and two more 109s were attacking me.

'I spiralled straight down to the sea at full throttle, and then weaved violently towards land with the two 109s still firing at me. I went under the fringe of the smokescreen to try to throw them off, but when I came out the other side I found them both sitting up top waiting for me. I therefore kept right down at nought feet and steep-turned towards them, noticing the smoke from their gun ports as I did so. After about five minutes of this, I managed to throw them off. I landed back at Takali and made out my report, claiming one 87 destroyed and one Me 109 damaged.'

That day was 10 May 1942. Spitfire sorties numbered 110 and Hurricane sorties fourteen. They destroyed fifteen attackers, while ack-ack accounted for a further eight. Three Spitfires were lost, but two of the pilots survived, so *Welshman* had been protected from enemy air attack at a cost of one pilot killed. After that the Germans made fewer daylight raids but more by night – rather like the Battle of Britain pattern. Their losses continued to be substantial, though.

Gradually a new plan was introduced of intercepting bombers before they could reach Malta, and this in time tilted the scales still further against the Germans. The inevitable result of this plan was that pilots and aeroplanes were liable to come down in the Mediterranean, and so the Air-Sea Rescue Service became more vital than ever. This is just one typical story from a high-speed launch log:

'At 1100 we had a call-out in HSL 128 for a Spitfire pilot, said to have baled out on a bearing of 160 Hal Far, about 100 yards out. Sounded like a piece of cake, for even though enemy fighters were plentiful in the vicinity, the position given was close to the island and we now had Spitfires on the job as well as Hurricanes. Getting on the given bearing, we steamed 100, 200, 300 yards – still nothing seen – and kept on going, though enemy activity was getting more and more lively overhead.

After we had steamed out about three miles, one of the escorting Hurricanes was shot down a couple of miles ahead of us. It was while we were investigating this wreckage that Jerry got closest to us, but even then the bullets only churned up the water over 100 feet away. As there was no survivor from this crash and still no sign of the original pilot for whom we had been called out, I decided to make for base, but on our way back we saw another fighter crash about six miles over to the westward and a parachute drifting down. We picked this pilot up within a few minutes of his hitting the water, and he turned out to be a Hun – a cheery soul who advised us to get back ashore before we were hurt.

'As we were then fairly well out, I decided to run out and then come in on our original bearing from a distance of about ten miles – as even the worst possible estimate of distance could hardly be over ten miles out. We actually found the Spitfire pilot in his dinghy about nine miles from the land, and the German pilot insisted upon shaking hands with him as he welcomed him aboard.'

War was strange.

Malta was still besieged, short of food, battered and bombed. The convoys still had to claw their tortuous way to and from the island. As

Beaufighters over Malta in the later stages of the air war

late as 11 October 1942, fifty-eight bombers blasted Malta, and during the next week there were nearly 250 raids by day. But on 23 October came El Alamein and sweeping success in the Western Desert. At long last, the siege of the island was raised.

And it was from Malta that Spitfire fighter-bombers first flew, carrying 250-pounders for bombing raids on enemy airfields in Sicily. The Allies were switching from the defensive to the offensive in the Mediterranean as elsewhere.

Continuing the story still further ahead, on 11 September 1943 came Sir Andrew Cunningham's classic signal to the Admiralty in London:

From: C IN C MEDITERRANEAN   To: ADMIRALTY

Be pleased to inform their Lordships that
the Italian battlefleet now lies at anchor
under the guns of the fortress of Malta.

13 *Air Escape from Java*

The sprawling 600-mile island of Java in the Dutch East Indies was falling to the Japanese. But in the rush, eighteen Americans were left behind. Then while they were wondering what to do about it, ten enemy Zeros dived down over their airfield, sent staccato machine-gun fire over the dusty ground, peeled off, and throbbed away into the distance. The hearts of the Yanks had been throbbing, too, as they lay on their stomachs, but now they limbered up again to survey the scarred airfield.

The only way out of Java was by air, and the only one of the Yanks able to fly was a young pilot, Cherry Mission. So he looked around the airfield after the raid to see what assets, if any, they had. The total: four crippled aeroplanes. Three Flying Fortresses and a B-18. Mission pointed to the B-18 and said, 'It's a wreck – but it's the only one I can fly.' Sergeant Hayes glanced up at the sky and said, 'Well, we've got to get out of here fast – somehow.'

Mission clambered into the aircraft to test the engine, as the others looked on silently, each with their own particular thoughts and feelings. Only a few minutes passed before he emerged to say, 'It won't work.'

Sergeant Hayes did not comment, but went over to the damaged aircraft, took a preliminary look at the engine, then stripped off his shirt and went to work on it. For the next two days he ate altogether just six sandwiches and drank some water, yet by the third day he had repaired the engine, and was able to say, 'It ought to fly now.'

But before they could celebrate, the whine of Zeros sent them for shelter again. The morse-code chatter from the enemy guns punctuated and punctured the field – and the B-18 – so that when they rushed up to examine the damage they found all Hayes' work had been ruined. They were back where they had been before. The situation became acute now, for among the group were civilians including Mission's young American wife.

Hayes had another idea in hand, however, as he sized up the three Flying Forts on the riddled airfield. 'I shan't be long', he called to the rest, and vanished.

A quarter of an hour later he returned with some sixty Dutchmen. He showed them the Fortresses. They appreciated the Americans' plight and agreed to help at once. Hayes decided which one of the Forts was least damaged and then he organised stripping the remaining two of everything that could be transferred to the chosen plane. Three days later, the engines were working, but the wings seemed in tatters. The tail had been shot away, while the wing flaps were non-existent.

'I don't think we can get her off the ground,' Mission said.

'But we've got to,' Hayes insisted.

'Somehow they fitted parts into the plane, which now looked like a crazy patchwork rather than a real flying machine. Next Hayes decided: 'We need space. Eighteen people take up a lot of room.'

So they stripped the interior of seats, parachutes, everything possible. At last they were ready, and Hayes called the group before him.

'I want you to know that you're putting your lives in my hands. I've never flown a plane before. I don't know how long this plane will stay together. I can't even promise you that she'll get off the ground. And if the Japs attack us while we're in the air, we won't have a chance. If anyone thinks they'll be safer here, they're quite free to stay.'

No-one wanted to stay.

Tensely they trooped into the aeroplane, sitting on the bare floor. Hayes and Mission took over the seats of pilot and co-pilot of the Flying Fortress. Neither knew how to fly her. Hayes started the engines, and as they warmed up he studied the maze of strange controls. Mission sat beside him. Mrs Mission was with the rest of the passengers.

Suddenly they sensed the rapid chug of machine gun bullets slapping into the side of the plane and piercing through its thin metal. They all dived for the floor.

Hayes' hand automatically, instinctively, moved to open the throttle. It was a natural reaction. But Mission stopped him, shouting, 'Don't take off now, for God's sake, or they'll shoot us down like an October duck.'

Hayes waited, itching to get airborne. For ten minutes, the four engines of the Flying Fort went on roaring, while seven Zeros trained a tracery of fire at the machine. Finally they must have thought they had finished it off, for one by one the Zeros zoomed away over the jungles of Java, leaving Hayes and Mission the familiar task of surveying the damage. Surprisingly, it proved negligible, and no one had been hit by the bullets. But something might have happened to the Fortress which would only show up when it was too late and they were taking off – or actually in the air. But it was literally now or never.

Hayes eased the throttle and the tattered ship shivered down the runway, gradually gathering momentum. Nothing collapsed. The Fortress gained speed, when Mission suddenly shouted in the pilot's ear, 'Hayes – even an empty Fort needs a 3,000-foot runway to lift. This is only 2,800 – and we're filled. Move the stick gently, boy: move it gently.'

The Fortress clambered off the ground, but bounced down. Mission watched the manifold pressure edge from danger point of 46 up to 50. Hayes' hands eased the controls back and the plane lifted. Wobbling like a wounded bird, she staggered forward over the forest. The passengers watched the foliage flash by them, much too near. Gradually she gained height, leaving the trees behind, till a few minutes later they shed the Java mainland, crossed the coastline, and thundered out over the Timor Sea.

But the sea bore a black, foreboding face: an endless blur beneath them. And the sky, too, had a darkness that could conceal Zeros at any

Hayes never got his B-17 high enough to make contrails like this one, but he flew from Java to Australia across the Timor Sea with eighteen people aboard, never having flown a 'plane before

time. It would need no more than a single accurate burst to finish off the 'Fort' in this vulnerable state.

Her engines wheezed away, as the passengers huddled themselves against the fuselage. They were without armament, without maps, without instruments. Mission kept his eyes on the dim horizon to give the pilot advice on navigation from time to time. Mrs Mission acted as observer.

Hayes himself, a man who had never flown an aeroplane before, kept the huge machine moving forward over the waters. Timor. The sea of fear.

Hour upon hour for a thousand miles or more. Mesmerised by the expanse and ellipse of sea and air, they had to concentrate to avoid losing control of things. Hayes was wonderful. All they knew was that they headed in approximately the right direction, but in these vastnesses it would be quite possible to miss Australia altogether. That was their goal.

More miles. Finally Mission pointed ahead and said simply, 'Land.'

The north coast of the continent scribbled and shaped up before them through the screen. A rustle of excitement was permitted to escape among them, though they knew first, that this might not be Australia at all but Japanese-held territory, and second, that the detail of landing the battered giant of a bomber would be hazardous. That was an understatement.

'Look,' said Mission, 'There's a clearing near that beach. Maybe you can set her down easy and run up the beach.'

Hayes nodded and the nose of the Fortress dipped, too, as if in agreement. The worst moment was coming up to meet them any minute, any second, now. They were only feet in the air. The 'Fort' hit hard, bounced off the beach, levelled off and stayed on the sands. It plopped and pounded along, then slowed and stopped. The propellers died until the blades became visible. Twenty people jumped down to the Australian ground, hardly yet able to appreciate the miracle that had whisked and borne them out of a much-razed Java airstrip and deposited them on a friendly shore. As they talked it over together afterwards, Sergeant Hayes said, 'I'd like to be a real pilot some day.'

14 *Bomber Offensive*

Soon after Fighter Command had won the Battle of Britain and beaten the Blitz, Bomber Command was on the offensive against Germany. These two examples typify the conditions encountered and overcome. One is the story of a single bomber; the other, an account of a 1,000-aircraft raid. Each is only a fragment of the whole air war.

First, the flight of Wellington T for Tommy. At 2330 hours one summer night in the middle years of the war, aircraft T2619 took off in thick darkness on an operational flight to Germany. Known to all concerned as T for Tommy, the Wellington had seven 500-pound bombs on board and its crew were all sergeants. Saich, who came from Dunmow, was the pilot; Telling, an Epsom man, the second pilot; the navigator was Smitten, a Canadian from Edmonton; while the remaining three were an Englishman, Trott, from Sheffield, and two more Canadians – Hooper from Vancouver, the front gunner, and English from Picton, Nova Scotia, the rear gunner. Their target lay in the German port of Bremen.

At first it seemed that they would have trouble finding the target at all. Just before T for Tommy reached the city, however, it flew out of the clouds into a clear sky intersected by the sharp beams of searchlights. A slight haze hung over the rooftops 11,000 feet below, but Sergeant Smitten found the target and Sergeant Saich began his bombing run. The time was 0140 hours. One bomb was released. Then the roving, probing lights caught and held T for Tommy in a cone which grew in size and intensity as more and more beams concentrated upon the aircraft.

As soon as the enemy ground defences got it in their sights and range, the bomber became the target of intense and accurate fire. Two shells burst at zero range, one just behind and below the rear turret, the other inside the fuselage itself, level with the leading edge of the tailplane.

The first shell wounded Sergeant English, the rear gunner, in the shoulder and hand, and cut the hydraulic controls to the turret, so that it could no longer be turned except by the slow process of cranking it. Fragments of the other shell riddled the rear part of the fuselage, and set on fire the fabric covering it and the tail fin, which was a special characteristic of the Wellington bomber.

In a few seconds, T for Tommy looked like a flying torch, thus presenting the kind of target that anti-aircraft gunners hoped for – and aircraft crews prayed against. The enemy jumped at it. The flames seemed to be the signal for every ground gun in the target zone to fire directly at them.

Wellington taking off

Air Chief Marshal Sir
Arthur Harris, C-in-C
Bomber Command RAF
from February 1942

And all this time, the rear gunner was in the blazing end of the torch.

Sergeant Saich, the pilot, took violent evasive action and actually managed to throw the German gunners off their aim – at least momentarily. While he was doing so, Smitten, the navigator, went to the help of English in the rear turret. He made his way down the rocking, shell-split fuselage till he was stopped short by the fire separating him from the turret. For the moment he could go no further.

He crawled back a little way, snatched a fire-extinguisher, and returned to the fire in the fuselage, which he somehow subdued. Above him the fin still flamed. He sprayed it with all that was left of the methyl-bromide in the extinguisher, thrusting it through the hot framework of the fuselage – from which the fabric had been burned. Eventually Smitten reached the turret.

By the time he got there, Sergeant English was making preparations to abandon the aircraft by swinging the turret round into the beam position. A rear gunner baled out by turning his turret until the steel doors, through which he entered and left it, faced the open air to port or starboard. Normally the doors faced the interior of the fuselage. He would then open the doors and throw himself out backwards.

English was about to do this when Smitten reached him. He had opened the doors, and now they refused to close. Smitten went back and returned with a light axe. He leaned out through a hole beneath the fin, which he had just saved from burning, and with the wind of the slipstream tearing at him, hacked away at the doors till they fell off. At that stage English was able to rotate his turret by the hand gear. As soon as the gaping hole coincided with the end of the fuselage, he extricated himself and entered the aircraft – or what was left of it.

While all this was going on astern, more trouble broke out forward. The Wellington was hit again, and a shell splinter set light to the flares carried in the port wing. These were for use in an emergency, when a forced landing might have to be made in darkness: the sort of emergency that actually existed at that precise time. The flares burned so brightly that Saich thought the port engine was on fire. He promptly turned off its petrol, opened the throttle fully and switched off. Soon the flames died down, for the flares had burned their way through the fabric of the main-plane and fallen from the aircraft.

Realising what had happened, Saich turned on the petrol again and restarted the engine. At his orders, Telling, the second pilot, crouched beside the main spar behind the wireless cabin, pumping all the oil that could be extracted from a riddled auxiliary tank. T for Tommy was still under the most massed ack-ack fire, and one of the shell splinters wounded Telling. Their hail continued to tear through the fuselage.

Already by this time many men would have thought it only sensible to abandon the aircraft, but yet a further misfortune was to befall the Wellington. At the moment when the Germans scored their first hit, the bomb doors were actually open. The aircraft had been completing its

Wellingtons taking off at dusk for another raid against Germany

first bombing run-up and one of the bombs had just gone down on Bremen.

That anti-aircraft shell caused such havoc that it became impossible either to close the bomb doors or to release the remaining six bombs – since the hydraulic pipes had been punctured and the electrical wiring to the slips severed. Each of the bombs weighed 500 pounds. As well as all this, and the damage to the fuselage, rear turret, rudder and fin, a shell had knocked a large hole in the starboard tank.

In this extraordinary condition, T for Tommy began to head for base. The chances of making it seemed slim. With the bomb doors open and a heavy load still on board, the aircraft was very hard to control. Saich's task was not made any easier by the hole in the wing. The draught hissed through this hole, blanketing the starboard aileron, which was virtually useless. Nevertheless, he held sternly to the homeward course given him by Smitten. T for Tommy choked its way back over the North Sea.

Its speed had been cut to an alarmingly low level, and the petrol gauges registered empty for some two hours out of the four on that memorable return route. They flew on and on, over nearly 300 miles of sea, until at 0535 hours, the Wellington crossed the East Anglian coast dead on track. With dry land beneath him once more, Saich determined to make a forced landing, for he thought that at any moment the engine would splutter to stop for lack of fuel.

The sky was beginning to take on a few pale pastels as Saich picked out a barley field where it seemed to him that a landing might be made. In the half-light he did not see the obstruction poles set up in the field to hinder an enemy airborne invasion.

Saich now set about making his perilous descent. The flaps would not work, and when he came to pump the undercarriage down with the emergency hydraulic hand-pump, he found that owing to loss of oil it would only push the tail wheel and one of the main wheels into their positions. T for Tommy came in to land, a little lopsided to take full advantage of the one sound wheel. On touching down, the aircraft swung round, but an obstruction pole violently arrested its progress. It shuddered and then came abruptly to rest on its belly with its back broken. Save for many bumps and bruises, none of the crew suffered further hurt.

But T for Tommy was little more than a wreck. It had flown back to that East Anglian barley field with a huge hole in its starboard wing, with uncounted smaller holes in its fuselage, with nine feet of fabric burned entirely away forward from the rear turret, with half the fin and half the rudder in the same condition. Yet it flew home.

The story of T for Tommy was not unique, nor even unusual. If it had been, the bomber build-up could not have continued as it did. Many other aircraft of Bomber Command sustained similar damage and survived at least long enough to bring their crews back to Britain to fly on other days and nights. Not only Wellingtons, but Blenheims, Hampdens, Whitleys, Stirlings, Halifaxes, Manchesters and Lancasters.

So from the story of one bomber to a 1,000-bomber blitz on Cologne. Such massive attacks required much planning and preparation. Bomber

Nearly 100 Lancasters in massed daylight raid

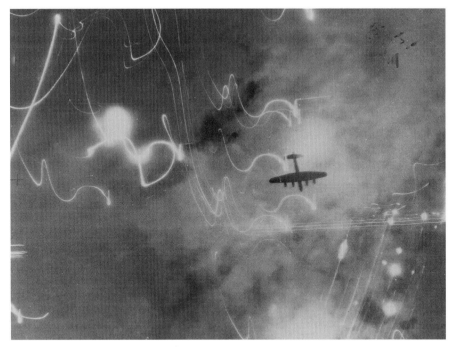

Abstracts in the night sky greet Lancasters over Germany

Bombers encountering impressive flak barrage

Command were using a new technique of concentrating a large force of aircraft for a short time over a single target. The effect of this was to dislocate, if not paralyse, all ground defences and air raid precautions. Before these raids, however, there was often a steady softening-up process.

The first example of these new stupendous-scale tactics was the attack on the Renault works in France. At this period, the Ruhr suffered eight heavy raids involving 1,555 aircraft altogether, besides three small attacks. In the same spell, Cologne was visited four times by a total of 559 aircraft. The damage done to the city was considerable. In the Nippes district, an industrial part, about 75,000 square yards occupied by workshops were damaged. Heavy bombs completely destroyed buildings nearby, covering an area of 6,000 square yards. The Franz Clouth rubber works, covering 168,000 square yards, were rendered useless, much of it being levelled to the ground. To the east of the Rhine, the bombers hit a chemical factory and buildings alongside. Severe damage was also done to the centre of Cologne. All this was confirmed by photographic evidence.

Then came the night of 30/31 May 1942. One thousand bombers brought chaos to Cologne. At the hour of take off the whole staff of one particular station was assembled around the aerodrome. The Station Commander himself sent off the aircraft. Two flare-paths were laid and the Wellingtons were dispatched simultaneously from both paths with only 300 yards between them. The first eleven got away in eight minutes: one every forty-four seconds. Some miles to the north, forty-three Halifaxes became airborne a little later. A few miles to the east, aircrews climbed into their Stirlings. Scenes such as these were taking place throughout eastern England. The Wellingtons arrived first over Cologne, followed closely by the Stirlings.

The CO of a squadron of Wellingtons said:

'When we got there, we saw many fires which had not yet taken real hold, but I thought it had all the makings of a successful raid. It was easy enough to see the city, for we could pick out the Rhine and the bridges quite clearly. There was little or no opposition over the target, I think because there were so many aircraft that the ground defences could not cope with them. We did meet with opposition on the outskirts but it was very indiscriminate. Before I left I saw fires growing larger and larger.'

It was then that the Stirlings arrived. Flying with them was Air Vice-Marshal Baldwin, commanding the Group to which they belonged:

'The weather forecast made it uncertain almost up to the last moment whether we should start. We had not been flying very long before we met much low cloud, and this depressed me. The front gunner got a pinpoint on an island off the Dutch coast but the weather was still somewhat thick and there was an Alpine range of cloud to starboard. Suddenly, 30 or 40 miles from Cologne, I saw the ground and then the flak. It grew clearer

Devastation of a German city caused by successive air attacks

and clearer until near the city visibility was perfect. First I saw a lake, gleaming in the moonlight, then I could see fires beginning to glow, and then searchlights which wavered and flak coming up in a haphazard manner.

'The sky was full of aircraft all heading for Cologne. I made out Wellingtons, Hampdens, a Whitley and other Stirlings. We sheared off the city for a moment, while the captain decided what would be the best way into the target. It was then that I caught sight of the twin towers of Cologne Cathedral, silhouetted against the light of three huge fires that looked as though they were streaming from open blast furnaces.

'We went in to bomb, having for company a Wellington to starboard and another Stirling to port. Coming out we circled the flak barrage and it was eight minutes after bombing that we set course for home. Looking back, the fires seemed like rising suns and this effect became more pronounced as we drew further away. Then, with the searchlights rising from the fires, it seemed that we were leaving behind us a huge representation of the Japanese banner. Within nine minutes of the coast we circled to take a last look. The fires then resembled distant volcanoes.'

When the Halifaxes arrived, the raid had already been going on for an hour. Latecomers could see the cauldron of Cologne sixty miles distant, first as a dull red glow over a large area of ground. The captain of one Halifax and his navigator both thought that the fire they were flying towards was too enormous to be anything but a specially elaborate diversion created by the Germans. The pilot of another Halifax thought that a heath or a whole forest must be ablaze.

But ten miles off they saw that the great glow came from a town on fire, and as they flew nearer still they could see more and more loads of incendiaries burning in long, narrow rectangles. These were composed of pinpoints of bright white patches, each of which swiftly blossomed into a rose of fire. Like the others, the Halifaxes identified the target easily by the bridges over the Rhine.

One captain reported:

> 'So vast was the burning that ordinary fires on the outskirts of the city or outside it, which I should usually describe as very big, looked quite unimportant. It was strange to see the flames reflected on our aircraft. It looked at times as though we were on fire ourselves, with the red glow dancing up and down on the wings.'

For several days, reconnaissance aircraft could not photograph Cologne. The smoke of the burning ruins was still too thick. It was not until 5 June that good pictures were taken. When intelligence examined these prints, the damage revealed was realised to be very great.

Cologne was a city of 750,000 people, the third largest in Germany. The total area of complete destruction caused on 30/31 May amounted to 2,904,000 square yards, compared to exactly ten per cent of that area damaged or destroyed in the four former raids. Of the area laid waste, about half was in the centre of the city. The cathedral appeared to be unscathed, except for damage to windows, but 250 factory buildings and workshops were either wiped out or badly damaged.

A significant feature of the photographs taken on 5 June was that they disclosed what appeared to be a dead city. An air raid warning would have cleared the streets while the pictures were actually being taken, but there were no signs of trains, trams, buses or cars. Apart from the material damage, the casualties caused to the population were bound to be heavy, too. But it must be borne in mind that by this stage it was total war on both sides.

The attack on Cologne was followed two nights later by a raid on the Ruhr in much the same strength. Here, too, Bomber Command caused catastrophic damage and fires. In these larger raids, our losses averaged under four per cent of the aircraft used. Although that sounds moderate enough, this represented forty aircraft, plus the precious lives of possibly over a hundred aircrew.

In the attack on the Ruhr, a Halifax was caught by searchlights over Essen and heavily shelled. The port outer engine went out of action and the aircraft was held for fifteen minutes in a cone of some fifty beams. A shell splinter broke the window in front of the captain and blinded him in one eye. On the way home, an Me 110 night fighter jumped on the crippled bomber, but the rear gunner drove off the intruder, setting his starboard engine aflame. Near Dunkirk, searchlights once more picked up the Halifax and flak knocked out the inner starboard engine. The bomber got back on two engines – typical of many episodes.

On the next night, the Ruhr received another attack. Then it was Bremen, then a night's pause, then the Ruhr again, then Emden, then Bremen again. So it went on night after night. This was the British bomber offensive.

15 *Duel in the Stratosphere*

Above 35,000 feet without a pressure cabin, a man must struggle to remain conscious – even with the help of oxygen. He can suffer not only from the intense cold but also from temporary paralysis of the limbs; expanding gases which distend the intestines; and sometimes from 'the bends'. The last condition is of course an affliction experienced by deep sea divers, where all the joints of the body are gripped by a pain said to be more intense than any other. Great height also has a temporary effect on a man's mind, plunging him into despondency against his will.

One day in the summer of 1942, Flying Officer G.W.H. Reynolds was flying a Spitfire which had been modified and stripped of most things save its guns. Reynolds had even dispensed with his Mae West and dinghy. He sighted a Junkers 86 reconnaissance aircraft with two men sitting securely in a pressure cabin in the nose. He was just north of Cairo and he pursued it towards Alexandria, then out to sea at an ever-increasing height. At 37,000 feet he almost reached it and began to zigzag back and forth just below in order not to overshoot. The Ju 86 zigzagged in the same manner, trying to stay just above the Spitfire and force it to lose a little height on each turn.

The long slow duel in the rarefied atmosphere proceeded in this way until Reynolds was at a height of 40,000 feet. He realised then that he could not get any higher until he had used some more petrol to lighten the aircraft. He started to calculate how much petrol he could use and how far out to sea he could go before he would be forced to turn back in order to reach home safely.

In the middle of these calculations he temporarily blacked out, having just sufficient time to turn his oxygen tap to full emergency to bring himself round again. He then slowly forced the Spitfire higher still. At a remarkable 42,000 feet he was practically level with the Ju 86, slowly closing. At a range of fifty yards he opened fire. Flame and grey smoke whipped backwards from the starboard engine of the enemy aircraft, which banked abruptly to the left.

Reynolds had intended to follow, but his Spitfire began not to function properly and he fell nearly 10,000 feet very quickly. The pilot's own physical endurance was in any case practically exhausted. He described his condition later: 'I had been experiencing great pain at that height, as I was over 40,000 feet for nearly half an hour and felt rather ill. Added to this, my petrol and oxygen were low and I wished to get home as quickly as possible. I landed at base with five gallons of petrol left.'

He did not know when he landed whether or not he had destroyed the

Ju 86, but its loss was confirmed afterwards. The first stratosphere reconnaissance aircraft had been shot down.

The destruction of this Ju 86 was the initial success in a struggle
between the German stratosphere reconnaissance aircraft of Egypt – such
reconnaissance was the only daylight activity over that country that the
Luftwaffe usually dared attempt – and a small group of test pilots and
engineers of the RAF who maintained that these high-flying Germans
could be reached and destroyed by a modified Spitfire. The Ju 86s were
certainly inaccessible to any other form of attack.

The pilots who undertook this task were not young men. Reynolds was
approaching forty years of age, yet he flew above 40,000 feet some
twenty-five times within a month. His first success came only after a lot
of trial and endurance, but the three other Ju 86 aircraft which the
Germans possessed for this reconnaissance work were soon to be
destroyed in the same way that the first had been.

However, the enemy flew at ever-increasing altitudes. The last one was
pursued to nearly 50,000 feet. This one also fell to Reynolds. He had been
higher than 45,000 feet for more than an hour; his whole cockpit, instrument panel, control column and perspex were thickly coated with ice;
his body was racked with pain and his arms were temporarily paralysed;
and his eyesight was also failing with weakness. When he met the Ju 86
at a distance of only 100 yards but at a height of 50,000 feet, he was physically incapable of firing his guns, yet the enemy turned and fled towards
the sea.

Reynolds manoeuvred his fighter to follow it by moving the position
of his body in the delicately balanced aircraft. He caught the enemy plane
once more, far out over the Mediterranean, and managed to move his
hands just sufficiently to press the firing button. The Ju 86 was destroyed.
The Spitfire completed much of its flight back to base in a powerless glide.

When the pilot started to glide home, he glanced around and below at
a remarkable panorama. He could see the whole of the eastern
Mediterranean spread out like a map beneath him. To the west he could
see past Benghazi into the Gulf of Sirte; to the east the coastline of
Palestine and Syria with the mountains beyond; behind him lay unrolled
the island-sprinkled Aegean; in front lay Egypt revealed at one glance
from the coast to beyond Cairo, and the length of the Suez Canal from
Port Said to Suez itself.

Down there in the North African desert, the army was fighting it out.
The decisive twelve months were from February 1942 to January 1943.
By the summer of 1942 the new air weapon had been tested and proved.
During the retreat to El Alamein, RAF Middle East held off the *Luftwaffe*,
shielded the army, and battled grimly to protect the seaborne convoys.
Then came El Alamein . . .

16 *The Air Battle of El Alamein*

The second battle of El Alamein was the turning point of the desert war in North Africa. Rommel's German and Italian army was routed. It was Britain's first great land victory of the war. In the run-up to the battle, and during it, air forces played a very significant role.

At 2200 hours on 23 October the first wave of more than seventy bombers and flare-dropping aircraft switched the nightly attack away from the enemy landing grounds and on to his troop positions all along the battle front. More than thirty Hurricanes, their pilots trained in night flying started at Alamein and strafed as far back as Fuka.

The bombers kept on throughout the night, and the usual fires and explosions broke out in the desert below. One fire in the south threw smoke up to 3,000 feet, while in the north a large ammunition dump was blown. At first the aircraft were met with strong anti-aircraft fire, but later in the night it dwindled appreciably. The enemy gunners' attention was distracted elsewhere. Suddenly the battle line sparkled with gun flashes. For twenty minutes, 800 Allied guns fired continuously along the front. The artillery had opened fire, and the sappers and infantry were moving steadily forwards into the enemy minefields, storming Miteiriya Ridge. By dawn they had made and held gaps in the minefields.

They had been assisted by a few light bombers which flew at a low level across the minefields and laid smokescreens at the points of assault. Others laid them at places where no assault was intended, so as to confuse the enemy. One laid a smokescreen along a beach off which some British warships were manoeuvring with a great show of gunfire and commotion. So well did they deceive the enemy that next day Rome radio reported repulsing with heavy losses a British landing which had not been attempted.

It had become a tradition of the Desert Air Force that on critical days of land warfare it should create a new record in the air. It did so on 24 October, the first full day of the land assault. The total number of sorties flown during that day was nearly 1,000. The whole weight was flying against the battle area, chiefly just west of the two gaps in the minefields. There were two smaller raids on Daba landing grounds. After the days and nights of attack sustained by the *Luftwaffe*, they thought more of warding off the bombs from their air dispersal areas than of intervening in this first day of full battle. Some Messerschmitts and Macchis made a few half-hearted attacks, but these amounted to nothing compared with the display of Allied air power. In fact, there were plenty of targets for the *Luftwaffe*, since all the Allied armour lay behind the minefields, waiting for the gaps to be enlarged sufficiently for it to pass through. But the Stukas did not come.

The chief opposition to the Allied bombers came from the German

Hurricane attacking enemy tank in the desert war. Hurricanes played a major role in the air battle of El Alamein

ground gunners. Having no tanks to meet at that stage, they swung their guns upwards and filled the sky with shells. Six bombers and five fighters were shot down. It was the heaviest bomber loss the British had ever suffered in fighter-escorted raids. On the other hand, it was the heaviest bombing assault the light squadrons had ever delivered.

All day long, dust clouds hung over the landing grounds, created by the wheels at take-off. Ground crews toiled on, while aircrews took scant rest. They had the moral fillip of knowing that this was the first ground assault assisted by an air offensive on such a scale. As they flew, the aircrews gazed down at countless flashes of gunfire. Little white puffs of exploding shells spattered the desert air below them like 'handfuls of flung rice' as someone said. By midday, pilots were already reporting areas of broken trucks, many ablaze, some burned out and still smouldering.

That night the Wellington crews could see battles being fought beneath them in the moonlight. Somewhere down there the infantry had widened the gaps, and the tanks and guns were passing through. Bombs started many fires ahead of them, one by the coast burning fiercely for five hours. It was a desert dawn before the last Wellington drew away. By then the tanks and guns were all west of the first line of the enemy minefields and the infantry solidly held the bridge in the rear.

Daylight on 25 October: the British Eighth Army held a bulge in the north of the Alamein line a mile or two away from the coast. This bulge was nicknamed 'the fist'. Away to the south, the attack had been sufficient to pin down the enemy airmen opposing it, but the commanding Himeimat Ridge had not been taken. From 'the fist' down to Qattara, the line ran more or less straight, due north to south.

On that day, the second of the land battles, the *Luftwaffe* did manage to make some sort of a challenge, but it cost them seven Messerschmitts destroyed and many more probables, while the British lost one Kittyhawk. The challenge was enough to switch a lot of the light bombing strength back on Daba and Fuka, but insufficient to cut down the overall programme by a single sortie. Nor was it enough to curb the Beaufighters which were ranging the back areas, shooting up enemy supplies.

Seven Beaufighters found a merchant ship and a destroyer which had nearly succeeded in reaching Tobruk. They lay only a mile offshore and a few miles west of the port. The cannon attack of the Beaufighters left both vessels with smoke drifting upwards, but did not sink them.

Having shot down two Ju 88s and a Dornier flying boat, the Beaufighters hurried back to their base to lead out a striking force of bombers and torpedo-carriers. The torpedoes missed, but a bomb from a Bisley blew the merchant ship to pieces and she sank in a few minutes. One of the Beaufighters shot down two Italian CR42s. These were actually obsolete fighters whose presence indicated the straits of the enemy air forces in the desert.

Shortly afterwards, another force of eight Beaufighters cut into the enemy air supply route from Crete to the battle. They found some thirty-five Ju 52 transports escorted by six twin-engine Me 110s a few miles north of Tobruk. Some of the RAF fighters held off the Me 110s, shooting one of them down, while the rest went after the Junkers. They destroyed at least four.

The battle on the ground was taking a definite shape by 26 October. 'The Fist' had thrust its way more firmly into the enemy's face, broadening out to the north and south. British troops held the whole of Miteiriya Ridge, and the tanks were embattled in strong defensive positions against which the enemy was permitted to wear out his armour. In the northern sector alone, some seventy enemy tanks had already been lost, one armoured division being reduced after only twenty-four hours' fighting to about five runners.

Another German division had been brought up from the south by a night march and was thrust into battle together with the 90th Light, veterans of Rommel's *Afrika Korps*. As they moved at night, they were bombed by the RAF and as they tried to form up by day they were bombed again. There were nine full-scale bombing raids during the day, not one bomber being lost, while numerous formations of fighter-bombers slipped down to the south, wiping out four tanks and two armoured cars.

High over the battle swept the Spitfires, still firmly holding their front line above Daba. The Kittyhawks darted far past that line, and fired several petrol convoys on the coast road around Sidi Barrani. The *Luftwaffe* was still trying and still losing. During the day, seventeen enemy aircraft were shot down by British fighters.

But the greatest achievement of that day, 26 October, lay out to sea off the Tobruk coast, where British air power destroyed a whole convoy. Next day ashore the enemy army were gathered together to attempt five counter-attacks. The 28th of October was probably the decisive day, even though the battle was fought furiously for several days after that. Within the space of two-and-a-half hours, the RAF carried out seven full-scale bombing raids on the *Afrika Korps*, dropping eighty tons of bombs in an area measuring some three miles by two. Pattern after pattern of bomb bursts spread from all directions across this area of concentration. Six times the German tank crews broke hastily and scattered across the desert; six times they reformed. The seventh time they did not reform. There was no counter-attack by the *Afrika Korps* on the Eighth Army. The enemy did not try to take the initiative again in the Battle of El Alamein.

About a week later, the enemy retreat was in full flood. One bomber pilot said, 'As we swept the road, we saw it packed with transport. But every vehicle was stopped, and everywhere there were tiny trails of dust where crews were running into the desert. Every bomber in our formation turned and flew down the road, spilling bombs on vehicles and men. I never saw such a scene of destruction'.

South of the Alamein position, in a few days RAF bombers would be searching for Italians, not to bomb them but to drop them water and food so that they would not die before they could be taken prisoner.

Meanwhile the main preoccupation was the road. By dusk whole lengths of it were blazing with fires bright enough for the Wellingtons to attack all night. This was the night they had been waiting for: they called it 'Bombers' Benefit'. The enemy vehicles were all concentrated around the thin ribbon of the coast road, lit by the fires that were destroying them. The Wellingtons started about sixty fresh fires along the stretch of road that runs through Daba. The truck columns continued to drive westwards throughout the night, traversing the area of fiercest attack under cover of darkness.

The road was so crowded that it reminded one pilot of Brighton road on August Bank Holiday in days of peace, or the Epsom road on Derby Day. The bombers came down low to drop their loads, then lower still to open fire with machine guns. According to one Wellington crew member:

> 'As we came in to drop our first stick the vehicles careered madly off the road. It looked absolutely crazy. I saw one overturn as it went over the bank. We could see troops leaping out and running away like cockroaches. They were colliding and jumping head first into patches of scrub or any hole they could find.
>
> 'Our first stick cracked right across the lorries at right angles. We could see some of the lorries coming up in the air . . . We went in low over a tented encampment and could see our tracer cutting through the canvas.'

It was then 4 November. After twelve days and nights, the retreat had become a rout. The Air Battle of El Alamein was over. And so was the land battle.

17 *The Story of Two Brothers*

Mark Mathis came from San Angelo, Texas, a town which, like all of Texas, seemed to specialise in fliers. With his brother Jack, who was four years younger, he grew up in the special Texas way – put a kid into cowboy boots until he was old enough for flying boots. The Mathis boys lived in town but put in a lot of time on their grandfather's ranch.

By the time they were ready to fly, both were over six foot tall. Mark, the taller, had a long neck and a hard jaw, and a reputation for spinning tall stories. Jack was an inch shorter, much darker, and quiet. But he was an irrepressible practical joker. In 1941, the brothers joined the Army, Mark from a job with Texas Light and Power, and Jack out of San Angelo Business College.

After a spell as enlisted men, the Mathis brothers passed the exams and went to preflight school at Ellington Field, Texas, early in 1942. When they were about to leave for bombardier courses, Mark did a little too much funny talking. That split up the brother team. The Mathis boys were razzing a maths instructor who became especially excited about Mark's barbs and reported him to the commandant of cadets. Although the brothers were equally good at maths, the CO made Mark stay three more weeks at school. Jack went to bombardier school at Victorville, California. Mark's setback put him into a later class at Midland, Texas. Then it happened that Jack became a bombardier in heavies and Mark and a bombardier-navigator in mediums.

One of Jack's fellow students, Lt Johnny Shoup of Boulder, Colorado, was staying with him at the Hilton Hotel in El Paso one time the cadets were on pass. Shoup told about one of Jack's gags that went too far for the perpetrator. Cadet Mathis, coming back to the hotel, saw some tough MPs herding a group of enlisted men into a truck. The fledgling officer asked them why. The MPs claimed the soldiers were drunk. Cadet Mathis said they weren't drunk; let them have their fun. Jack couldn't help it; he started to gag it up and act drunk himself. Lurching wildly he declaimed in a loud voice the innocence of all soldiers and the intolerance of MPs. Jack ended up in the 'dangdang' wagon among his enlisted pals.

In a few months a full-fledged bombardier, 2nd Lt Jack Mathis was slightly embarrassed one day when his CO got a much-forwarded letter asking what action had been taken on Cadet Mathis's drunkenness and disgracing the uniform. But Bill Calhoun, Jack's squadron CO, knew his man and his gags, and Jack lived it down. When the grand echelon moved out on overseas orders, twenty-year-old Jack became acting squadron adjutant. Bill Calhoun said he was 'a damned good executive'.

Then the B-17s flew to England.

This shot of a B-17 shows the nose guns and bomb-bay that were Jack Mathis' domain

Jack's first raid was the first one in which the Eighth Air Force penetrated Germany – Wilhelmshafen, 27 January 1943. Bill Calhoun said, 'Jack never had any nerves,' but the tall Texan became a man over Wilhelmshafen.

Jack began combat service with a 'superior' rating at his job; now he was giving something more than superior service. He set a quiet example to his squadron one day after returning from a mission. His crew armourers came into the ship as Jack swung down out of the hatch to go to debriefing. Jack said, 'Leave the guns the way they are – mine and Elliott's. We're going to clean them ourselves. From now on I'm taking care of my own guns'. It was the custom for ground crew members to clean and maintain the fifty-calibre nose guns of the busy bombardiers and navigators. But Jack and his navigator, Jesse H. Elliott of Jacksonville, Florida, began taking care of their own guns, spending two hours with the enlisted gunners in the armoury after a mission, cleaning, wiping, oiling, and storing the guns that brought the ship home.

Captain Calhoun let the idea percolate to other bombardiers and navigators, and ordered it then as an official policy of the squadron. The Group Commanding Officer followed.

Jack also inaugurated the practice of the bombardier inspecting the bomb doors before a mission. What good was it for a half-million-dollar ship, loaded with trained young men, painfully and perilously airborne by the sweat of a whole people, to arrive perfectly on the bomb run, hit the aiming point on the crosshairs, and have a careless dab of oil freeze the bomb bays shut? Jack Mathis considered that his job was to hit the target. There were many other jobs on the ship and on the ground and across the sea to the factory, that went into bombing Hitler from a Flying Fortress, but the act of Jack Mathis's index finger was the climax of all this labour. Nothing was to be overlooked if he could help it.

On rainy days, Jack was most likely to be working on the bomb trainer. Johnny Shoup, with whom Jack roomed, was often drawn into discussions of more accurate methods of computation; the bombardier is a mathematician in action.

There was another reason why Jack wanted to hit the aiming point. Like the other Americans who were in the killing business temporarily, he was proud of bombing military objectives only. He hated the Nazis, but he considered the people of France who lived near captive factories and ports harbouring Nazi submarines. One of his friends, Capt. Joe Strickland, a tall, sandy navigator from Liberty, Mississippi, told about some Fortress men who arrived mysteriously at the station after being on the missing list for months. How they got back was one of the deepest riddles of the war: it can only be said that they were helped home through France. Jack wanted to ask them all about the French people: he questioned them with the kind of look he had in his eyes when someone mentioned San Angelo. Joe Strickland voted Jack as 'a very conscientious bombardier'.

Brother Mark was pining away in the States, sweating out his orders to come overseas, while Jack's missions piled up: St Nazaire submarine pens, Rouen railway yards, and the sanguinary mission to Hamm by a handful of B-17s which flew into German railway yards far beyond any previous targets. The combat men who came home from Hamm had distorted faces. All they said was, 'Man, that was *rough*,' and they shook their heads.

One day Jack got a sizzling telegram. Mark had arrived! Jack asked Bill Calhoun to get him a jeep so he could pick up Mark and bring him back to the station.

The Mathis brothers arrived at Jack's station in the evening of 17 March in high old boyish spirits. Gags went flying and Mark had the guys looking at him sideways on account of the tall ones he was spinning. 'I never saw anyone catch on faster than Mark,' said Calhoun, 'In a couple of hours he was one of the fellows; seemed like he'd been around all the time'.

After dinner the combat men heard there was an attack order out. The Forts were going out the next day. The tall brothers from Texas had 'half the squadron' around them in the club that night. Mark claimed he once had five monkeys. When he got tired of the little monkeys he traded them in for a big one – a gorilla. This gorilla used to go along with him when he was a deputy sheriff in Texas. The reminiscences got down to earth after a while. Remember the time we threw that champagne party in the Rice Hotel when Shorty got married? How about the razzin' we gave that civilian maths instructor at Ellington Field? The Mathis boys, who hadn't seen each other for over a year, remembered their cadet days and when they were kids together in Texas.

No-one drank much – a few beers and early to bed. Thinking of the next day's job, Mark asked Bill Calhoun if he could go along with Jack. He got excited about the idea but Bill had to say he couldn't go: too much red tape getting permission from Wing and on up to Bomber Command. 'The way it would turn out,' said Jack, 'is that President Roosevelt wouldn't let you'.

It was mission number 14 for bombardier Jack Mathis of the B-17 *Duchess*, piloted by Capt. Harold L. Stouse of Spokane, Washington. The Forts were going to Vegesack, to the *Untersee* shipbuilding yards up the river from Bremen. The men said, 'another D.P. job – deep penetration raid.

In the truck going to the disperal area, Jack said, 'I want you to get into this outfit, Mark. I'll be going home soon for pilot training. This is the best station and ours is the best crew. I want you to take my place in *Duchess*.' Mark was more than half convinced that he liked Jack's gang.

Jesse Elliott, the navigator, installed Jack's guns in the ship so Jack and Mark would have a little more time to visit before the take-off. As Jack climbed in, Mark yelled up, 'See you boys at six o'clock'. Jack yelled back, 'Sweat us out on this one, boy'.

Mark watched the take-off with Joe Strickland, who was grounded that day. They played a little snooker in the club and went over to the tower early to watch the ships come in. 'Mark was happy as hell when he saw the first ship to land was *Duchess*,' said Bill Calhoun.

But *Duchess* did a funny thing, came in on the wrong runway without circling the aerodrome, or buzzing it the way the boys did after a tough job. *Duchess* came in abruptly and shot a red flare. The waiting ambulance dashed for the ship at the signal. Wounded aboard. Mark and Bill Calhoun went out in a jeep and got there after the ambulance had been loaded and had roared back to the station surgery. Capt. Stouse and Jesse Elliott faced Mark gravely and told him his brother had been wounded.

At the infirmary, Chaplain 'Holy Joe' Skoner of Chicago told Mark his brother was dead. He had died over Vegesack in a moment of grace of which legends were made.

Jesse Elliott was with Jack Mathis in the nose of the *Duchess*. This is his story as it was recorded in the deposition accompanying the citation of Lt Jack Mathis for the Congressional Medal of Honor, and also as related to Walter Cronkite of United Press.

'We ran into very little trouble on our raid on Vegesack until we started on the bombing run. A very heavy and accurate barrage of flak was thrown up at us just as we reached the target. Flak hit our ship and sounded like hail on the roof. I glanced at Lt Mathis who was crouched over his bombsight lining up the target. Jack was an easy-going guy and the flak didn't bother him. He wasn't saying a word – just sticking there over his bombsight, doing his job.

'Bomb bay doors are open,' I heard Jack call up to Capt. Stouse, and then instructions to climb a little more to reach bombing altitude.

'On the bomb run – that flak hit us. We were just seconds short of the bomb release point when a whole barrage of flak hit our squadron, which we were leading.

'One of the shells burst out to the right and a little below the nose. It couldn't have been over 30 feet away when it burst. If it had been much closer it would have knocked the whole plane over.

'A hunk of flak came tearing through the side of the nose. It shattered the glass on the right side and broke through with a loud crash.

'I saw Jack falling back toward me and threw up my arm to ward off the fall. By that time both of us were way back in the rear of the nose – blown back I guess by the flak flying in.

'I was sort of half-standing, half-lying against the back wall and Jack was leaning up against me. I didn't know he was injured at the time.

'Without any assistance from me he pulled himself back to his bomb-sight. His little seat had been knocked out from under him by the flak. It was way back in the ship and he sort of knelt over the bombsight.

'Part of my job as navigator is to keep the log of the flight, so I looked at my watch to start timing the fall of the bombs.

'I heard Jack call out on the intercom, "Bombs . . .". He usually called it out in a sort of singsong. But he never finished the phrase this time. The words just sort of trickled off, and I thought his throat mike had slipped out of place, so I finished out the phrase, 'Bombs away' for him. We don't start our evasive action to avoid the flak until those words go up to the pilot – and we all love that evasive action.

'I looked up and saw Jack reaching over to grab the bomb bay door handle. Just as he pushed the handle he slumped over backwards – I caught him. That was the first indication that anything was wrong. I saw his arm which was pretty badly shot.

'I guess they got you that time, old boy,' I remember saying, but then his head slumped over and I saw that the injuries were more serious than just some flak in the arm. I knew then that he was dead. I closed the bomb bay and returned to my post.

'He knew that as bombardier of the lead ship the results of the whole squadron might depend on his accuracy. And he didn't let anything stop him.'

Johnny Shoup was in the leading ship of the second element over Vegesack. The leading bombardier of the first element was Jack Mathis. Johnny saw Jack's bomb fall away at the exact moment he released his own. 'Our string fell right across the target. That's considered good bombing.'

The target photographs proved it conclusively. Jack's bombs were shown striking right on the aiming point. 'They hit the target,' said Mark Mathis. 'Jack had a reputation for that because he never would drop them until he was sure.'

In the hospital Mark Mathis looked at his brother and wept for a moment. Then he said to Chaplain Skoner, 'I'll get those dirty bastards for this'. He went to Bill Calhoun and said he wanted to take Jack's place; get a transfer as soon as possible. Bill said he would see what he could do. *Duchess*'s crew went to a rest home for a few days and Bill suggested that Mark go with them. When General Haywood S. Hansell of Bomber Command visited the rest centre, Mark asked him to help get a transfer. In record time Mark was transferred and assigned to *Duchess*.

He moved in with Johnny Shoup in Jack's bed and went on his first mission to Bremen. He bombed it with Jack's bombsight, still scarred by the shrapnel burst at Vegesack. Mark said, 'I reckon to do some good bombing because I expect I shall have Jack with me, like he was that Saturday'.

After a mission to Meaulte, *Duchess*'s crew entered the combat man's heaven – Mission 'X', the operation which completed the tour of combat duty. There was talk of Mark Mathis being sent home with them to tour the States. He insisted on staying until he had finished his 'X' mission. Meaulte was at the beginning of siege week. The Eighth Air Force was blooded. It had proved the case for daylight bombing from scratch – from the bitter days of the first raid on Germany, in which the rookie bombardier Jack Mathis saw his first flak.

Mark transferred into a new B-17 which had arrived on the President's birthday and had been lettered up with a big FDR. The big bombs of siege week were echoing over the Third Reich. FDR went to Antwerp and then to Kiel. Mark Mathis failed to return from his fourth mission.

Bill Calhoun was leading the squadron on the return from the target. Mark Mathis's bombs had fallen square on the aiming point which the striking pictures later proved. *FDR* was badly hit on the elevator and had begun to straggle. Bill Calhoun disobeyed common sense – and pulled his squadron back to cover *FDR*. The ship was hit but it was going strong – just a little slower than the rest. There were no Aldis lamp signals from *FDR*, so Calhoun believed the ship had a good chance.

FDR began losing altitude off the coast of Europe. Out of the clouds came the yellow-noses of enemy fighters and knocked out two engines on Mark Mathis's ship. The B-17 gunners were still blazing away at the attacking FW 190s, when the pilot evidently rang the bale-out gong.

Bill Calhoun left the pilot's seat of his ship, 8-Ball, and went back to the waist of the bomber to watch *FDR*. Seven parachutes opened away below him and began falling into the sea mists. The ship pancaked in the water, in what might have been a deliberate ditching by her pilot.

For a long time Bill Calhoun saw a pillar of smoke above *FDR*, which was a good sign, the ship had stayed afloat for minutes, time to get the dinghies out and provision them. His own formation went steadily home and Bill stayed at the waist until he could see no more of the tiny plume of smoke.

Was Mark Mathis still alive, he wondered.

18 *Tangerine – She Is All They Claim*

The left-waist gunner of the Flying Fortress, Sgt Bob Knight, of Schenectady, NY, was lying in his barracks bunk, his mind half on the bacon and eggs he had just finished and half on the fine weather outside. It was no surprise when the voice came over the loudspeaker: 'Stand by for announcement. All combat flying personnel will report to the briefing room at once.'

Knight glanced over in the corner where Smitty was sleeping. He woke the top turret man. In the briefing room they joined the assembled crews. Knight learned what was ahead: a routine raid. During the briefing he noticed that his hands were cold and clammy. The only time he was really scared was when he sat there listening to that calm voice telling what lay ahead.

The Flying Fortress took off. Knight settled down for the ride over. It would be a while before anything started popping. Down there, a crazy quilt of fields – neat little English farms. Charley Nease, at the right-waist gun, came in with his Savannah drawl. 'You'd think those farms would raise some good fryin' chickens, wouldn't you?' Smitty up in the turret kidded one of the boys about the little blonde in town. Somebody asked how the Dodgers did the previous day. T/Sgt Johnny Burger mused that it was corn time back in the States and how it would be to have a half dozen ears just dripping with butter. Even sex reared its pretty head as well.

Lieutenant James Balaban cut in: 'Here comes the Spits, boys.' They were a pretty sight. Long and slim and simple. Coming from all directions. Knight was glad to see them. A Fortress had a formidable pack of guns sticking out of it, but it could not do the tricks a Spitfire could. The Channel was below and then the Continent. The conversation on the interphone died down. Knight was looking all over the sky for the enemy and wondering whether he had seen a Spitfire or an Me 109 over there at one o'clock.

'Here he comes – 10 o'clock about 15,000.'

It came over the interphone and Knight swung his guns toward 10 o'clock. While he was doing so he thought of Sven Hansen, another Californian boy, who was on radio. Sven was facing the tail and could not see 10 o'clock. It was no fun to be there – and wonder how close the enemy was and when the bullets might start ploughing through at the rear. Three Messerschmitts coming up fast on the left but too far away.

Then the flak began. Much too far to do any damage. It did not even rock the bomber. But it made Knight look – diverted his attention. Then he heard someone on the interphone say that more Mes were in sight,

B-17 showing the
starboard waist gun
position, similar to the
port one manned by
Sgt Bob Knight

about 2 o'clock at 20,000. And then more. The boys all over the ship
sounded them off, one by one, as they came in. The voices were subdued,
almost monotonous, as if reading off stock quotations. After each
sentence they paused to give the next guy a chance. It sounded like this:
'There are a couple at 4 o'clock; watch 'em . . . See that one at 11 o'clock,
Hooks? Coming up from about 15,000 . . . Let them have it, boys . . .'

Knight thought of his buddies in the ships to the right and left. The
same thing was going on over there, only instead of using 4 o'clock and
11 o'clock and so on, they might have been saying: '10,000 feet on the
green beam,' or 'Get 'im, Alec, high in front of the red beam,' and they
would know which way to look because there was a green line painted
along the right wing and a red one along the left. Or maybe they were
using plain old port and starboard. His gang, though, stuck to the one
o'clock system, as on the rifle range, because it seemed easiest to follow.
And also quickest, which was important.

They were coming in now, plenty of them and fast. They had yellow
bellies. Goering's prize squadron. Pick of the *Luftwaffe*, out to get the
Fortresses. Okay. Let them come; they would find out.

It was not smooth riding now. Old *Mayme* was weaving from side to
side and rolling up and down as if she were hedge-hopping. Knight's guns
were leading the three enemy. They were closing in from 10 o'clock:
2,000 yards . . . 1,500 . . . 1,000. He let go and watched the tracers fade
off. He wished to hell the tracers had carried just a little farther. The Mes
peeled off as two Spitfires dived in. A wisp of smoke curled from one of
the enemy's engine; then he was falling fast.

Almost to the target now. He had not thought about it, but he could hear the navigator talking to the pilot and the bombardier – almost as if they were discussing a business deal. Then:

'Pilots, bombardier. Watch your 4 o'clock.'

Bombardier. That's Lieut A.D. Blair, an Alabama boy. In a second or two Knight heard Blair's guns open up. Blair loved his machine guns – practically fondled them – and now he was working them for all he was worth. A Messerschmitt came in from below, guns chattering. An alien accent. No hit yet, on either side. The enemy peeled off and circled for another try. Then came the warning:

'Navigator to bombardier – target coming up.'

Time to sweat now. The enemy on their right, on their left, ready for the kill – and the Fortress had to level off and fly as straight as a commercial airliner for long enough to dump the bomb load.

The Me circled and was coming in again – 400 miles an hour. Blair, he knew was busy with the bombsight. He had a pretty good notion of what was going through Blair's mind. Knight could see himself in the same spot: two good machine guns in front of him with belts of .50 calibre bullets, and the enemy coming up with his guns spitting at the plane – and Blair had to ignore the fighter and get those bombs away. Rivers of sweat flowed down his body . . .

Thirty to forty seconds for the bombing run . . . thirty to forty seconds of the roughest smooth flying he had ever put in. Blair sang out:

'Bombs away!'

Knight visualised them floating toward the target. He heard Blair's verdict: 'Direct hit, smack on the railroad tracks.' But Knight was not thinking of Blair any more now. He was thinking of Eddie Smith up in the top turret. He had just heard over the interphone: 'Here he comes, Smitty – in high at 11 o'clock.'

Smitty swung the turret to 11 o'clock. The enemy was only 1,000 yards away, and the turret man could not tell whether they were the target or the ship to the left. But his guns were blazing so furiously the fighter looked as if it were on fire. A thousand yards was a long way, but Smitty had a burst anyway. He scored a hit. Smoke trailed from the enemy but still he came on. His whole fighter was afire yet the guns blazed out of the smoke. It was suicide.

The ship to the left shuddered and the wing made a sickly dip. The enemy bullets had clipped one engine. Knight saw it out of the corner of his eye as he kept pouring bullets at the enemy. The fighter's nose dipped. He started to spin leaving a coil of smoke behind him . . . The interphone was talking again.

'Tail gunner. Watch the red beam. He's circling around, Johnny, watch him.'

Johnny Burger, astride his bicycle seat in the tail, knees planted firmly on the floor, muttered an unintelligible answer. Now the enemy snapped out of his bank and came in fast at 4.30 o'clock.

The enemy was the grim counterpart of a humming bird, poised at a flower and suddenly darting away. That was how he looked – so fast he could hardly be seen. There was a flash of flaming wings – his guns – and the flare of sunlight on his propellers. Then he was gone.

Burger was just as quick this time, though. His guns fired. Smoke curled up from the enemy's cowling. He snapped upward, and then down, and he was through . . .

It was quiet momentarily, and Knight glanced down. To his surprise, the Channel was looming ahead. He had hardly noticed that the Fortress had even swung around. He looked at his watch. Forty minutes since he first saw the formation of Mes off there at 10 o'clock. Now no sign. Knight started singing into the interphone. The others joined in. It was the song they always harmonised on the way back.

'Tangerine. She is all they claim . . .'

Good harmony number, too.

19 *The Dam Busters*

On 17 March 1943, Headquarters No. 5 Bomber Group received a letter from Bomber Command telling them of a new mine weapon intended to be used against 'a large dam in Germany'. The attack had to be made during May, and a new squadron was formed to carry out the attack.

Four days later, this squadron started to take shape at Scampton, while the twenty Lancasters it would receive were being built. The whole project was both top secret and top priority. Everyone picked for it had to be top grade, too, air and ground crews alike. The personnel had to be chosen first of all, before the modified Lancasters were ready. The man chosen to command the new squadron was Guy Gibson. All he himself knew about the project at that stage was that it would involve low-level flying across country, and training started along these lines at once on standard Lancasters. All twenty crews reached Scampton before the end of the month, within ten days of the squadron being born.

Wing Commander Guy Gibson, leader of the nineteen Lancasters in the Dam Buster's Raid

All they had yet learned was that they would have to fly at 100 feet and at 240 miles an hour. A mine would have to be dropped from each bomber within forty yards of the precise point of release. They went into training over reservoir lakes in Wales and the Midlands, for only six weeks were left to perfect this demanding technique. This ability to fly at 100 to 150 feet over water in the dark, and to navigate and drop mines accurately as well, was the first key factor in the operation. There were many more, not the least of them being able to avoid enemy fighters and ack-ack in the actual target area.

But even Gibson did not yet know this target area, so he was literally flying in the dark. Then he met the inventor of the mines, Mr B.N. Wallis – later famous as Barnes Wallis – who told him roughly how the mines would work. They would bounce along the water towards their target. The whole project became daily more fantastic.

Meanwhile, Gibson and his crew practised flying over Derwent Water reservoir in Cumbria, which bore resemblances to the conditions expected over the ultimate targets. After some trial runs by day, Gibson discovered that he could estimate his altitude and direct a bomb at the specified speed of aircraft with reasonable accuracy. But by night he only barely escaped actually striking the gloomy invisible water of the reservoir. And the attack was of course to be carried out at night. They would have to learn a lot in the coming few weeks. One of the many problems involved was solved when an accurate range-finder was devised which enabled the squadron to keep within a rough twenty-five yards of their target, and so within the forty yards' tolerance allowed by Barnes Wallis.

The following day, Gibson was finally let into the secret. They were to attack the great Ruhr dams of Germany: Mohne, Sorpe and Eder. The main target would be the Mohne Dam, 830 yards long, 150 feet high and 40 feet thick at its base – of sheer concrete and masonry. If Gibson and his squadron could smash one or more of these dams, the havoc caused to the enemy industries and communications would be tremendous.

Apart from the difficulty of flying to the rigid requirements vital for the success of the plan, there was one other problem: the mine had not yet had its full-scale trials! The first such trial came in mid-April when an inert mine was dropped from one of the modified Lancasters at the required height of 150 feet over water. The outer casing of the mine disintegrated as soon as it struck the sea off the Dorset coast. No time was lost in strengthening the casing, but this made no difference to the trials and the mine still shattered.

Gibson, too, had his worries, just as fundamental as the setbacks for Barnes Wallis. They found it impossible to fly at exactly 150 feet over the water and maintain that height accurately. Then one of the backroom 'boffins' found an answer: to train two spotlights downwards from the nose and belly of the bomber so that their beams would meet at 150 feet below the Lancaster, making a spot where they intersected. In this way, with the help of a couple of Aldis lamps, the aircraft could be flown within a few

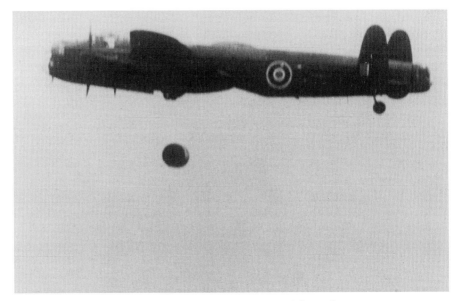

Bouncing bomb being dropped by a Lancaster in one of the trials

feet of any required height simply by keeping the spotlight at water level.

The next panic came when the inventor found that they could only expect effectiveness from the modified mine if it were dropped from sixty feet instead of 150 feet. Without the spotlight device, this would have been quite out of the question. By the time they had put in some practice at sixty feet, the month of May had arrived.

Early in May, an inert mine was dropped from the new height of sixty feet and operated successfully; then an active mine went off exactly as expected. While this aspect went well, just one more problem presented itself at the operational end. A complicated signalling system had to be worked out to control about twenty bombers over several tricky targets. The answer was very high frequency radio-telephone sets, twenty in number. These arrived on 7 May, but a lot of routine testing and procedure had to be accomplished before the actual attack. This had been done by 9 May, except for minor adjustments.

The nearness of the operation had suddenly been brought home to them all by the dress rehearsals, the first of which was timed for the night of 6 May. A film company was actually called on to assist by building dummy structures in the Uppingham and Colchester reservoirs, so that the squadron had something tangible for a target as they roared in during their dress rehearsal raid.

Even this stage had not been reached without further hazards and headaches, for a few days earlier half of the dozen Lancasters in one trial had sustained bad damage – with rear turrets dented, elevators broken, and fins bent. The trouble occurred because the aircraft had been flying a few feet too low, and though the mines they dropped were only inert, they had caused gigantic splashes as they struck the water, which had affected the bombers flying at 232 miles an hour.

On 15 May, Gibson got word at last: 'Be prepared to take off tomorrow.' He sat up later that night committing the detailed operation to paper – just in case none of them got back. They had been so busy training that the danger of the mission might have partially escaped some of them, especially since it was only on the following morning that the aircrews knew the complete plan.

The first of nineteen Lancasters took off at 2128 hours on 16 May. The main force of nine would go for the Mohne Dam and then, if it was destroyed before all their mines had gone, they would fly to the Eder. The second force of five was to head for the Sorpe Dam, while a third force of five was to form a reserve to fill in any gap, according to how the operation progressed.

They skimmed over the sea towards the Continent at a mere sixty feet or so, and went still lower after they crossed the Dutch coast. Moonlight helped them, but navigation at that altitude proved hard.

Gibson and the other two Lancasters in his immediate section of three hurtled overland, rolling right and left to confuse the defences. No guns opened fire. But in a couple of minutes they found themselves over the sea again! They had flown over one of the several islands they had tried

At the top of the ladder, Guy Gibson leading his crew on the day before the Dam Buster's Raid in May 1943

to avoid, and instead of being inland were only now crossing the real Dutch coast. By good chance, none of the ack-ack guns on the island had opened fire on them. On their fresh course, Gibson's bomb-aimer had to shout to them regularly over the intercom, to lift the aircraft to avoid trees or high-tension cables. All three aircraft in the section kept formation right until the Rhine came into view. Then it was found to everyone's alarm that Gibson's Lancaster, leading the whole flight, was no less than six miles too far to the south and heading for Duisburg, one of the most heavily defended towns in the whole of the industrial Ruhr. Gibson made a sharp turn to remedy the potential danger of the situation and flew along the line of the Rhine, under heavy fire from barges on the river equipped with quick-firing weapons.

On to the Ruhr Valley, with half an hour to go before the Mohne Dam. Ceaseless anti-aircraft fire forced Gibson to take evasive action. The three were also being continually caught by searchlights, some of which Gibson managed to avoid or shake off by 'dodging behind trees' as he colourfully put it.

Then they flew over a new and heavily defended airfield near Dorsten, not marked on their maps, where all three were held by searchlights. Gibson's rear-gunner fired at the beams but stopped when some tall trees came between the lights and the aircraft. Suddenly the searchlights were extinguished by a long burst from the rear turret of one of the other two Lancasters.

It was about here that one of the aircraft of the first wave of nine was lost. Gibson sent a radio warning of this new airfield to following aircraft. Lancasters B, N and Z formed the second section. Shortly before it was lost, aircraft B broke formation, presumably for the pilot to check his position. The pilot of Lancaster N, then flying at 100 feet, reported that soon afterwards he saw a bomber being shot at by anti-aircraft guns and returning their fire. Then he saw an explosion on the ground. The inference was that Lancaster B had crashed, its mine probably exploding at the same time. The other eight Lancasters flew on, past Dortmund and Hamm, avoiding more fire from the ground. Then hills rose ahead, and open country apparently without defences. Gibson gained height to get over a hill and then saw the Mohne Dam lake ahead – and in a moment the dam itself. From all along the dam, which looked, Gibson said, rather like a battleship, guns were firing, as well as from a powerhouse below the dam; but there were no searchlights. Gibson estimated that tracer was coming from five positions, and probably a dozen guns in all. The Lancasters all circled around getting their bearings, and each time one of them came within range of the guns on the dam, they received accurate fire. One of the eight aircraft was hit, though not fatally.

The attack on the Sorpe Dam had been planned for this precise time, as an effective diversion from the efforts of the main force of Lancasters against the Mohne. But only one of the five aircraft aiming for the Sorpe Dam had in fact reached it. They had met heavy opposition early on.

Lancasters K and E had both been shot down near the Dutch coast; H had hit the sea and lost its mine in the process, so had returned to Scampton; W had been hit by flak which disrupted the intercom., so that the pilot had had to return home. Only Lancaster T attacked the Sorpe Dam, a minute or two before 0300 hours on 17 May.

Back at the Mohne Dam, the Lancasters had scattered, ready for the attack. Gibson was due in first. He made a wide circle, and then came down over the hills at the eastern end of the Mohne lake. He dived towards the water and flew at exactly sixty feet, with the spotlights meeting on the water below. With these lights on, the bomber made a still simpler target for the gunners on the dam, who could see it coming from more than two miles away. Tracer shells converged towards it as Gibson flew straight and level towards the dam. The bomber's gunners replied. Gibson said afterwards that he expected to die at any moment. But the Lancaster was not hit anywhere. The mine was released, and Gibson flew in a circle.

Looking back at the lake, the crew saw fountains of water, white in the moonlight and 1,000 feet high. The surface of the lake had been broken, and sheets of water were pouring over the dam. At first, Gibson thought it had burst at the initial attempt, but he soon realised that it was only water churned up by the explosion. The mine had gone off five yards from the dam, but Gibson had to signal home that there was no apparent breach. Back in England, 'Bomber' Harris, Barnes Wallis and the rest received the news breathlessly, and waited for the next report. They had to hang on for fully thirteen minutes.

Gibson waited for the water to subside, and then signalled to Lancaster M to make its attack. The same thing happened all over again. The enemy guns focused on the lone bomber, which looked very vulnerable. Some 100 yards from the dam, a jet of flame sprang from the aircraft. Gibson inferred that the bomb-aimer had been wounded because the mine fell late and onto the powerhouse below.

The pilot was striving desperately to gain height for his crew to bale out of the blazing bomber. He got up to 500 feet, and then there was a flash in the sky, and one wing fell off. The whole aircraft came apart in the air, and fell to the ground in fragments. Almost immediately afterwards the mine that had fallen on the powerhouse exploded. This caused so much smoke that Gibson had to wait some minutes for it to clear before he could direct the next aircraft to attack.

For this third attempt, Guy Gibson had a plan. As Lancaster P flew towards the dam, Gibson went alongside, a little ahead of it, and then turned. His rear gunner fired at the flak position on the dam and at the same time helped to draw off their fire from the bomber about to attack the dam.

Lancaster P was hit several times despite Gibson's help, and all the petrol drained from one of the wing tanks – but the mine was accurately released and exploded fifty yards from the dam. Again circling near the scene, Gibson thought he saw some movement of the wall itself, but although the same huge fountain of water was thrust up, it was

The morning after – the Mohne Dam breached

disappointingly clear that the dam had not yet been breached.

Now it came to Lancaster A's turn. Gibson developed his diversionary tactics still further this time, and as the bomber began its run in towards the dam, Gibson flew up and down on the farther side of the dam and told his gunners to fire on the enemy's positions. To make sure that they would concentrate on him rather than Lancaster A, Gibson had his identification lights switched on. The plan was successful, and the enemy did in fact keep their guns trained on his Lancaster while the attacking one flew straight towards the dam. As the mine exploded a huge wave went over the dam, but although it had gone off in contact with the wall they were still unable to report any apparent breach. Back at headquarters the tension was becoming increasingly unbearable as each attack failed to bring about the desired effect.

Gibson ordered Lancaster J to attack. The fifth mine went up almost exactly in the correct spot. Just before the moment of release, however, the pilot reported seeing a breach in the centre. The bomber's own mine flung up the by-now-usual fantastic fountain, and then the aircraft became badly harried by enemy gunfire. Gibson himself could not see the dam at that moment, so was in no position to confirm a breach. He knew that time was running out, however, so decided to send the next bomber into the attack at once. Just as he had ordered Lancaster L to start, he turned and came close to the wall of the dam.

But it had rolled over.

Quickly he told Lancaster L to turn away. Gibson flew close and looked again. Then he saw plainly that there was a breach in the dam 150 yards wide. A huge cataract of water was churning through the breach. At 0056 hours, Gibson signalled to Group Headquarters the prearranged code-word 'Nigger', meaning that the Mohne Dam had been breached. Nigger, his dog, had been run over and killed the evening of the day before the attack.

The valley below the dam was filling with fog, evaporating from the water that was pouring down it. It was moving in an unbelievable wave, and in front of this Gibson could see the headlights of cars racing to safety. These headlights changed colour, first to green, and then eventually to dark purple, as the water overtook some of them. The water surged on towards the eastern end of the Ruhr Valley. The powerhouse beside the dam was by now completely submerged.

Gibson circled for three minutes and then called up the rest of his force. He told aircraft J and P to make for home. Lancaster M had been shot down. The rest of the force Gibson ordered to set course for the Eder Dam. Gibson's own G and Lancaster A no longer had their mines, but they went as well; L, Z and N still carried their mines intact.

It was getting late in the night by the time they all reached the Eder Dam, which lay in a deep valley among wooded hills, and at the far end of the lake was a hill about 1,000 feet high with a castle on top of it. They had to approach the dam by flying over this hill, and then diving steeply from above the castle, down to sixty feet over the water. Lancaster L made three runs before the bomb-aimer released his mine. A great spurt of water was followed by a small gap towards the east side of the dam. Next followed Z, after two tries Gibson saw a vivid explosion on the parapet of the dam itself, which lit up the whole valley. Then no more was seen of the Lancaster, which must have been blown up by its own mine on the parapet . . .

At 0152 hours Lancaster N attacked, successfully this time. A cone of water rose up, then a thirty-foot breach appeared below the top of the dam, leaving the top intact for a moment. A torrent of water cascaded downwards and rushed in a tidal wave to the valley below. Gibson's wireless operator signalled the code-word 'Dinghy'. The Eder Dam had been breached, too.

So the five aircraft set course for home, with the enemy's fighter force now fully aroused. Lancaster A failed to return. Some time on the way back, Gibson's rear gunner warned him that there was an enemy aircraft behind. Gibson lost height, though he was already flying very low, and made towards the west, where the sky was darkest; by this manoeuvre he evaded the enemy.

One of the reserve Lancasters managed to get through to attack the Sorpe Dam at 0314 hours.

Eight of the Lancasters making this historic Dam Busters raid were lost: eight bombers, and more distressing, eight crews. But without Gibson's heroism, both at Mohne and Eder, in drawing enemy fire on his own plane, the losses would have been even heavier.

There is no need to repeat the catastrophe and chaos caused by the result of the raid. The headlines have told the story before:

'Growing devastation in the Ruhr.'

'Flood waters sweep into Kassel.'

'Damage to German war industries.'

'Dam floods stretch for sixty miles.'

Later it came to light that the dams had not been as badly hit as believed – but it was still a heroic operation. After it, Churchill asked Guy Gibson to tour the United States on behalf of Britain, and he was of course feted wherever he went. Gibson returned to flying duties and there is a school of thought that suggests he became over-confident and was not sufficiently experienced with the Mosquito he was flying on 19 September 1944. He led one last raid on Rheydt, in the Rhineland, a strongly defended rail centre and traffic terminus for the Ruhr.

He was flying below the main force, guiding the bombing, talking to his fellow pilots, telling them where and when to strike. Over the target, his bombers, coming in to bomb high above him, heard his voice on the radio telephone, calm, unhurried. His instructions came clearly, and they followed his orders. The bombs hit an ammunition train and started a series of fires and explosions. The crews heard his final orders. His plane crashed near Bergen-op-Zoom, on the East Scheldt estuary, where his body was found and buried.

20 *The Saga of* Suzy-Q

By the end of 1942 the United States Army Air Force spanned a substantial part of the world. Distilling its achievements and ordeals during that first year of the Americans' war was the saga of the scarred *Suzy-Q* Flying Fortress. In a year of constant combat, she encircled the globe and fought in the battles of the Coral Sea, Java, Macassar Straits, the Celebes and the Solomon Islands. She was hit literally countless times, and her four engines were knocked out and renewed.

It was New Year's Day 1942 when *Suzy-Q* left Seattle for Tampa, Florida thence to fly to Trinidad, Brazil, West Africa, the Nile, the Middle East, the Indian Ocean, Ceylon, and finally to Java.

The battle for Java had just begun when she touched down there and she bombed the Japanese horde advancing by land, sea and air. But at last her pilot and commander, Major Felix Hardison realised that there were too many of the enemy. When the order came to abandon Java, *Suzy-Q* went out with three other Flying Fortresses on a last raid from

Another B-17 showing signs of long service on operations

Japanese Zero
fighter burning
on the ground
at Lae

Bomb explodes
off port bow of
enemy destroyer
during the Battle
of the Bismarck
Sea

Japanese
merchant ship
under fire during
the Battle of the
Bismarck Sea

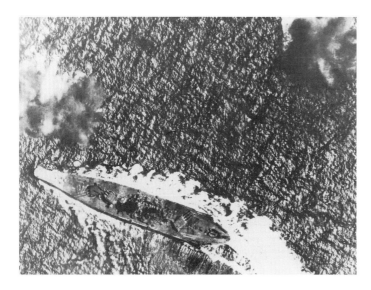

Japanese battle-
ship *Musashi*
attacked on 24
October 1944.
It sank later
after receiving
hits from 19
torpedoes and
17 bombs

their airfield. After bombing two ships and invading forces, she flew around for hours, hiding in the clouds, until she could return to her base safely by night. By the time she finally got away the enemy were within fifteen miles of the airfield.

By the end of that year, the Major and all eight of his crew had been decorated at least twice. Hardison himself was wearing a Silver Star with three clusters and the Order of the Purple Heart. This last decoration he earned in saving the life of *Suzy-Q* herself. It was on that Java runway that the enemy screeched down to bomb and strafe in a fanatical attempt to hit her. Hardison and his co-pilot were naturally not aboard as the raid broke, but they raced down the runway under a metallic maelstrom of bullet and bomb fragments, climbed aboard *Suzy-Q* and took her off.

'You get very attached to a plane,' Hardison explained later. 'You don't like people going around taking pot shots at her, especially while the lady's on the ground and can't defend herself.'

Of course the crew were wonderful, too, in this round-the-world trip. Men like T/Sgt William E. Bostwick, from Arizona, who was up in the top turret pounding away during one action when some ack-ack burst right inside the bomb bay. Bostwick was wearing only shorts at the time, and borrowed ones at that. He got the flak right in the seat, and was afraid to look down because he felt covered in blood. He could not sit down for days after that; the crew thought it a good joke.

From Java they flew to Australia. Using this friendly territory as a base, they operated over the Pacific in their first major encounter, the Battle of the Coral Sea. On 26 and 27 August, at Milne Bay, *Suzy-Q* hit and damaged a warship, sank or damaged a cruiser, and sank a transport ship.

Returning one night from Rabaul, *Suzy-Q* had two engines already gone when she ran into a tropic headwind. The fuel gauge showed so low that Hardison told the crew to bale out before he tried to put her down over the Australian bush. But all of them insisted on staying aboard *Suzy-Q*. Hardison was secretly pleased at their decision and determined to do his best to get her down safely. He lost altitude over the wild Australian landscape, a tree-covered wilderness with few open areas. This would really be a forced landing, bringing a Flying Fortress down on the only open patch he could see for miles. Lower and lower she fell, till she was almost touching the 'melon hole' land, so-called by the natives as it was pitted with large apertures. Somehow Hardison dodged these dangerous holes and skimmed *Suzy-Q* to a halt.

For three whole days in the North Australian wilderness they went without water, existing only on their iron rations. To vary these they shot a wild boar before it decided to make a meal of *them*. Then on the third day, not far from being dead from thirst, they found water. Master Sgt John Ceckeler thought of water throughout those 72 hours: lakes, rivers, pools, kitchen tap. By then they were filling in the melon holes for take-off, and repairing the radio set to contact the base. Things rapidly improved after that. Aeroplanes flew over to drop supplies, while bush natives volunteered to help with the holes to make a runway. On the eighth day, stripped of her heavy armour and guns, *Suzy-Q* revved up and her wheels gritted into the earth. Then she inched forward, gripping it and spraying up tracks of dust. In no time she was airborne and back at base ready for the battle of the Solomons.

Finally as she flew into Duncan Field, Texas, for repairs and overhaul, *Suzy-Q* had crossed the Equator four times and flown 350,000 miles, not counting her combat mileage.

21 *The U Boat War – British*

The aeroplane was one of the submarine's deadliest enemies and the running battle waged by Coastal Command against the German U boats proved of incalculable assistance to the vital Atlantic convoys. At first Coastal Command seemed to be getting the upper hand, but then the U boats began hunting in packs – wolf packs as they were known – and they were fitted with new and heavier anti-aircraft guns. No longer did the U boat commanders order an urgent dive when a Liberator or other bomber was sighted. Instead, the vessels stayed on the surface and could put up such a strong barrage that the attacking aircraft stood a substantial chance of being hit if not shot down.

Unless the aircrews showed a high order of heroism, all the scientific aids they possessed, such as advanced depth-charges and other anti-

Mosquito attacking and sinking U boat in the bitter Battle of the Atlantic

Sunderland flying boat depth-charging U boat in 1944

submarine projectiles, would be useless. There was nothing for it but to 'fly down the barrels of the U boat guns' – not a pleasant assignment even in fast aeroplanes such as the Beauforts and Mosquitoes. But the long-range crews had to handle heavy cumbersome flying boats or bombers, designed to operate from high altitudes. Moreover, these air attacks inevitably occurred several hundred miles out to sea, where rescue was rare. The result would often be the exchange of an aircraft for a sub-marine. And yet the aircrews did not complain. They accepted the new strategy of the enemy and set about beating him at it.

The submarines obstinately stayed on the surface, hoping to deter the Allied airmen from attacking. But they were not to be put off. Time and time again one aircraft would dive on a pack of the enemy and thunder right into the convergent shells. Often the aircraft scored successes. Just as often the Germans got the aircraft as well. The crews just hoped to survive somehow. Some did, others did not.

For instance, Wing Commander R.B. Thompson, captaining an RAF Fortress, was lucky. They sank a U boat but crashed into the sea beside the wreckage of the vessel they had just destroyed. They managed to get themselves and a dinghy clear of the Fortress, and then set about staying afloat and alive. Thompson and his crew drifted for four days and nights before they were rescued.

Flying Officer A.A. Bishop in an RAF Sunderland flying boat forced his attack home on a U boat and sank it. But the front turret of the flying boat was half shot away before the U boat finally went down. The wings, galley and bomb-bay were all blazing badly, and the flying boat was forced down on to the sea. The end of this episode was also a happy one: the survivors of both the Sunderland and the U boat were picked up sodden and shivering by a British destroyer.

Flying Officer Lloyd Trigg had rendered outstanding service on convoy escort duty and also against U boats. He had completed forty-six sorties. On 11 August 1943 he undertook a patrol in a Liberator bomber as captain and pilot, although he had not previously made any operational sorties in this type of aircraft. Number 200 Squadron had only recently switched over from Hudsons to Liberators.

Trigg took off with a crew of four fellow New Zealanders and two Englishmen. They left the airfield of Yundum, near Bathurst, west Africa, and set course westwards. Their destination was an area where several Coastal Comman bombers and flying boats had recently been shot down. Hour after hour the Liberator flew back and forth, covering the sea where the U boats were most expected.

After eight hours' flying they spotted a U boat on the surface, fitted with the latest large-bore anti-aircraft guns. Trigg prepared to attack at once. He nosed the Liberator down to be sure of getting into a good position, but in so doing the aircraft met the full focus of these new weapons, especially the forward gun. Trigg made his first run right across the U boat. Then he wheeled round and came in again. Bombs burst on each flank of the submarine, spuming water over her. The Liberator in return received many hits. Fire broke out, and a further hit after the second run caught its tail. Flames engulfed the tail rapidly.

This was a critical moment for Trigg. He had to decide whether to break off the attack and try to alight on the sea. All question was already past of keeping the Liberator airborne to fly back to base. If Trigg continued the engagement, the Liberator would offer a 'no-deflection' target to the anti-aircraft fire, while every second spent in the air would increase the extent and intensity of the flames now coursing inside and out. The decision to continue would also obviously diminish the chances of survival of himself and his crew. It was a heavy responsibility.

Without hesitation, Trigg maintained their course, in spite of the precarious condition of the aircraft, and proceeded to carry out a masterly attack on the already smouldering U boat. Skimming over the water at less than fifty feet, with anti-aircraft fire now entering his open bomb doors, he dropped his weapons on and around the U boat, where they exploded with undoubted effect. The Liberator limped clear of the submarine and a little way further on it dived into the sea, taking Trigg and his crew with it.

But the U boat was already doomed. In twenty minutes it sank. Some of her crew struggled through the water to swim clear of their vessel and towards the wreckage of the Liberator. They saw the bomber's rubber dinghy, which had broken loose, and got aboard it. When the Germans were rescued two days later by the corvette HMS *Clark* they told the story of the attack and their own subsequent ordeal.

Sunderland sinking U boat in the Bay of Biscay in 1943

On its third attack the Liberator had been hit full and square by a shell, but continuing on its course it dropped its bombs near the hull of the submarine, damaging the vessel so severely that the batteries began to release chlorine gas. The aircraft flew on at over 200 miles an hour, hit the sea, and sank in a few seconds . . .

Half the German crew were overcome by gas, but twenty-four survivors were left in the water when the U boat sank. One German sighted the Liberator's rubber dinghy, and it was this man who reached it half an hour after the U boat disappeared. He then paddled in the direction of his companions. But only six men, including the captain, were able to reach the dinghy, and although they paddled round the spot for a long time they found no further trace of their companions.

Next day an RAF aircraft circled them and dropped supplies. At that time the Germans were thought to be survivors of the Liberator, for which a search had been made as soon as it had been posted overdue. When the *Clark* finally found the U boat survivors, the Germans were generous in their praise of the captain and crew of the Liberator, for the daring and courage which had brought them victory at the cost of their lives. Lloyd Trigg and his crew were 'expendable' in the ceaseless Battle of the Atlantic, but without them and all the other Coastal Command crews it could not have been won.

Flying Officer John 'Joe' Cruickshank was struck in seventy-two places by pieces of flak while piloting a Catalina flying boat. It seems incredible that a man could survive such injuries, but he did. A staunch-looking Scot with a dark moustache, Cruickshank started flying with Coastal

Catalina similar to that flown by Flying Officer Cruickshank

Command in 1943. On 17 July 1944 he was piloting his Catalina between 69 and 70° NW of the Lofoten Islands on a normal anti-submarine patrol, when his navigator on the radar roused him with a shout of 'Blip up, about sixteen miles away'. They were now inside the Arctic Circle: no place to be ditched even in mid-summer.

The Catalina flew towards the spot, and then slightly to starboard the crew saw the tell-tale plume of foam. The submarine surfaced. It was one of the latest type of U boat with a tonnage five times as great as the standard model. From his pilot's seat, Cruickshank could see 37 mm and 20 mm anti-aircraft cannon behind the conning tower. He took his aircraft in to attack, flying into the wind so that the engine noise would be carried away from the U boat. There was not a sign that they had been spotted. The bomb-aimer's thumb stabbed the release button, but nothing happened. The depth-charge had jammed. A double danger at once, from the U boat and from their own weapon.

By now they had been seen. The enemy guns blasted the air around the Catalina. Levelling up at fifty feet above the Arctic, Cruickshank began a turn for another run. He had not thought of giving up at that stage. Within seconds the shells were punctuating the airspace near the cumbersome Catalina as she made her turn. He banked heavily.

'Hold on, we're going back,' he shouted into the mouthpiece of his intercom. It was his twenty-fifth patrol and the first time he had sighted a U boat. He began his second turn over the vessel. The whole enemy armoury belched up as they came down to depth-charge-dropping height, right in the teeth of the cannon. The shells could hardly have missed them.

Dickson, the navigator and bomb-aimer, was killed outright. The twenty-year-old wireless operator, Flight Sergeant John Appleton, described what happened next: 'The skipper called "Everybody ready?" and then "In we go again". We made a perfect run-in at low level. When almost on top of the U boat another shell burst in the aircraft. Everything seemed to happen in a flash. I was hit in my head and hands. Cruickshank took no notice. He continued straight on.'

There were explosions in the Catalina, and the second pilot and two others of the crew fell injured. The nose-gunner had his leg riddled with scalding shrapnel. Fire broke out, and the aircraft filled with the fumes of exploding shells. The whole frame of the aircraft was devastated.

Cruickshank was hit in seventy-two places by seventy-two separate pieces of flak. He received two serious wounds in the lungs and ten penetrations in the lower limbs. But he did not falter. He flew the Catalina right over the enemy, released the depth-charges himself, and straddled the submarine perfectly. A gunner fought the flames with an extinguisher all the time Cruickshank was making his attack. The U boat sank, vanishing in a soap-like froth.

But the fire was still burning. At this moment, Cruickshank collapsed and the second pilot took over the controls. He was Flight Sergeant Jack Garnett, and though wounded he managed to steady the Catalina sufficiently to keep it airborne. Soon afterwards, Cruickshank came round again, and although he was bleeding profusely he insisted on resuming command and actually taking over the controls. He did take over and retained his hold until he felt satisfied that the damaged aircraft could be kept under control; that they had set a course for base; and that all the necessary signals had been sent. Only after all this could Garnett persuade him to accept medical aid. Despite the seventy-two wounds, he refused morphia in case it prevented him from carrying on if he was needed.

Then came the long run home. The attack had been made at almost maximum range from base. Now the two main questions were: could the Catalina keep going and could Cruickshank live long enough to get back for proper medical attention?

They carried him aft and put him on the only serviceable bunk. The others had been on fire. Fortunately all the fires were under control fairly soon. Wireless Operator Appleton dressed his wounds and they kept him warm with their Irvin jackets. He recovered again and asked for something to drink and a cigarette. He was very thirsty. He kept asking if everything was all right, and insisted on periodic checks.

As the hours of flying passed, they left the Lofotens behind and headed for the Shetlands. Several times Cruickshank lapsed into unconsciousness and he lost a lot of blood. Yet when he came round each time, his first thought was for the safety of the aircraft and crew. It still seemed touch and go whether he could last out till they reached the Shetlands.

The hobbling Catalina flew right through the evening till about 2200 hours double British Summer Time. It was dusk, and the Shetlands were dimmed. Cruickshank rallied enough to realise that with the aircraft in its present condition they would have to take great care in bringing her down on the water, especially since the second pilot had also been injured. Cruickshank could only breathe now with agony, but he insisted on being carried forward and propped up in the second pilot's seat. Somehow he stayed conscious by will-power.

Sullom Voe lay below now; they had only to get down. But Cruickshank refused to let them rush it. For a full hour he gave orders as they were needed. He would not bring down the Catalina until the conditions of light and sea made it possible with the minimum of risk. With his help the aircraft eventually landed on the friendly waters off Sullom Voe. Even then Cruickshank directed it while they taxied across the bay and beached, so that it could be easily salvaged.

The base had received their signals and a medical officer was waiting to go on board as soon as the big flying boat ground to a stop on the shingle of the Shetlands. As it did so, Cruickshank collapsed. He should have done so hours earlier; only indomitable will-power had kept him going. The medical officer gave him a blood transfusion on the spot, and life flowed slowly back again. Then they removed him gently to hospital, where he had to remain for several months, before he was well again – not surprising in view of the number of his wounds. The surprising thing was that he survived at all.

22 *The U boat War – American*

In the beginning of 1943, the war under the seas steadily grew more merciless. There ensued a long series of actions against U boats, some by planes, others by ships. For instance, when a U boat surfaced in the Atlantic to tackle the SS *Columbian*, a thirty-year-old US merchant vessel, machine guns swept the submarine's decks clean while bigger weapons hit her conning tower, causing an explosion that sank the submarine even before the merchantman had steamed safely away.

The next phase of the campaign against U boats was carried on by aircraft of all kinds. To the surprise of the Navy, a heavy bomber of the USAAF caught and claimed a U boat in the Caribbean. The plane, piloted by Captain Howard Burhanna, Jr, was on a patrol flight that promised to be very uneventful, when he sighted the submarine surfaced eight miles away. Changing his course, he trapped the sub. before she could dive and he released depth charges carried for just such an unlikely

Catalina long-range bomber was a famous flying-boat associated with war against U boats. It was flown by both British and American crews. Among its distinguishing features were the twin engines perched high and clear of the fuselage. Nearly 4,000 were built

encounter. As soon as these exploded, air and oil bubbles began rising from the water with volcanic intensity. When the bomber crew spotted the familiar dark circle of oil on the surface, indicating that the sea had forced itself into the main compartments of the undersea raider, they knew their victory was complete.

At least one member of the submarine survived, to be spotted by the aircrew as they flew off. They radioed his position to a nearby US destroyer, which was only too glad to speed to his rescue – secure in the knowledge that there was one less U boat lurking about those waters.

But it was the Navy naturally which found most U boats. Lieutenant Richard E. Schreder, of Toledo, Ohio, kept his usual rigid control of a Catalina patrol bomber over the Atlantic one day when his radioman reported seeing a large submarine basking on the surface. Schreder immediately changed course and in a matter of moments prepared his plan of attack. With meticulous piloting precision, he kept the sun directly behind him to blind the lookouts on the submarine. The heavy plane responded well to his manoeuvres as he put its nose into a sharp dive.

The bomber roared down, right between the raider and the sun, and a depth-charge exploded just under the submarine's stern. A frantic, futile attempt to crash-dive, and then a second depth-charge was released. This zoomed downward and struck squarely on the deck, exploding in full view of the bomber's crew as they climbed into a patch of cloud. Wreckage sprayed over the ocean and the navy plane headed for home.

The endless routine brought its own danger, too, because of the sheer number of missions the pilots flew. For while Schreder scored his success, Machinist Leland L. Davis, piloting a Consolidated Catalina patrol bomber off the Aleutians, similarly sank a Japanese submarine. But on another patrol flight later the same day, Davis did not return. He was awarded the Navy Cross.

Another sad story of submarines in the Pacific came to light when news was released of a US submarine under the command of Commander Howard W. Gilmore. During a surface attack on a Japanese gunboat, Gilmore directed operations from the bridge of the submarine. Just as the gunboat was hit by the sub, enemy machine-gun fire hit him. Although mortally wounded, he saw the danger of keeping the submarine surfaced a second longer. So he gave the order to dive, while he was still on the bridge.

So it went on. Sometimes the results were spectacular, like the time a U boat in the South Atlantic was literally blown in two by depth charges from a Catalina while the crew appeared to be taking sun baths on deck. After the explosion, which blew the craft out of the water, the American fliers saw it break up, and several objects looking like long cylindrical tanks floated among the spouting debris. The submarine's stern rose vertically ten feet out of the water, bobbed up and down a bit, and then sank in a rough sea, as if drawn down by some unseen force.

Again it was a Catalina flying boat that made the kill: an especially skilful piece of piloting by Lieutenant John Dryden, Jr. Patrolling among the West Indies islands, not far from the previous Caribbean victory over a U boat by the army bomber, Dryden came on an enemy sub. eight miles distant. This was a large submarine having substantial surface armament so an air attack was by no means assured of success. Dryden brought his plane down from 4,500 to 1,200 feet on the run-in, and then a mere quarter-mile off he pushed the great flying boat into a 45-degree dive. it shuddered slightly as if in protest, but took them down safely to 300 yards from the submarine.

The 200-foot vessel still moved on at a little under 10 knots, blissfully ignorant of its possible fate. Two Germans were basking on deck, breathing fresh air after the stale substitute they had when submerged. But they would never need to breathe that again, for a 100-round burst of machine-gun fire from the flying boat killed them both. One threw up his hands as he headed for the sub's gun, and then he pitched forward.

As the plane pulled out of its dive, Dryden and Lieutenant Stetson Beal, the co-pilot, jerked the switches releasing four depth charges in salvo from an altitude of less than a hundred feet. The two port charges left their racks and hit the water ten to fifteen feet to starboard of the U boat and just aft of the conning tower. A few seconds later, the whole sub. lifted and broke in two amidships. The centre sections went under water first, then the bow and stern rose in the air and submerged. The familiar explosion sent debris, smoke and water forty feet into the air.

Two hundred feet had been the length of the U boat. This was also the

Airfield construction made a significant contribution to the air war including the anti U boat war, particularly in the Far East and Pacific The picture shows an American airfield constructed on the tiny island of Middlesburgh – only 300 miles from the Philippines

extent of the patch of frothing foam that stayed on the surface for four or five minutes. In its place then appeared a shining green oil slick expanding in the following hour and a half until it was three-quarters of a mile long and a quarter-mile wide.

The Catalina could only wait, circling around overhead. Then, emerging miraculously from the wreckage, were eleven of the submarine's crew clinging pitifully for life to debris.

Dryden did not hesitate. He cruised low over the struggling men, while the crew of the Catalina dropped life rafts along with some emergency rations tied to life jackets. The Germans were waving frantically for the flying boat to land, but the rough sea put any rescue attempt out of the question.

The Americans looked out of the Catalina, down into the rolling sea, and saw six of the Germans gradually lose their grasp on fragments of wreckage. Covered from head to waist with the horrible thick green liquid, they slipped beneath the oily waters, choking in their death-throes as the oil entered their lungs.

The five others somehow heaved themselves by life-or-death efforts onto one of the rafts. But although the Catalina cruised the area for nearly two hours waiting for the weather to calm, a dwindling fuel supply forced it to give up and return to base.

'That's it then. They've had it – poor devils.'

23 *The Regensburg Raid*

The Regensburg raid was just one of many over Europe by the USAAF in 1943. The mission was to hit the Messerschmitt factory at Regensburg, carry on to Africa to refuel, and then bomb Bordeaux on the way back to Britain. That day, 17 August, was to be memorable, for official opinion reckoned afterwards that at least one quarter of Nazi day fighter production had been destroyed in the raid. But to the crews returning tired – or those not returning at all – figures did not mean much. The raid leaps to life more in the memories of three men in three of the armada of Flying Fortresses.

Staff Sergeant Roger Palmer spent two years in the infantry before flying. He felt lucky to be a tail-gunner that day: It was the best spot in the ship, he thought. His particular Fortress flew the lowest in their formation. Palmer liked being tail-gunner better than ball-turret gunner. In the tail he could see all that went on from there: spread out nice and neatly. They knew they would have a hectic time because it was such a beautiful day: and they were right.

In the first quarter of an hour after crossing the enemy coast, all remained undisturbed. Five minutes later, the interphone relayed a confused variety of voices.

'Fighter at six o'clock.'

'Fighter at ten o'clock.'

That was it from then on, four solid hours of it. The Nazis sent up their special yellow nose fighters to try and stop the Fortresses. The Yanks knew that when they saw Goering's Yellow Noses the enemy took the raid especially seriously. The Yellow Noses were the *Luftwaffe*'s first fighter team – more experienced pilots and willing to take more chances. They had learned a lot of old tricks and frequently some new ones. They came in close, but one of them could not flop over quickly enough, and Palmer pressed his gun to get in a few rounds. The wing of the Messerschmitt tore away. That was the first of the day.

No time to get excited at scoring a hit, for those hours on the run-in to Regensburg marked the roughest ever known to bomber crews. Fighters by the hundred – and bombers, too. Everything except gliders, Palmer thought, in a more quiet second.

Then he saw *them*. Advancing across the landscape lying ahead. In relays. Row after row. Palmer was firing at one fighter and lining up another out of the corner of his eye at the identical instant. He had been too busy to notice smoke below, and too busy to notice that they were 'going on downstairs': flying lower for the final run-in and raid. The smoke meant target approaching.

The opposition reached its hottest just about then, before they were actually over the target. The *Luftwaffe* flung in twin-engined aircraft as well, not caring about losses in a last shot to save the factory. Twice at least it seemed as if their pilots deliberately tried to ram Fortresses. They were set on breaking up the formation, whatever it meant. But the B-17s ducked out of the way of fighters, and Palmer thought it an amazing sight to witness.

Palmer's bomber got right over the target area and was just straightening out for the run when his fire hit a Junkers 88 squarely in the centre. The aeroplane must have been all burned up before it struck the ground. Next came Palmer's third score. Even after their bombs had gone, this fighter was determined to catch the Fortress, and he came in very close from behind like a wasp or some such stinging creature. Palmer could watch him coming, and got the aircraft straight in the sight.

Its engine caught fire and Palmer assumed that was that. But then the pilot baled out. He seemed fated not to survive, though, for his parachute became caught on the wingtip of the Fortress flying right behind Palmer's own. The pilot was dragged along like that for some time, hanging in the air, but then when Palmer managed to take another look at him, he was no longer there . . .

Regensburg raid on 17 August 1943. Taken from a B-17 of the US 8th Army Air Force during the attack on the Messerschmitt factory

Staff Sergeant A.R. Bartholomew, ball-turret gunner in another Fortress, takes up the story of the Regensburg raid.

It was the same with his bomber: over the target the enemy seemed to be desperate, demented. After the bombing, the German fighters would not let the Yanks go, but followed them part of the way towards the wild wastes of the Alps. The crews could see the mountains while they were actually on the bombing run, and they knew that once they got over those peaks they would be comparatively safe. And the enemy knew it, too.

To make matters worse in Bartholomew's case – he fell out of the door!

The other gunners kidded him about it afterwards. They said he must have been nudging the Fortress along to the Alps by pushing against the back of his seat, where the door was located. But Bartholomew maintained that they were all doing some nudging. The prayers going on over the interphone made the bomber sound like a flying church.

Just after they had dropped their load, Bartholomew was firing at an Fw fighter trying to come in behind them, so he happened to be facing the tail of the Fortress. Which was fortunate for him. Suddenly the back of the seat gave way, as if someone had sneaked up behind him and pushed a chair off balance while he was sitting on the two rear legs.

He heard no noise; just fell backwards. The wind hit him like a solid board across him while he grabbed at anything for a hold. The seconds seemed multiplied many times while he groped about. The wind helped him haul himself up into the turret again. At the time he did not realise that he had in fact fallen out of the aeroplane, with only his right foot holding him into it. A gunner in a ball-turret operated a lot of devices with pedals, and his foot must have got caught in them somehow. For that was literally all that saved him from being swept away to sudden extinction. His safety belt had not been buckled, either, so he certainly had a near miss.

The radio operator relieved him for a while in the ball-turret while Bartholomew recalled some of the earlier episodes in that mammoth raid – before the door incident. He had seen an enemy fighter dive into one of the dark forests far below, and spatter and scatter flame all over the trees. And he recalled the last fighter pilot they encountered, who would not give up, even after his engine had started to smoke and he knew he could never get back to his base. The pilot attacked them four times before his aircraft fell away into the mountains. The smoke from it seemed to stay suspended in the icy air . . .

Still the epic raid went on. Lieutenant John Keeley, Jnr, pilot of another Fortress, got past the Alps at last, just as his remaining dregs of oxygen gave out. He let the bomber down to 13,000 feet and turned it over to the co-pilot, Harry Coomes.

A life-raft had become entangled with the vertical stabiliser of the bomber, but Keeley thought they could get rid of it. The raft had been shot from its housing and wrapped itself around their tail surfaces. They tried everything they knew to dislodge it, but nothing worked. The bomber was vibrating violently now and they had to drop out of formation. And, of course, as they had passed the sanctuary of the Alps, enemy fighters flew at them from all sides. They shot down four almost in seconds.

The raft kept flapping around so much that Keeley felt afraid it might tear off the whole tail, but worrying him still more was the way it caused them to burn up their meagre remaining fuel: only just enough to get them across the Mediterranean to the North African airfield where they hoped to land.

They were over the water now. The only good thing about that was an absence of any more fighters. But Keeley did not fancy the idea of the Mediterranean, so he passed the controls over to Coomes and went back to see what, if anything, could be done about the life-raft. One of the crew tried to lasso the raft from the waist-gun window, and another made an effort to shoot it clear. Keeley even let them chop holes in the fuselage to get at it, but the thing seemed to be positively *fused* there. They had to give up hope of freeing it.

Thirty miles from the coast of Corsica. Nothing to do but sit and wait for the red lights to start blinking on the panel-board. Sure enough, it did not take long.

One engine spluttered and went dead. Nearly all the gasoline was gone. In fact it was only a matter of counting before the next engine died, though sweating away it all seemed outside time to them. Then the third engine. Three out and one to go. Keeley told everyone to get into the radio compartment.

The last engine quit.

They got down all right. The water was very smooth, like the Mediterranean should be in mid-August. They got the remaining life-raft afloat and piled on everything they thought they would need. The one detail: ten of them and the raft held five. So it meant five inside and five hanging on outside. They did not mind that so much, as long as they could still see the B-17. For forty-five minutes they paddled around just watching it. They had nothing to say. There was nothing to say. She was a swell plane. They had her in the States first and she had done seven missions over Europe. She seemed to hate to leave them. Keeley never thought he would get sentimental about a plane, but he did.

It got dark after the Fortress sank. Dark and lonely and chillingly cold. A ghastly night. Keeley could not remember just when it happened, but in the middle of that icy wet night they all became aware of a dark object drifting for them. They did not know if sharks lived in the Mediterranean, but they feared that this might be one just the same. Nearer it approached. It turned out to be somebody's flying jacket floating under the water. They felt distinct anticlimax after that, even hoping for something to happen to break the freezing monotony. They hung on, took turns in and out of the raft, watched, waited.

They all felt better with the lemon dawn and then the sun. They laughed a little at how they looked. It was rather remarkable, for the dinghy by this time had become completely submerged, so they were ten men apparently sitting or crouching on water. Almost a miracle.

They all felt fairly confident of being found, for ever since ditching their little automatic transmitter had been in touch with their base. Yes, things seemed to be going fairly well. Considering. Then the transmitter gave out. They all started to pray. Harry Coomes managed to fish out his rosary and they prayed.

A B-26 spotted them during that afternoon. Tired cheers greeted its silhouette. It flew around and stayed right there overhead until a British air-sea rescue launch churned up to collect them. The crew of the launch took off their own clothes to help get the Americans warm again after the night in the Mediterranean. Twenty-one hours down in the drink. That was the end of the Regensburg raid . . .

24 *Bale-Out Over India*

Even when an aircraft went, the crew sometimes survived. Sometimes. Nine men of the USAAF had a concentrated experience over Rangoon that they would not forget. Fifteen minutes short of the target area a fire broke out in the nose of the B-24 – a parachute had been stowed too near an electric heater. First Lieutenant Francis Thompson's fire extinguisher dealt with that.

The bomber reached right over the target when all four of her engines cut out. She faltered and then slowly started losing height towards the ack-ack as the pilot, First Lieutenant William Berkeley, contorted himself and the controls. The engines came on again as suddenly as they had stopped and he levelled off quickly. It looked like a jinx flight.

Master Sergeant Howard Darby dropped his bomb load of thousand-pounders on cue and Berkeley scooped her around for home, with the only damage as yet one burned parachute. If they had known it, though, the mission had not even begun . . . Their route back to base lay over the sea and the B-24 was still a hundred miles from the coast in the dark, when the whole electrical system went out; so did the auxiliary system; so did the batteries.

The bomber had no electrical power at all, which meant no electrical

The valuable and versatile Liberator was especially suited to conditions in the Far East and Pacific theatres of war

governor for the propellers – fast approaching the red-for-danger line on the rpm gauge. They could not put out distress signals, nor communicate by radio, nor put on landing lights. Otherwise things were fine. The bomber flew on for a few minutes, as the engineer, T/Sgt William Frost, frantically tried to produce some power: but it was hopeless. Berkeley kept the aeroplane hammering for home and before anything further happened, she crossed the coast. That was one hazard averted – the sea.

But they must have been hit badly to cause so much wreckage to the system. They circled over a city – they did not know which one – without landing lights and were scanning the solid dark ground below for a possible airfield, when they were spotted by a Hurricane who thought of them as an enemy bomber. Luckily the fighter pilot recognised the shape of the B-24 before he decided to attack.

Their time was running out now. The No. 3 engine was running out, too. Not stopping but rising to 3,300 rpm, beyond the danger level. When this engine, as expected, started to splutter, Berkeley was ready with his decision.

'Okay – bale-out.'

But he could not give the crew time to adjust their parachutes properly. Nine 'chutes blossomed out irregularly like night-flowering plants. Opening instead of closing seven thousand feet up. Seven of the crew were knocked out by the flailing buckles of their chest straps, just seconds after they had pulled their ripcords. This happened because they could not adjust the parachutes. The seven 'chutes swayed crazily, with the riser lines flowing without guidance from the unconscious men strapped to their rubber seats. When they reached the cool layer of air at about 5,000 feet, they stirred to find themselves drifting down in the darkness. Not a nice moment.

Frost jumped ready for action, carrying a tommy gun, 125 rounds of ammunition and a camera. But he had reckoned without that strap buckle. When he felt the coolness on his face, he had only his flight cap left in his hands. Darby had his .45 with him and was uninjured. So he took his delayed descent in comparative comfort, pulling a pack of cigarettes from his pocket and actually lighting it on the way down.

The others had a rougher time. Waist gunner, S/Sgt Edward Salley, landed in a tree, complete with a lip wound where the strap buckle had driven two teeth through his lip. He shook his parachute loose and fell to the ground without further harm.

Staff Sergeant John Craigie, bleeding badly from a broken cartilage in his nose, landed in a lake. He had to swim and wade through mud for nine hours before being rescued by an Indian boatman. He had half-swum, half-walked, right through the darkness in a real nightmare situation. Some of the crew landed in rice paddies, others in swamps. All except Second Lieutenant Thomas Murphy, Darby and Craigie spent the night where they landed, utilising their parachutes as pillows.

When the sun filtered through the jungle, all nine of the B-24 crew started for a nearby Indian city by different routes, some of them meeting along the line. Craigie and Salley ran into each other at a native village and boarded an aged train together. At the next station, S/Sgt Bernard Bennet got on. Staff Sergeants Adolph Scolavino and Thompson had already caught an earlier one, each at a separate station. Frost met Darby along the river and got a boat to take them to the city. Berkeley himself was also travelling by boat when Murphy hailed him from one of the riverside villages. The two of them connected with a train to town and the entire crew met that same night at a hotel!

They stayed there for eight days waiting for travel orders back to base, and then at the end of that time they had to pay their own bills! But they were all alive, that was the main thing. And quite remarkable, really.

25 *Gunner over Lorient*

What was a bombing raid *really* like? Come over Europe to Lorient in a B-17 with Sergeant Denton Scott. This is how he felt.

'The moment you climb past the bomb bay, you forget, forget altogether once you shudder involuntarily at the monstrous, sinister cases, fused ready to explode. You shudder, but you force yourself not to think about that, and you know that you are a prisoner of this ship, this gaunt fuselage, a ward of those four motors – for many long and tedious hours to come. That imprisonment can be broken only by three factors, and they are, in order: Disaster by explosion and parachuting to another prison; death; or a safe return.

'The nose of a B-17 is cramped and small, and once there you know you are no longer a part of anything except this ship.

'You look out at the black tarmac, at the camouflaged hangars, and they are remote and distant. They are a part of a world which does not concern you in the slightest. They are a part of a world, seen in a dream, securely moored to the safety of the earth itself – a world you are leaving for eight hours, perhaps forever.

'This is your world now; the tarmac flashing by on take-off, the emptiness of the sky, the vertigo caused by looking straight down at the earth below with only glass supporting you. It is a sparsely populated world; the only men in it are the men imprisoned with you. This is your world: the strong faces around you, the acrid smell of sweating flesh, the gun you man. This is a world in which four motors are a human, tangible part of your crew, because motors can be temperamental and therefore assume a personality – a personality at which you can curse if they fail, which you can beseech if they falter, which you can almost subconsciously praise if they beat forever strong. This is your world.

'We move out to sea in perfect formation. Men speak among themselves in this world not as men speak in the world we know. Speech is an automatic reflex, born of fear and excitement. Speech in our world is the speech of Dutch Schultz when the gangster delivered his death-bed soliloquy. The tongue speaks before the mind thinks. It is almost a world of subconscious reactions. A man cannot, and will not, stop to rationalize his way into the arms of death, or of Jerry.

'This is why Santoro, the bombardier, turns to me and says: "For Christ's sake, don't get rattled. Just do what I do."

'Now Santoro is a mild fellow, ordinarily, patient and untiring. On the ground he would have said: "Now, Scotty, the main thing is to take it easy and relax. It is just like any other game where you need quick reflexes. Tensing only slows you up."

'But now, we are over the Channel, and it's "For Christ's sake . . ."'

'All questions and answers are clipped and grievously accentuated by the circumstances, as another voice through the interphone: "Scotty, don't pay any attention to that son of a bitch. All bombardiers are nuts."'

'We are told to test our guns. There again, spontaneous reactions. I had pressed the trigger of the .50 calibre and had watched the tracers stream down toward the sea, had accomplished this order as an automatic reflex, without hesitation, without thinking. The last bullet had sliced its red-hot path into the cold waters below before I realized specifically and rationally that I had been given an order and had complied with that order.

'We are nearing the coast, nearing the flak and the fighters, the targets, into a clean and sunlit battlefield, a land of quiet, swift violence, on which the traces of violence leave no mark save for a vanishing cloud of smoke, or the white, pathetic shroud of a parachute blooming against the blue skies and slowly leaving this battleground that refuses to be despoiled by war.

'We are nearing the coast, flying low now at just 1,500 feet. And now we begin the long haul up to the front, up through the mist, into a land of broken patches of light and darkness and then entirely above the clouds into the clear. The sun is bright in the nose, and warm. There is a natural feeling of security in sunlight, but when that sense of warmth and security is tempered first by the knowledge that the air outside is cold and sterile and then by the knowledge that the sunlight is your enemy, it produces an effect far more eerie than fear in the night, since the primary association of fear is with darkness.

'If men sing in the sky, going into battle, as they say men sing, it is the singing of a small boy who finds in passing a graveyard by night that the action of his lungs reduces the tingling in his spine and the awkward involuntary tendency of his legs to break into a fast run and get out as fast as he can.

'We did not sing.

' "Fighters at nine o'clock! Fighters at nine o'clock! Oh, you little . . ."'

'They are Fw 109s, and they are rubbed down and polished so they glitter in the sky, and they are hard to see. They come right at us. Hausman opens up. I look straight into their props; they come straight towards us. They then veer away, leave by lowering a wing and just sliding off and away from us, turning slowly up and over, exposing their slick Nazi bellies to the sky above, and then just floating off. There is no sensation of speed, strangely; I always thought there would be a sensation of speed; but they just float away like feathers in a breeze.

'We are coming over Lorient now, Lorient with its docks and quaysides and its sinister submarine pens. We come steadily, thundering relentlessly toward the target. The charge of the light brigade is no more impressive than the firm, sure run through blast troubled skies of a

B-17 showing gun positions

bombing run. The city spreads out far below us through the nose. Santoro, the bombardier, squints through his sights. The windows are glazed with ice, and Santoro curses. He presses the button and the bombs go tumbling from the opened bomb bay doors, down through the clear blue skies, down through five solid miles of space, gathering velocity, becoming steadily smaller and smaller and finally falling out of sight. Then the brief eruption down below.

'I look ahead. One B-17 slips out of the group, faltering and crippled, helpless. Its right wing, riveted with science and the delicate touch of experts, begins shredding off. Chunks of metal flutter through the sky, caught up sometimes in the prop-wash of oncoming planes. She loses speed, and then gains it. The rights wing is breaking into bits. Then the parachutes, one by one, billowing out against the blue sky.

'The flak is becoming hot and heavy, black deadly puffs of the stuff erupting all around the ship. Santoro rages back and forth in the restricted confines of the nose, cursing the men for not cleaning the windows. He curses the Germans. He hurls vile implications at the men. He curses the major in the leading plane for flying too high, for giving the wrong kind of evasive action. The Jerry fighters come in through the ripening fields of flak, and he curses them too. The red tracers stream past the ship. Two red balls of flame rise in front of the nose and disappear. Me. cannon blasts, somebody yells, and we look through the frosted windows. The two Me 109s are coming in at 300 miles an hour. I grab my gun and let go. The sweat is pouring from my face. Once, the oxygen mask loosens and I stop to fix it on my face. Somebody is yelling through the intercom. that the supercharger on the number three engine has blown. We have driven the Mes back, and now our problem is to stay in the protecting line of our formation or risk getting picked off by fighters.

'We streak out across the Channel. The fighters don't follow. The sweat dries on our faces. It is cool and quiet now, and the sky is peaceful. We come down again, slowly, surely from our great height to 1,500 feet once more. At times, we can see water. It seemed very blue. The tension had been broken but we did not sing. Until we landed we still would not have established contact with that world we had left on take-off. Even when we made landfall once more, the sight of men's houses, and the farm-lands, and the green Cornish hills below were nothing more than impersonal landscape, a painting that held nothing but objectivity.

'What I did feel was a sudden physical release from strain, but more acutely a deep affinity to every man on this ship, my fellow prisoners. The swearing and the violence in the sky had only brought ten men closer together in eight hours than eight years might have in that other, more normal world, such being the inevitable bonds between men who have suffered fear together and fought against it. This is perhaps the strongest of all ties among men; but that affinity now was only of the confines of our ship; for the moment, it did not extend to those outside the circle of those experiences we had just lived through.

'We had been to a battlefield, not of this earth and not of the men in it. There is a chasm greater than 25,000 feet of bright blue altitude between those two worlds.

'It is a hard and terrible transition to come back. I hope we all make it . . . after so much sweating and swearing and swallowing our hearts.'

26   *The Legless Survivor*

For a couple of days he pretended not to know. Finally he reached down painfully and flipped the blankets aside. He could see enough to be certain that both his legs were gone. The crash killed everyone else in the plane, and it smashed Kenny Class so badly the doctors had to amputate both legs, one just above the knee, the other just below. And for a long time Kenny lay in silence and pain; but after he knew for sure about his legs, he snapped out of his silence, and since then he didn't ask for a word of sympathy.

Kenny Class was turret-gunner on a B-26 Marauder that raided a Nazi airfield in France during early autumn 1943. They bombed the target but one of the bombs did not release; so Kenny climbed down from his turret and went into the bomb-bay. The bomb weighed 135 lb, so it was quite a struggle, but he lifted the bomb and let it fall safely into the Channel.

Flying so long with the bomb-bay doors open meant that they lost the formation, and by the time they got over their home field, a sudden English fog had closed in tight. Thinking to find it clear at a nearby field,

Marauder medium bomber went into mass-production in 1941 and 5,000 were built by the end of the war

they flew on but when they got to the new field, conditions were 'zero-zero' and the Marauder crashed. All members of the crew were killed except Kenny. He had climbed back into his turret after he got the bomb away, and when they found him he was still in the turret – and the turret was 200 feet from the rest of the plane.

Kenny was young and blond and hailed from Sioux City, Iowa. The day he crashed was his seventh wedding anniversary – seven months. And it was his eleventh mission, and eleven had always been his lucky number.

He liked flying in combat. He was never scared. He didn't brag about it, but everyone who knew him said he wasn't scared. He had confidence in his Marauder and in his pilot. And he was sure that the top turret of a Marauder was about the safest place to be to fight a war. He said, 'Sometimes I wanted to reach right up and grab the brim of my helmet and pull it down clear over me, but usually about that time I started looking around for Jerry'.

He kept hoping he would get a crack at an Fw 190 or an Me 109. Sometimes he would see them start for the Marauders and get cut off by the vigilant Spitfires before they had a chance to fire a shot. And then Kenny would feel himself being disappointed. For Kenny wanted to fight. When they got over the target, he would steal a quick second or two to look down and see the sticks of bombs puffing across the runway, he felt his heart pounding and he grinned through clenched teeth.

Kenny got married in February 1943. Dee used to come and live in an hotel near the field right after the first of the month and for about three weeks they would have a fine time of it. Then Kenny would go broke and Dee would go home to stay until the next pay day. Kenny was not being heroic when he said that he was looking forward to dancing again with Dee. While he was still recovering, he insisted, 'She's particular about dancing, and we'll be out on the floor with the best of them when I get used to my new legs'.

When they got Kenny out of his turret, 200 feet away from the snarled wreckage of the Marauder, they rushed him to hospital. For a while they did not operate on him because he was suffering from shock and they were afraid of what the operation might do to him. But they soon realised that infection was setting in, so they gave him plasma and transfusions; and they amputated.

'The boys in the squadron gave me something like six quarts of blood,' he said, 'I've got so many people's blood in me I hardly know who I am.'

After the operation, infection did set in. But with the then-new drug penicillin he got better. Lying there in the long, narrow room, day after day, he watched the English seasons change, marked by the changing colours of the light streaming in from the windows – from the bright yellow of summer to the saffron of autumn. He had a long time to think. To remember.

As soon as the hospital would allow, Kenny began to get visitors, their ranks from private to colonel. Colonel Thatcher came, and he brought with him a Purple Heart ribbon. Thatcher was a group commander flying Marauders. After a few words of greeting, Thatcher pinned the ribbon on the front of Kenny's pyjamas and shook his hand and then walked out of the room.

Kenny saluted the colonel's back as he was going out of the door, and his nurse Miss Southerland, who had been standing behind the colonel, looked at Kenny and looked at the empty door. She half-ran out of the room and caught up with Colonel Thatcher in the hall, grabbed him by the elbow and turned him round. Colonel Thatcher stopped and turned and Miss Southerland reached up and took him by the lapels of his blouse.

'You can't do it that way!' she said tensely. 'You can't just walk in there and pin a little ribbon on his chest and walk out. That boy's all the heroes of this war wrapped into one. He deserves all the medals in the world. That boy is wonderful. You can't just pat him on the back and then walk away and forget it.'

Colonel Thatcher let her finish, and then looked at her for a minute.

'I know,' he said at last. 'I know all about Kenny. And Kenny knows that I know. There's no need for talk between Kenny and me. We understand each other. I'd be making things difficult for him if I stayed to talk with him, because he'd be working hard to keep me from feeling sorry for him.'

Miss Southerland turned away uncertainly and went back into Kenny's room. She still wasn't sure. She didn't look at Kenny when she went into the room. Kenny spoke first.

'He's certainly a wonderful guy,' Kenny said, and Miss Southerland looked at him, hoping Colonel Thatcher had been right in what he said.

'He's the finest man I'll ever know,' Kenny continued. 'He always reminds me of something I read somewhere.'

'What was it?' Miss Southerland asked.

Kenny quoted: 'They shook from their wings the dust of their bodies.'

As he finished speaking, Miss Southerland heard an aeroplane in the far distance. Kenny was listening, too.

'That's a B-26,' he said.

27 *Target Schweinfurt*

It was still dark when they woke the crews. The briefing had been timed for 0730 hours. The men got dressed quietly, trying not to disturb those who could sleep till later, and secretly envying them.

The briefing-room was bright and also noisy until the mild-mannered intelligence captain rose to speak. He had a long ruler in his hand. It moved out over the North Sea and into Belgium, then slowly and deeply across Germany until it eventually stopped.

'This, gentlemen,' the captain said, 'is your target for today – Schweinfurt.'

The men listened intently, leaning forward in the long rows of chairs. The air was clouded now with cigarette smoke. The captain continued:

'Schweinfurt is the most important target of all in Germany today. We cannot go ahead with other targets until it is seriously crippled. Half of Germany's ball-bearings are produced at Schweinfurt, and ball-bearings are important to Hitler. If we destroy these factories, we will have crippled the enemy's production of tanks and planes and submarines to a very great degree.'

The captain went on to give some technical information concerning the target, wind and weather, and the briefing was over.

Outside, it was quite light now, a peaceful English morning. The sun was beginning to dissipate the fog, although chunks of it still lay between the trees and in spots it still hung over the airfield itself. Outside the briefing-room they were given chewing gum and candy, one of the solemn rituals of a raid.

'I think this Schweinfurt is named after a very special kind of a pig,' one of the radio operators said, as they headed towards the trucks.

They rode up the taxi-strips to their hard-stand, and the crews stood around the ship. Station time was thirty minutes ahead, and the guns, ammunition, radio and bomb-bays had been checked.

The name of one particular Fortress was *Yank*. Its skipper was a 21-year-old giant from Monterey, California, Captain Ivan Klohe. While waiting for the take-off, he pitted his hulk against two of the waist gunners, Sgts Charlie Hill and Edward Cavanaugh. Standing only just a little over five feet, Cavanaugh succeeded in pinning the captain's shoulders to the ground; Hill had a deadly lock on his legs. The remainder of the crew stood by and cheered for the gunners.

Station time was announced. The men became suddenly serious as they took their positions in the ship. Sgt Walter Peters climbed into the nose with Lt Howard J. Zorn, the navigator, and Lt Richard J. Roth, the bombardier.

'The right gun is yours, Pete,' Roth said.

The *Yank* queued up by the runway. Lt Herbert Heuser, the co-pilot, announced through the interphone, 'There goes the *Piccadilly Queen*'. They watched her as she sped down the black runway – 50, 60, 90 miles an hour. It was a beautiful take-off. So was theirs.

At about 11,000 feet the pilot told them to check their oxygen masks. They did so and then put them on. Heuser was still on the interphone making an imitation fireside chat a la Roosevelt – and the crew ate it up. Then he began to sing, and Cavanaugh and Zorn chimed in occasionally with a raspberry, a vocal trick hard to achieve on an interphone. There were more songs, from Hill, Roy (Tex) Blansit, who was their top-turret gunner, and from Sweeney. The war was beautiful . . .

The formation across the North Sea was perfect. They led the 'purple heart' element and before them the sky was clouded by B-17s. They counted up to 190. Then they quit counting.

Zorn directed their attention to a long file of P-47s to their right. They sped so fast it seemed the Fortress was standing still, and they left a silver vapour trail. The view from the nose was great, thought Peters.

At 1302 hours the captain warned that they were approaching enemy territory. They were above 20,000 feet and suddenly, over the interphone somebody announced the presence of unidentified vessels in the sea below them. A couple of seconds later somebody said these vessels were shooting at them. 'Why, the silly bastards,' another voice replied.

At 1330 hours the captain said they were over enemy territory and as he did Heuser announced the presence of unidentified fighters. It turned out to be all right, though. The fighters were theirs.

When they were over Luxembourg, the sun was still with them. The nose became so hot that there was no need to use the electric suit; a pair of white silk gloves proved enough to keep their hands warm. Enemy fighters got hot about that time, too. Heuser did most of the calling, singing out their positions in a voice that was cool and undisturbed. He sat where he could see them all, and he didn't miss one. 'Fighter at 5 o'clock high.' 'Fighter 10 o'clock' 'Fighter 8 o'clock low.' 'Fighter 3 o'clock.' 'Fighter 12 o'clock.'

There were fighters everywhere, but mostly on their tail – or so it seemed. 'The whole goddam *Luftwaffe* is out today,' somebody said over the interphone. There were the single-engine Me 109s and twin-engine Me 110s; there were Ju 88s and Fw 190s; there were also Me 210s and even Dornier bombers. The only things they didn't throw at the division were the plane factories themselves.

'This is nothing,' Zorn reassured. 'We've seen worse in other raids. About twenty-five more minutes to the target.'

The captain took a little evasive action. The bomber banked to the left, then to the right. To the right they sighted a huge column of smoke, which

The ball bearing centre of Schweinfurt, attacked in daylight on the same day as Regensburg. The losses of 51 aircraft for the two raids were rightly considered unsupportable

looked at first like a big black cloud. It was the target.

Liberators and Forts had already passed the ball-bearing works and hit the plants solidly. *Yank* would soon be there, and they wondered just how soon. The passage of time appeared a little different up there.

The navigator told Peters to look out of the left side. There were a couple of planes burning there, a Fort and an enemy fighter. Three white 'chutes and one brown one floated in the sky. The whites belonged to the Americans. Under the brown one floated a German.

Time was passing so slowly. When in hell were they getting to the target? They were all beginning to wonder. Heuser was still calling them off. The fighters came from all sides now, but not too close. Maybe about 500 yards away, often as much as 1,000.

Peters looked back toward the fuselage. There was Tex, his left foot planted in a box of calibre 50s, his right foot lazily dangling in space. From the interphone they knew Tex was a very busy top-turret gunner. His gun kept tracking fighters all around the clock. Occasionally he concentrated his gun to the tail, where his friend Sweeney was busy firing at the enemy as they queued up from the rear.

A Ju 88 and a 190 attacked Sweeney's position from 4 and 8 o'clock, and high. Tex's guns worked fast. Both planes peeled off. The 190 shied away but the 88 came back from about 500 yards to the rear, flying smack into the ex-tyre salesman. Sweeney calmly pressed his triggers. Meanwhile Tex directed his fire. 'You're shooting at him just a little high. Get him lower. A little lower.' Sweeney did; the 88 came closer, and lobbed out two of the rockets the Germans had started using. They were deadly looking affairs as they shot out like flames.

Tex still guided his pal over the interphone. 'A little lower, Bill,' he said. A little lower Bill aimed. The 88 wavered, flipped over and as it did so they could see that it was afire, trailing smoke. Then there was one less Ju 88; also one less Ju 88 crew of two. They did not get out.

Klohe headed the Fort north-east, hitting a straight course for the tall column of smoke 6,000 feet high, marking the target. At their level and even higher, flak sooted the sky. Roth was ready. It was only a matter of twenty seconds before he released the bombs. Then came the flak, great black balls of it all around them. It seemed almost impossible to escape the barrage.

They weren't having fighter trouble now; their enemy was flak, and there was nothing they could do about it – except take evasive action. Klohe did just that, beautifully. Suddenly they heard a loud, jangling noise, even above their four engines. They looked toward the navigator. The plate glass on his side was broken. A fragment of flak had found its mark there. Zorn lifted his head quickly, took off his gloves and his fur cap and felt around that part of his face not covered by the oxygen mask. He winked. He was okay. Peters took a deep breath – of oxygen.

The flak ceased, but the enemy fighters and fighter-bombers returned. Heuser was back on the job, his cool tones calling them off again. He reminded Peters of the stick-man at a dice game in a gambling house, but his voice had the confidence that the croupier's doesn't.

'Fighter 11 o'clock,' Heuser said. The navigator tracked the plane down with 50s until he was out of sight. 'Fighter 5 o'clock,' and Sweeney was back at his guns. 'Fighter 2 o'clock.' Peters grabbed his gun, and tracked the German until Heuser bawled him out for using too much ammunition. He stopped fast.

Heuser's voice again: 'Fighter 3 o'clock high.' Tex saw him, recognised it as a 190, waited until it came closer and then let loose with a barrage. Sweeney congratulated him. From where Sweeney was he could see the 190 spiral down; he saw the pilot bale out, brown parachute and all. That was the end of Jerry number two for the boys of *Yank*. The third was claimed by Sgt Cavanaugh, the left-waist gunner. Cavanaugh bagged an 88, the crew of two baling out.

All the time Hill and Sgt Ralph Baxter, the ball-turret gunner, were engaging two 88s. These had been attacking a lone B-17 forced out of formation with a feathered engine. Baxter saw the Germans dive after the B-17 and appealed to Hill to give him a hand from the right waist. Between them they saved the Fort from destruction.

It was now 1615 hours by the watch. But the watch was no longer running. They cursed. More fighters came at them. They cursed some more.

Half an hour later, more flak. It wasn't as heavy as the stuff at Schweinfurt. Zorn said he thought they were near Amiens, France. Just then they heard another loud jangle of broken glass as flak hit the left front plate. Roth ducked. Zorn went calmly about his business of navigating. Peters put on his helmet, then took it off a few seconds later. A helmet was not very conducive to good sight – and he wanted to see what was happening.

Roth picked up a piece of flak.

They tried guessing the time. Peters figured it must be about 1730 hours. They were well across the English Channel and in a few minutes they could see the English coast. Klohe began dropping altitude. At 17,000 feet Roth and Zorn took off their masks. So did Peters. Zorn smiled.

Tired but happy voices began coming over the interphone. They were kidding again. Heuser sang. Zorn told them how sharpshooter Sweeney couldn't hit one skeet out of fifteen a year ago. Somebody else threw digs at Tex because he was once turned down by the Army with flat feet. Cavanaugh kidded the captain over the interphone and Klohe dished it back to him. Peters sat back and relaxed. He pulled out a cigarette and lit it. The mission was over.

28 *Berlin or Bust*

Captain (then Lt) Rosenthal and his crew came overseas quietly enough in September 1943. They brought with them their own crew name, of course, Rosie's Riveters, to be duly inscribed on the nose of a Fort by some weary Joe who had seen all kinds of names tagged on to B-17s that can't answer back.

The pilot was a quiet, inconspicuous young man of twenty-six, who wore his visor cap clamped down on his head and walked in the shambling gait of a countryman, though he hailed from the farmlands of Flatbush, Brooklyn. With him was one of those typical American mongrel crews that the Army arranged so well. For their backgrounds were German, Irish, Scottish, Italian and others – and their home places scattered from the Eastern seaboard to the Far West.

In Dyersburg, Tennessee, 'Rosie' had quietly canvassed among his crew to find out how they felt about combat. No-one backed out. Yet no-one could possibly have wanted combat as they got it in their first three days of flying in the European theatre. As S/Sgt Ray Robinson, the ball-turret gunner, from Arkansas City, Kansas, put it, 'The first night, after Bremen we were too scared to sleep; the second night, after Marienburg we were too tired; and the third night, after Munster, we were just through – finished'.

Bremen was bad. On that one, the squadron 'lead crew' piloted by Captain Everett E. Blakely had hell smashed out of it; on the Operations blackboard Sgt Jennings could write after all plane numbers – 'Severe battle damage.' Marienburg, with only a few hours' sleep intervening, was one of the longest flights ever undertaken in this theatre – and then came Munster, the very next morning.

The haggard, griping crew of *Rosie's Riveters* went down to the briefing that morning in the company of experienced crews – men who had been on the first Regensburg shuttle raid to Africa and on 'the longest flight in the ETO,' to Trondheim.

In the late afternoon, as fog settled over East Anglia, the drone of the two remaining engines of a single Fort was a mournful elegy for the men who had been to Regensburg and Trondheim. The careful landing procedure for formations was unnecessary. There was only one plane coming in – actually half a plane – with two engines out. Thirteen planes had failed to return. The debriefing was very exclusive, like a consultation with a private physician. There was only the evidence of the dazed, battered members of *Rosie's Riveters*. It had been a ferocious and concentrated attack. One by one the planes of the group had gone down. So had part of the *Luftwaffe*.

Left alone, it had been Lt Rosenthal's decision to go in on his bombing run. The bombardier kept asking, 'Shall I drop them now, Rosie?'

'Not yet.'

'Now?'

'No.'

'We're over Munster,' said Lt C.J. Milburn, the bombardier.

'Now,' said Lt Rosenthal.

And from Munster to the French Coast trying to get home, enemy fighters queuing up like wolves. Another engine was knocked out. Staff Sergeant L.F. Darling, of Sioux City, Iowa, crept up to the nose to help Lt Ronald C. Bailey, the navigator, spot the landing field. At last the landing.

'Rosie' came down through the bomb-bay to look over his crew and his wounded. Besides Darling there was the other waist-gunner, S/Sgt J.H. Shaffer. And as 'Rosie' stepped out, and went along in the ambulance with his wounded, he got a glimpse of something new – the torn-down skin of the right wing where a rocket shell looping from above had ploughed through between empty gas tanks, cutting out a hole a foot across.

Mike Bocuzzi, tumbling out white-faced, yelled, 'I'm through flying these things. That's enough.'

'CJ', the bombardier, round-faced, amiable, who was a little quieter than Mike, didn't say that but thought about it. 'I thought, well, if this is the way it is, they must get you sooner or later, but I'll go along until it catches up with me.'

That was Munster and it was five months more to Berlin. Young Bill DeBlasio, the tail-gunner, wrote in his battle diary, 'By the grace of God we were the only ship to come back. Our pilot brought us home safely.'

Mike Bocuzzi, yelling, as he tumbled out, that he was going to quit was to gripe that way many more times – and never quit. Technical Sergeant C.C. Hall, of Perry, Florida, a pleasant guy who camouflaged it behind a sourpuss, would go on shooting down fighters for which he was reluctant to put in claims. And 'Rosie', the pilot, would go on making his laconic reports to debriefing officers trying to pump him.

'The flak was meagre,' he would say. 'We landed with our flaps out.'

'Flaps out? Were you hit?'

'A little bit. But if you get back it's a milk run.'

They flew to Bremen, Rostock, Brunswick. On the 'second Regensburg', the target was snow-covered. Lieutenant Bailey, the navigator, commented to the crew on European history and geography. Here were the Alps. Over that way was Switzerland. Those long, wide lanes below were the 'six-laned highways built by the Germans for this war'. And here was where the Germans had broken through in an earlier war with France, in 1870.

Before Rostock, Bocuzzi was tired and jumpy. 'Rosie' said, 'What's the matter, Mike? We're all nervous. I'm always scared stiff myself. What's the matter?'

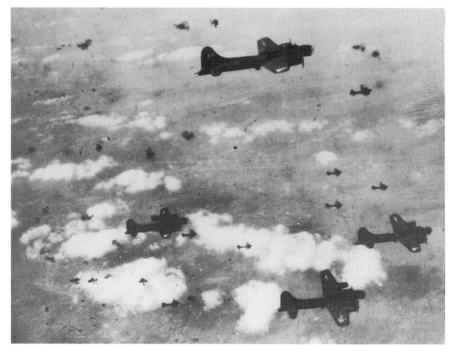

B-17s met fierce flak on their way to bomb Berlin

'Nothing,' said Mike.

In his battle diary, DeBlasio wrote darkly, 'They better give us a rest and a few short raids. I am very tired now'.

Everything had mounted up – enemy planes shot down, pep talks . . . 'By this time we'd had a hundred and two of them since Dyersburg,' said Ray Robinson. 'I counted them. "Rosie" always gave us them before the mission. After that you never heard him speak on the raid, except when he had to.'

For Berlin, the briefing was like all the others. But it was Berlin, the 'Big B' – to be hit in daylight. The previous August, as a gag, someone had put up the red ribbon across to Berlin, and no return route indicated. Now it was no gag, and there *was* a return route. Through the briefing room there sounded the scuffle of heavy boots, cigarettes were lighted. Bocuzzi said to somebody, 'Who got drunk last night and dreamed this one up?' as the pointer touched Berlin.

They went out down to the line. Behind them was more than a score of raids. They dived into the ground crew's kitty of cigarettes in the tent. Bocuzzi borrowed a pencil from the ground crew. 'Number 12, this is. I owe you twelve pencils,' said Mike.

It was a cloudy day. Berlin could always be postponed, couldn't it? Couldn't it wait for tomorrow? They looked toward the tower where the

Lieutenant Colonel
Harry Mumford receives
the Silver Star for
leading the first B-17
daylight raid on Berlin,
6 March 1944

flare might go up announcing, 'mission scrubbed'. There was no flare, only the dull grey sky.

A new navigator was along, not Lt Bailey riding the bike, with his navigator's briefcase under his arm, looking like a professor – but a new man, to be put at ease by 'Rosie'.

Then Lt Winfrey 'Pappy' Lewis, of Houston, Texas, came down, did his pre-mission job of checking up on equipment and then dived for the cot in the tent – a regular thing with him, this sack-time before a mission. Staff Sergeant Marion J. 'Junior' Sheldon, of Arkansas, who had replaced Darling, carefully, hung his two rag dolls, 'Blood' and 'Guts' to the receiver of his gun. All the little things had been done, and pep talk No. 103 took place – 'Rosie's' usual delivery: 'You worry about your guns, and let me worry about the plane.'

The only change after more than a score of missions was that they got into the plane a little earlier than usual. That same old take-off, but the silence over the interphone was greater than usual. Interphone discipline had always been strict, but this was quieter than it had ever been.

'We were a shipload of nerves,' said Ray Robinson.

As they came over the German coast, the clouds began to lighten. Moving into Germany it was getting clearer. 'Pappy' Lewis, the co-pilot

– the 'bald eagle' – looked over towards 'Rosie' – the 'legal eagle' – the lawyer who hadn't ever practised. Everything the same. 'Rosie' beginning to sweat.

'It was only thirty below,' said Mike, 'not too cold.'

They came over the 'Big B' and it was clear below them. Things had been done here because smoke billowed high in the air. Flak was thick about them – 'but not worse than Bremen,' said DeBlasio. Nervousness disappeared with the first fighters.

'On this one,' said Mike, 'we didn't want them to get in close.'

The bombardier got one and so did the top-turret. They made their turn past the target.

The enemy coast behind them. Over the interphone 'Rosie' said, 'Interphone discipline is now a sack of something.' Voices broke in a frenzy of babbling, laughing noises. There was a hell of a squabble in the waist and DeBlasio was refereeing between S/Sgt Jimmy Mack and 'Junior'.

England again. They buzzed the field. It was a private victory, but in this roaring excitement, there was the knowledge of the men who had not come back. In four raids on the 'Big B' it had been dished out, but they had taken it, too.

One evening, a week later, they went to get decorations at the Officers' Club. There was Captain Rosenthal, Bill DeBlasio, Ray Robinson and Mike Bocuzzi. They sat quietly shoulder to shoulder dressed in Class As. Generals Spaatz and Doolittle spoke.

Afterwards 'Rosie' went out, walking down towards his hut in the dark. Captain Putnam, a close and good friend, had gone down a few weeks before . . .

'Rosie' hit the sack.

29 *Fighters in the Fray*

This particular dogfight over Frankfurt was blistering hot. German and American planes, hopelessly intermeshed, twisted all over the flak-specked, Fortress-filled sky. In the midst of the dogfight, a single classic duel developed. It was between a Messerschmitt 410 and an American Mustang. In the German fighter was a man obviously one of their aces. In the Mustang was 27-year-old Colonel Kenneth R. Martin, a nice-looking, medium-built man with light brown hair, who had joined the Marines as a private in 1937 and had gravitated into the Army Air Corps.

The fight progressed for minutes – an eternity in aerial combat. Both pilots threw their planes into impossible manoeuvres. Neither could get in a solid burst. Then suddenly watchers saw the Me lunge fiercely at Martin's Mustang. The two planes ripped toward each other. Martin refused to pull out. There was no accounting for this. It seemed to be just the expression of a cold inexpressible anger. The planes crashed head-on at 23,000 feet. The Me disintegrated in a flash of exploding gasoline and ammunition. Martin's tough, shattered Mustang fluttered to earth in a long, uncontrolled glide.

Martin survived the crash. It was later reported by Berlin Radio that he was recovering from a broken arm and leg in the same hospital with the German pilot he had brought down with him.

Elsewhere at a well known Ninth Air Force Tactical Mustang Group, the pilots stood around in the sun waiting for missions to be called. There was the peculiar similarity about them of objects that had passed through the same crucible and the same mould.

It was against this background that a combat wing of Flying Fortresses was coming back from a big raid on Oschersleben. Twenty minutes after the target was bombed, the *Luftwaffe* struck. At least a hundred Nazi fighters smashed in from all sides. Two squadrons of Mustangs engaged the enemy at the vulnerable rear boxes. Then with cunning precision, the Germans switched their attack. Forty fighters struck at the forward boxes. There wasn't an American fighter in sight ahead of the formation.

The Fortress crews swore and manned their guns. Then they blinked in disbelief. A single Mustang had come up from nowhere and was zooming in and out of the box, attacking five and six German fighters at a time. Whenever the Nazis queued up for an attack on the bombers, the little Mustang would tear into them and break them up. The Mustang kept diving, attacking and climbing back to bomber level. He actually was engaging forty Nazi planes singlehanded. Time and time again he forced the attacking fighters to break off and dive away. But on his third combat encounter, the Mustang pilot had only two guns firing. On his fifth, his last gun went out. He kept up a pretence of attack without guns and the Fortress crews last saw the Mustang diving through the clouds, on the tail of an Fw. As the Mustang disappeared, Major Allison Brooks, leading one of the Fortress formations, muttered: 'That was the greatest exhibition I have ever seen. I hope to God he makes it.'

That afternoon a Mustang limped back to the group's base. It bumped along the landing strip. It came to a stop and out stepped Major (now Colonel) James Howard, a 31-year-old ex-medical student, who left school to fly with the Navy and shot down more than six Japanese planes in China, where his parents were missionaries. Major Howard was weak with exhaustion, but he went through the regular procedure.

He spoke with his crew chief, reported two claims and two probables to the intelligence officer. Then he went into the pilots' room and had some fruit salad, bread, peanut butter and coffee at the snack bar. He mentioned to the other pilots that he 'ran into quite a few enemy planes and got in a few good shots'. Not until the next day did it come out that Howard was the lone fighter pilot all the Fortress crews were talking about. He didn't even realise the suicidal heights to which the emotional stress of the dogfight had almost automatically driven him.

In the church of a little English town there is a monument to another

The Mustang has been called the most effective American fighter aircraft of World War II. Mustangs with Rolls-Royce Merlin engines arrived in Britain for the USAAF in December 1943

American fighter pilot of this same Mustang group. The pilot's name was Lt Charles F. Gumm. Before the war Gumm was working in a grocery store in Spokane, Washington, and studying law at night. He was mild and quiet on the ground. In the air he became a terror. He was the first ace of the group and probably would rank among the leading fighter pilots of the theatre today. Once, eight German fighters lured him into a trap where he should have been annihilated by the converging fire of their guns. If he was lucky, he might have pulled out and escaped. He didn't even try. He tore into the eight enemy aircraft with such fury that it was the Germans who pulled out. Four of the eight Nazi planes went down.

On another occasion, Gumm, flying at 25,000 feet, saw an Me 109 firing at a Fort that had lowered its wheels, signifying that the crew was going to bale out. Cursing furiously over the RT, he dived to 22,000 feet, raking the Me 109 most of the way. His guns kept firing at the harmless fragments of the Me long after the Nazi fighter had blown up.

One day Gumm took his plane up to test it for his mechanic. His engine started to go out while the plane was heading directly for the little town of Nayland, and he couldn't change his course. Gumm stuck with it. Fighting all the way, Gumm lifted the plane over the rooftops, not touching a thing. Then he headed toward a clearing blocked by two young oak trees. The Mustang caught the trees and blew up. Gumm was thrown from the plane. He was killed instantly.

Captain Richard Turner brought his flight of Mustangs home with four planes missing. They had become lost in a heavy overcast sky above Southern France. Without waiting to refuel, Turner hopped back into his plane and went out to look for the missing four. He cruised at 37,000 feet and tried to contact the missing men by radio. But they were too far south, nearly to Spain, to hear him. Suddenly Turner blacked out. His oxygen supply was exhausted. The Mustang spun all the way down to 10,000 feet before he regained consciousness. Just as he recovered he heard the voice of one of the missing pilots, Lt Mailon Gillis, talking over the RT to Lt Leonard Jackson, another of the strays. 'That looks like the Isle of Jersey down there,' Gillis was saying. Turner called to them, and in a few minutes they were flying formation behind him.

Gillis and Jackson were the only ones left of the original missing four. The other two Mustangs had run out of gas and the pilots had long since baled out over France. Now Gillis, Jackson and Turner were nearly out of gas, too. And they were hundreds of miles from home. Talking a continuous stream of verbal encouragement over the RT, Turner shepherded the two lost pilots home. They made landfall at the Isle of Wight. They landed on an emergency field. Then they looked at the gas tanks. They were all bone dry. The planes had been flying on little more than fumes. Turner had known this all the time.

Lieutenant John Mattie, another quiet, mild guy, was the leading train-buster of the group. When Mattie got on the trail of a train in enemy territory he had been known to follow it, guns blazing, right into railroad stations and the teeth of enemy flak. Captain Robert Brooks, after the excitement of a dogfight, flew back and crash-landed perfectly a plane that had no right to fly. Half of one wing had been shot away. The ship was riddled and in tatters from nose to tail. Brooks' only explanation was: 'I hardly knew what I was doing.' He almost fainted from the strain when he stepped from the ship. The same thing happened to Lt Willie Y. Anderson when a five-inch piece of molten flak ripped through the floor of his cockpit, tore and scorched his trouser leg, and set the plane on fire. He put out the fire, kept flying and brought the Mustang home.

As Capt. Richard Turner explained:

'Ninety per cent of the time we're scared stiff. The other ten per cent is split up between terrific extremes of exultation or anger. When you're in the air, trying to control a 400-mile-an-hour machine in the face of the unknown, even a little thing like your squadron leader getting out of line gets you wildly browned off . . . You get on a Jerry's tail and you clobber him, and you feel a tremendous, unreasonable joy inside. Then you turn into Jerry and your guns miss him, and you cuss and swear like a crazy man. Every second you're up there, you're trying to figure out how to save your own skin and do your job at the same time. The speed and the tremendous extremes of emotion leave you wrung out, mentally and physically.'

30 *My Battle* from *Britain*

Fred Huston called his war in the air 'My Battle *from* Britain.'

'The mission was compounded of two main ingredients, boredom and terror, depending on how it went. Towards the end of my tour the forming-up contributed more than its fair share of terror. One can only witness so many mid-airs. You can only take so often the sight of a sheet of flame consuming eighteen men or so at a time. After the twentieth mission I began to get very jumpy and took to wearing my 'chute during the form-up. Yet we never even had a close shave. But just being physically near so many aircraft took its toll on my nerves.

'Rex Maluy was well aware of the feeling I had. He used to watch me putting the thing on with a bemused look on his face. If it had come to the real thing, it might have helped – but it was good for my sagging morale. When we started out, a tour was twenty-five missions and then Stateside. That was until the advent of General Jimmy Doolittle, who soon ran the tour up until it became thirty-five. After that we lost interest because nobody ever made that many . . . !

'For the majority of each mission the bombardier had little to do. It was sort of like being semi-retired. I could sit and stare at the sky; nap; or do whatever suited me, like writing the notes that form the bedrock of this story. When we got issued with a B-17 model G it had a little seat fitted that, as far as I am able to judge, would fit no part of the human anatomy. So I had it removed and got a 'biscuit' from supply. I could then lounge in considerable comfort, to the envy of the rest of the crew.

'From the time we crossed the enemy coast in to target and out again, I had to stay alert. Actually, part of my duties was to run oxygen checks on the crew every ten minutes from the time we went on the stuff. Hardly an onerous chore. I also learned early in operational life to keep an eye out for enemy fighters. When we started our tour we learned fast that any fighter we saw was bound to be on the wrong side. I did get a few rounds in now and then, but no confirmed kills – not even a shared one.

'I guess I was lucky in that most missions I flew happened at the time when the *Luftwaffe* was on the defensive. In the early days of 1942 they would come across the Channel to meet you, harry you all the way into the target – and almost home again. When I was flying, however, they waited over 'Hunland' and jumped you for all they were worth. It was short, sharp and furious while it lasted. Of course, once our fighters got their long legs and escorted us both ways, life became that much easier. Actually I didn't mind the fighters as much as I minded the flak. You could at least shoot at a fighter, even if it might have been ineffectual. With flak

A formation of B-17s making their own cloud

you could only sit there and take it and hope that their aiming number was bad that day. Sometimes it was; mostly it wasn't.

'Being in the lead formation was a bonus in that you couldn't see what was happening behind you unless you deliberately chose to look. Thus you didn't see airplanes blowing up or flying into each other. You didn't have to agonise as you counted the 'chutes go out. And you didn't have to swallow a lump as you watched one ship after another turn slowly over and over on its way to destruction. There was something really poignant in watching the death of a Fort – more than any other ship I ever saw. They died hard. When they went down, they did so grudgingly, under protest, and metaphorically with all their flags flying.

'Even today, just once in a while, I'll see a Fort flying some place and it never fails to bring a lump into my throat. Flying lead formation spared you all that. But we were seldom spared. Flak is funny. It sounds and smells funny. The books talk about box barrages, predicted barrages, tracking barrages. They all look and sound alike from inside a Fort. Little black tar babies most of the time, their fragments would rattle against the ship, sounding like hail on a tin roof. When the gunners wanted the fighters back in, they would fire some shells with different coloured smoke. Mostly the German fighters paid scant heed to what the colour was – they just came boring straight in, no matter what. They were pretty brave guys really, for a flock of Forts must have

Contrails from Britain. A B-17 formation en route from somewhere in England to somewhere in Germany

looked pretty inhibiting seen from the cockpit of a fighter.

'Twenty-seven thousand feet. At around this point in the action, flak and cannon holes would appear and anxiety for our safety would mount accordingly. Voices would be heard on the interphone.

"We've lost number four . . ."

"One gear is down . . ."

"We're losing oil . . ."

"Feather the fan . . ."

"Christ – we're burning in number four . . ."

"Pull the bottle . . ."

'Things would get really hairy about this time and the pilots would earn their pay by trying to keep the crippled aeroplane up. No longer is it the graceful thing full of power that has brought you this far. Now it's a crippled beast that's trying its best to kill all of us.

'When it's like that, there's no time to get scared. You do what you have to do. It's not until afterwards that you realise your legs are shaking – or that you can't breathe properly. The pilots have gotten the beast under control again. It's behaving like an aeroplane again. Except for the gear down and number four still smoking despite the bottle being pulled.

'The pilots decided to follow the CO's advice. We don't abort the mission. We struggle along with the formation and we'll all keep vigil beside the guns, praying that three or four fighters don't pick on us. Maybe the gear down will make them think that we're surrendering. We did hear tales that if you lower the gear they will leave you alone. I don't recall that they attacked us after the gear went down.

'There's no way to explain to someone else exactly how you feel when you've been sucking oxygen for four or five hours. You aren't the same guy as when you took off, that's for sure. You are chilled to the bone, despite the suit. Your eyes burn and your throat aches. Your ears feel like they are welded to your head. Once again it pays to be friendly with the 'chute boys – they got me a set of rubber-foam cups for my headset. Meanwhile, too, your mask is scratching your face and you feel you've got frostbite. The filler tubes of your Mae West will have worn a sore spot on your jaw, and man, you are tired. Totally exhausted from what might go down on the returns as a milk run. Everything might have gone like clockwork, no leaks, all the fans turning, and no fighters or flak. Makes no difference, you are still completely worn out and ready for the sack.

'The real worry after dropping your bombs is not so much the return journey or the Channel – it's what the weather will be doing over the field and the approaches. As we let down over the Channel you can pull off the mask and start breathing real air again. If you were lucky that morning they might have issued you with a Royal Air Force high carbohydrate ration to eat. These were real tasty bits. If you weren't lucky you got a PING bar. Food it wasn't.

'Back over England, if you were lucky the weather was open. B24s occupied the next field to our own. If they were already down, so much the better – one hazard less for us. We would break formation, land and roll past ambulances tending to the damaged and ground-looped ships that had gone in before us. This was always a chastening sight and we never got used to it. Soon as we stopped rolling and reached the hard-stand, we tried not to listen to the shocked remarks of the crew chief when he saw what we'd done to his airplane. It was always our fault. He would never believe that the Germans had done it.

'We got out of the ship, stretched our legs, took out the guns, and headed for the debriefing, where a shot of something resembling whisky awaited our pleasure. Then you told your story to intelligence and the weather folk and headed for the mess hall, where even goat meat and mashed potatoes with hair in them looked good! We had a cook called Whitey and you could always tell when he was on duty. Then it was back to the hut and sack out. There was never any point in trying to take a hot shower. I don't know why, but we never did get down in time. They were always cold.

'I have long since promised myself a trip back to England to see if she still looks as good. Of Snetterton I read that today racing motor-cycles and cars roar down what were once our runways. Of the hangars and hard-stands where our big birds once stood, there is now no trace. Like our youth they have vanished . . . Yet our youth is still there really, at least in our minds.'

31 *Nuremburg and Schweinfurt*

On 30 March 1944 no fewer than ninety-six bombers were reported missing from the night's raid on Germany. It was one of the Allies' heaviest losses in a bomber attack.

Cyril Barton was captain and pilot of a Halifax bomber detailed to attack Nuremburg. Seventy miles short of the target, a Junkers 88 swooped on the aircraft. The very first burst of fire from it put the entire intercom. system right out of action. A Messerschmitt 210 joined in and damaged one engine. The bomber's machine guns went out of use, so the gunners could not return the German fighter's fire.

Somehow Barton managed to keep his Halifax on course, covering those seventy miles to Nuremburg, although fighters continued to target him all the way. But in the confusion caused by the failure of the intercom. system at the height of the battle, a signal had been misinterpreted, and

Halifax heavy bomber as captained by Pilot Officer Cyril Barton in his raid on Nuremburg

the navigator, air bomber and wireless operator all left the aircraft by parachute.

Barton then faced a situation of dire peril. His aircraft was damaged, his navigational team had gone, and he could not communicate with the rest of the crew. If he continued his mission he could be at the mercy of hostile fighters when silhouetted against the fires in the target area. And if he happened to survive that, he would have to make a four-and-a-half hour flight home on three engines across heavily defended enemy territory. Barton determined to press on, however. He reached his target, and released the bombs himself.

As he wrenched the Halifax round to aim for home, the propeller of the damaged engine flew off. It had already been vibrating badly. Two of the bomber's petrol tanks had also suffered damage and were leaking precious fuel. But Barton remained aloof from all these dangers and concentrated on the task of holding to his course without any navigational aids and against strong headwinds. Somehow he avoided the most strongly defended areas on his return route.

Using just his own judgment, he eventually crossed the English coast only ninety miles north of his base. Now the worst part was about to begin. As a result of the leaks in the tanks, fuel was virtually non-existent. The port engines stopped with a sickening, intermittent coughing. Seeing a suitable landing place, Barton told the three remaining members of the Halifax crew to take up crash stations. The aircraft was then too low to be abandoned successfully. It lost height rapidly. With only one engine functioning, he struggled to land clear of a group of houses just below them.

The three members of the crew survived the ensuing crash, but Barton was killed. The three who baled out over Germany were safe, too, as prisoners-of-war. So Barton alone died, while the other six members of his crew survived.

Mrs Barton read the letter Cyril had written in case this ever happened to him:

Dear Mum,

I hope you never receive this, but I quite expect you will. I'm expecting to do my first operational trip in a few days. I know what ops over Germany mean, and I have no illusions about it. By my own calculations the average life of a crew is 20 ops, and we have 30 to do in our first tour.

I'm writing this for two reasons. One to tell you how I would like my money spent that I have left behind me: two to tell you how I feel about meeting my Maker.

1. I intended as you know taking a university course with my savings. Well, I would like it to be spent over the education of my brothers and sisters.

2. All I can say about this is that I am quite prepared to die. It holds no terror for me.

Pilot Officer Cyril Barton

At times I've wondered whether I've been right in believing what I do, and just recently I've doubted the veracity of the Bible, but in the little time I've had to sort out intellectual problems I've been left with a bias in favour of the Bible.

Apart from this though, I have the inner conviction as I write, of a force outside myself, and my brain tells me that I have not trusted in vain. All I am anxious about is that you and the rest of the family will also come to know Him. Ken, I know, already does. I commend my Saviour to you.

I am writing to Doreen separately. I expect you will have guessed by now that we are quite in love with each other.

Well, that's covered everything now I guess, so love to Dad and all.

Your loving son

Cyril

It was nearly four weeks later. On the morning of 26 April 1944, Norman Jackson, flight engineer of a Lancaster, got a telegram telling him of the birth of a son to his wife. He and the rest of the crew were jubilant and excited about this – especially since the night's operation against Schweinfurt was due to be the last of Jackson's Bomber Command tour. He had already completed a Coastal Command tour. Once the night of 26–27 April was over, that would be two tours over as well.

Despite the expected opposition, they had a reasonable approach to their target of Schweinfurt and dropped their bombs successfully. The Lancaster had climbed out of the inferno of the target area and reached 20,000 feet when an enemy fighter pounced on it. The captain reacted instinctively and took evasive action, but the fighter secured several hits on the less agile four-engine bomber. Fire crept dangerously near a petrol tank on the upper surface of the starboard wing – between the fuselage and the inner engine.

The evasive tactics during the engagement had thrown Jackson to the floor of the plane, where he sustained a whole series of wounds from shell splinters in his right leg and shoulder. He recovered himself quickly and got the captain's permission to try and put out the flames. He knew they could not fly back to England in that state; indeed, they could not fly for long at all unless something were done.

Stuffing a hand fire-extinguisher into the top of his life-saving jacket, and clipping on his parachute pack, Jackson jettisoned the escape hatch above the pilot's head. Then he started to climb out of the cockpit and back along the top of the fuselage to the starboard wing. But before he could leave the fuselage his parachute pack opened, and the whole canopy and rigging lines streamed and spilled into the cockpit.

Undeterred he went on. The pilot, bomb-aimer and navigator all gathered the parachute together, paying it out as the sergeant climbed aft: all this, still four miles above hostile country. Eventually Jackson slipped, but falling from the fuselage to the starboard wing he somehow grasped an air intake on the leading edge of the Lancaster's wing. Every sinew strained beyond the normal limits. Jackson succeeded in clinging on, but inevitably lost the extinguisher, which was sucked away with the piercing windstream.

By this time the fire had spread alarmingly, and continued to do so progressively. Jackson himself became directly involved in it, affected by it. His face, hands and clothes were severely burned. Charred and in pain, he could not keep his hold, and was swept through the flames and over the trailing edge of the wing. When the rest of the crew glimpsed him, he was dragging his parachute behind him. It was only partly inflated, and burning in a number of places.

The captain realised that the fire could not possibly be controlled now, and gave the order: 'Abandon ship.' Four members of the crew baled out safely, and were taken prisoner, but the captain and rear gunner failed to get out. So Flying Officer Fred Mifflin and Flight Sergeant Hugh Johnson died as the Lancaster crashed.

Meanwhile, the wind gasped through the nylon and the rigging lines of Jackson's parachute, spreading the patches of fire as he fell. His speed increased. Jackson could not control his descent at all, but thankfully it did not reach a fatal rate. He landed heavily, breaking his ankle; so with this injury, his right eye closed through burns, other burns still hurting him, and his hands useless, he could only wait for daybreak, when he crawled to the nearest village.

He rapped on the door of the smallest cottage he could see, and an old woman and her daughter gave him first aid. Then, after rough medical treatment at a nearby hospital, he was paraded through the village. People turned out to jeer and throw stones at him, but he was too far gone to care.

Jackson was made a prisoner-of-war and there followed ten months in hospital, where he made a good recovery. But long before all this, the whole Lancaster crew had been posted as missing. Two-and-a-half weeks went by before German radio announced that Jackson was a prisoner with the four others.

All that remained in 1945 was for them to be returned home soon after VE-Day, when it was found that Jackson's hands needed still further treatment, and that they were only of limited use to him. It was also only at this late stage that the whole story was pieced together by the reports of the rest of the crew: how he had ventured out of the Lancaster at a great height and in intense cold; how he had ignored the extra hazard of his spilled parachute; and how, if he had managed to subdue the flames, there would have been little or no prospect of his getting back into the cockpit.

After the war, Jackson and his wife found a bungalow for themselves and their baby son in Hampton Hill, Middlesex. Outside it at night, passers-by could see the silhouette of a Lancaster lit up in a porthole-shaped window. There was no need to ask Jackson what it meant, or why he had put it there.

32 *Softening-up for D-Day*

The air attack on Europe was intensified in spring 1944 to unprecedented proportions. Zero-hour bombing it became called, in preparation for the long-awaited invasion. The American A-20s, in fact, were flying two missions a day in the non-stop assault against targets in France and else-where, such as marshalling yards, railroads and bridges, and were a crucial constituent of the softening-up process for D-Day.

Take a day in April, for instance; wonderful weather that was perfect for baseball – and bombing. The A-20s had set out early and were due home soon to give the crews a rest and to load another cargo of bombs, bound for the other side of the English Channel. The airfield seemed strangely quiet, as it always did when most of the planes were away. Then quite suddenly the ground crews heard the distant drone before the formation showed up over the field. These men below sat on a high

A-20 showing D-Day black and white bands on wings. This light attack day bomber and night fighter intruder had over a dozen variations between 1941 and 1945. Known first for the RAF as the Boston, it became the Havoc in USAAF service. It was one of the major successes among American aircraft for allied use, with a speed exceeding 300 mph.

mound of ground overlooking the whole field and eagerly counted-in the aircraft. The engines died, the propellers gave their final few twists, and the crews were soon rushing and roaring into the briefing room, generating the electric excitement that invariably accompanied this after-mission moment.

Lieutenant Wilbert Sawyer's plane had got a couple of bullet holes through the fuselage. 'When I saw the blue smoke' Sawyer said, paying tribute to the enemy fighter, 'I said "that guy's fortune's made" . . .'

Another pilot, Lt Charles Thomas, had an experience that really ranked as a close call: a shell ripped across his chest and cut his mike cord, severing interphone touch between him and his crew for the rest of the flight.

Lieutenant P.G. Benson announced somewhat sheepishly that he was all alone because the rest of the crew had baled out over France. The flak had been thick. He had been bounced upward by blast, and thought that the men must have assumed the ship was out of control – because they all jumped. Every one of their 'chutes opened, so it might have been much worse.

On this twice-a-day assignment, representing the pulverising pace of the western air offensive, the men then tried to get in some sack time before their next flight. Gunners and pilots alike dozed on benches in the locker room.

Squadron Commander Major Arthur Milow, Jr, flew in that afternoon mission. The major hailed from Omaha, but a lot of time spent in the South had lent a slow rhythm to his speech. His bombardier-navigator, Lt John 'Moose' Ertler, was an exuberant ex-amateur boxer from Cleveland, and really keen on seeing that his bombs got to their goal.

At briefing they heard the same things that made all briefings classics of understatement – and even downright funny.

'You may expect flak at X and again at Y . . . This should be light flak, but the Germans as you know employ mobile flak guns . . . Coming out at the coast, navigators should make sure they avoid Z which is a big town. You should have no trouble coming out, if you follow the course laid out.'

Different from last year, Milow thought. Last April they did not wear flak suits, while escort fighters were still practically non-existent. This year they wore the suits, and today there would be Spitfires in the sky, both ways. Spring, 1944. One that would be remembered forever by all of them.

The planes got up fast, climbing in a hurry. They set up the formation in no time, it seemed, and then below them curved the friendly, familiar English coast, symbol of so much to so many. Right behind Major Milow's plane there pounded Lt Charles Reed's: so near underneath their fuselage that they might have been doing close order infantry drill. They could actually see Reed chewing gum and grinning in his cockpit.

Then the French shoreline lay etched below, curving quietly, less friendly. Over land now, and the spring shades of yellow and lime on the patterned countryside. The little farms seemed to be slumbering, yet the Americans knew that German guns were lurking there, too. On the formation flew.

The first flak blossomed behind them. They were moving very fast now, with the escorting Spitfires outside the boxes of heavy A-20s. The target was the railroad marshalling yards at Busigny and they would be coming in there any minute.

The 'Moose' prepared to drop his bombs. Lying flat on their stomachs, some of the other crew members saw the sticks of bombs fall away from the belly of the A-20s, swarming off like a school of fish instinctively staying together. Then they were lost for a few seconds against the cloudy confusion over the target, before the erupting puffs of smoke signalled hits. The bomb pattern fell in rows, one after the other, exactly as if someone were planting seeds in a furrow. One stick from another aircraft smashed squarely across the centre of the yards, each bomb sparking a sheet of flame ten feet high.

They told this to the 'Moose' over the interphone, but he was not so sure that his own had hit and was already beginning to fret about it.

They were heading homeward even more quickly now, lightened of their load. The blue ditch, the sacred moat, of the English Channel appeared. A freighter seemed to be utterly still on its surface. The 'Moose' was singing into the interphone, which he did on every mission at this particular stage. Major Milow's A-20 landed like the smooth, fast aircraft it was – and one more routine raid had been completed. Just one of the two-a-day series of pre-invasion attacks. Once they actually flew three in one day, which they reckoned must have been some sort of record.

After it was over, the 'Moose' played the Warsaw Concerto on the piano, and later slid into some soft rhythms. The Americans had come a long way from their first raid over the Continent on 4 July 1942 – a happily apt date.

Parallel with the offensive on French targets was the ceaseless strategic bombing against German centres of industry and aircraft production. For each of the five months from November 1943 to March 1944 less than half the planned production of single-engine enemy fighters was actually achieved. Yet all this involved heartbreaking sacrifice by both the British and American air forces. On the notorious night of 30/31 March 1944, ninety-four aircraft of British Bomber Command failed to return from the air attack on Nuremburg.

By this time, however, the new American long-range fighters had mastered those of the enemy during the day, and Allied bombers made powerful precision attacks, protected by American Thunderbolts, Lightnings, and later, Mustangs.

Throughout the preliminary period before the ultimate fling for

D-Day, air attacks also had to be maintained on 'Noball' targets, the code name for the German flying bomb and rocket-launching sites.

Important as all these objectives obviously were, the main aim was to stop enemy supplies from reaching the invasion area once the battle was on. To do this, the railway-bombing plan started in April. So the railway centres of northern France and the Low Countries were hit by 66,000 tons of bombs in three months, with the avowed aim of creating a 'railway desert' around the Germans in Normandy. Secondary targets were the main marshalling yards, while another part of the plan covered the destruction of road and rail bridges. Eighty targets were attacked in this plan, fifty-one being heavily damaged, twenty-five damaged, and four little affected.

Gradually a paralysis extended over the whole northern network of railroads; stupendous-scale fighter sweeps intercepted locomotives all over northern France. On 21 May, over 500 British-manned Thunderbolts with 233 Spitfires claimed sixty-seven locos destroyed with ninety-one damaged. The Americans claimed ninety-one locomotives destroyed on the very same day.

Lines, locos, and rail and road bridges leading into the assault area were preferred targets. This bombing of bridges had a twofold object: to check troops and supplies entering the battle, and to prevent their making a rapid retreat should it become necessary to the enemy. Yet the Allies had to take care not to betray any special interest in the routes to Normandy, so bridges over the Seine became the first targets, together with others which did not commit the Allies to any specific assault area. So the steady air attacks went on – and forty-nine coastal batteries, capable of firing on shipping approaching the assault area, were bombed and blasted.

The final figures for the two-months' softening-up operations of April, May, and to 5th June, were 200,000 individual sorties of the combined Allied air forces, distinguished among which was the USAAF. So it became a question of offence and defence. As the spring sped on, more and more of the D-Day armada were gathering, inevitably very vulnerable, around the coast. All this time, protection against attack by air had to come partly from the Allied fighter force. For over 6,000 craft were to be employed in operation Overlord, the liberation of Europe.

The Germans had 450 heavy bombers still on hand to hammer at invasion preparations, but for some reason a raid on any never materialised. Then suddenly they were too late anyway. D-Day was here.

Out of the morning mist broke a barrage mightier than sound itself, the concerted crescendo of almost a thousand guns firing in shattering sequence. Across the sea the shells quivered their way to the Normandy shores, leaving the decks of the ships shuddering with the recoil.

Here was history being made, as cloudy columns of suffocating, smudgy smoke rose in a grey-black blot along the fringe of France. D for

On the night before D-Day, 'window' radar countermeasures being dropped by Lancasters to confuse enemy defences

Deliverance. Men's hearts hung in their mouths, or their throats – or their stomachs. A glance at a watch; muted mutterings; parched tongues; a prayer.

The Yanks went in at two areas, designated Utah and Omaha. At Utah, things went comparatively well, but they were drastically different at Omaha.

33 *First Blood to the Skymen*

THE CHANNEL STOPPED YOU, BUT NOT US was chalked in foot-high letters on an airborne glider during the evening of D-1. The blackened faces of troops contrasted with the white chalk. And they did not seem to mind that the glider was numbered 13. Camouflage sprouted through the netting over their tin helmets. In smaller letters beside the main message, one of them had written carefully, 'Rember Coventry, Plymouth, Bristol, London. Now it's our turn.'

Over at another airfield, preparing for a flight on D-Day, troops sweated and heaved as they shoved a jeep up a ramp into a glider. Anti-aircraft guns were also loaded, together with a mass of equipment needed to ward off German counter-attacks.

Earlier Eisenhower had talked to American airborne forces as they quit their canvas tents to get ready for the flight. And Air Chief Marshal Leigh-Mallory went round to every airfield from which Allied airborne forces would be taking off later that night of June 5.

At 2230 hours that night sixty men of the 22nd Independent Parachute Company were drinking tea out of mugs from a mobile canteen, and smoking beside half a dozen Albemarle aircraft on the runway of Harwell. These men were to be the pathfinders for the 6th Airborne Division, commanded by Major-General Richard Gale. Not only black but brown and green paint darkened their faces, and among as much as 100 lb. of gear they carried Stens, ammunition, knives, and grenades, plus a bag of Radar beacons and lights strapped to one leg of each man for marking the dropping-zones.

Another twenty minutes, and the paratroops filed into their planes. Darkness now, as at 2203 hours the first Albemarle taxied down the runway, cleared the hedges at the perimeter, and droned south. The other five followed rapidly. Seventy-seven minutes later, at 0020 hours on D-Day, they were over the three dropping-zones. Despite the advantage of moonlight, and that half the aircraft ran in twice or more, only one stick of paratroops landed correctly on the three zones. All the visual beacons for one zone were lost or damaged in the drop.

The pathfinders parachuting down near Ranville were scattered – principally by the high wind, which carried them east of the intended zone. Since the main force they were to guide would be due in under half an hour they had no time to attempt a recovery. Instead, they lit their beacons where they landed.

Due to drop at the same time as the pathfinders was a *coup de main* force (six platoons of the 2nd Battalion of the Oxford and Buckinghamshire Light Infantry) under the command of Major R. J. Howard. Their task was to capture intact two vital bridges: the one on the only through-road over the Orne river, the other over the canal between Caen and the sea. Theirs was an airborne assault by gliders. Like the later main force, towed by Halifax bombers acting as tugs. At exactly 0015 hours the bombers slipped their tows and then went on to attack Caen, while the gliders circled silently down. Their audacious assault plan was to crash-land on their actual objectives. Howard was in the leading glider headed for the canal bridge, and its wheels gripped into the ground only 47 yards (who measured that?) from the eastern end of the bridge. It grasshoppered the rest of the way, ending in barbed-wire, with its nose broken. Howard and his men had to grope their way out via the cockpit instead of through the door. The two other gliders aimed at the canal bridge crash-landed close behind them. The enemy was sheltering from the sudden crescendo on Caen by the Halifaxes, so Howard's men raced on to take the bridge. A spatter of machine-gun fire from the far side killed the commander of the first platoon. They ousted the defenders from a pill-box and a near-by network of trenches, and ensured that the bridge would not be blown up by the enemy.

Eight hundred yards to the east, at about the same time, the other gliders landed less accurately. But two of the three platoons got to their bridge over the Orne within minutes, and found it undefended.

Consolidating the captures, the pathfinders found that, although the enemy had prepared both bridges for blowing, no alarm of invasion had reached them, and so the charges were not in position.

So the bridgeheads had been won. Now the pathfinders must hold them until the main forces reinforced and relieved them.

Half an hour after the pathfinder-drops, and at just about the moment the two bridges fell, the 5th Parachute Brigade joined the invasion. Their story started at 2000 hours on the evening of June 5 when the 7th Parachute Battalion was called from a pre-battle rest. Few of them could sleep. All identification by letters or other evidence was surrendered, and 620 men went out to the airfield in thirty-three lorries, one lorryful for each Stirling plane. An occasional quiet song floated across the stilled airfield. Then they went through the routine of sipping mugs of tea and smearing dark camouflage on their faces so that no sniper should pick them out against the night sky. Even collapsible dinghies were crammed into some of their kitbags, since they would be operating near two rivers and might need to get across.

The briefing over now, watches were synchronized as they stood near propellers waiting to turn. Then they stepped off English earth, and the Stirlings climbed into the sky of that immortal night and flew high over the Channel. People still awake in coastal homes murmured to themselves, 'Another raid over there.' But this time they were wrong.

At a quarter to one low cloud blew over the dropping-zone. This obscured some of the beacons and made accurate air navigation impossible. The Stirlings circled, trying to find the exact spot. Suddenly the anti-aircraft defences sprang to life, spitting shells and tracer upward. Flak hit two of the thirty-three planes. The night wind fanned the fires, and a deadly drone presaged the start of two spirals down, down into the French fields they sought to liberate. Two Stirlings, their crews, and forty precious paratroops.

Promptly at 0050 hours the other thirty-one aircraft came in low over the zone and dropped their human loads. The descent took only about ten seconds, but to the paratroops, exposed to a tracery of fire from below, it seemed something out of time altogether.

Lieutenant-Colonel Pine-Coffin was commanding this drop, but, due to the pathfinders' problems and the low cloud, the battalion landed badly scattered. As they neared the ground the scene grew dangerously lighter each moment. With a succession of bumps they were down, but, although they landed quite near the dropping-zone, many were unable to find it. Luckily, Pine-Coffin managed to get his bearings when a flare from one of the aircraft silhouetted the old church at Ranville, which had stood serenely in the village for six centuries. Now he knew which way to go.

Pine-Coffin found Lieutenant Rogers, and together they assembled some men. This was a slow business, but expedited by Rogers' Aldis lamp, which blinked out as a pre-arranged signal to the troops. For Rogers himself, however, it could have been fatal if it had attracted enemy fire towards him. In the confusion he had little time to dwell on this.

They were not exactly keeping their arrival secret, as another means of attracting men to the commander was by their regimental call blown on a bugle! This combination of blinking and bugling mustered about one-third of the 620 men dropped from the thirty-one aircraft. By 0215 hours the number rose to some 250. They dared not delay any longer, as firing from the canal bridge suggested that they were already needed there. When they reached the bridge, however, they found with relief that the firing had been no more than ammunition exploding in a German tank; and soon Major R. J. Howard's radio code signals of 'Ham and Jam' told them that both bridges were in fact safely in British hands. With real relief they ditched their dinghies, and by 0300 hours were in the planned positions near the bridges. Many of the men were without their special weapons, lost somewhere in the French fields as a result of the unlucky air drop.

Two hundred and fifty men with a few pistols and Stens, but no 3-inch mortars or medium machine-guns. No wonder Pine-Coffin was not too happy about their ability to hold the bridges. But before long A Company settled into the village of Benouville, and B Company in the hamlet of Le Port, keeping one platoon actually on the bridge over the Orne. Pine-Coffin had C Company in reserve.

'The hour before the dawn' will always mean to A Company the moment at Benouville when the enemy suddenly attacked them on three sides simultaneously. Carrying across the air to the other companies came sounds suggesting that the attack was in some strength, so Lieutenant MacDonald led twenty men from the reserve C Company, ill-armed for such a task, to get through to Benouville. This they did, fighting all the way till they found A Company still warding off attacks on all three sides.

Two platoons of B Company, meanwhile, dug – not literally – into the escarpment of Le Port, while the third platoon wrapped itself around the canal bridge. One platoon for a vital canal bridge was scarcely what the planners had intended; sporadic fire kept the men alert for their lives every second, and made them wish for those paratroops who had been dropped far from the right zone. One of their two particular aircraft discharged its troops no less than 12 miles from the centre of the zone. They might just as well have been 1,200 miles away at this precise moment.

At 2330 hours on June 5 the first of the Stirlings to carry the 12th Parachute Battalion gave a mechanical cough as its engines spluttered into life. The battalion's objective was the village of Le Bas de Ranville, and, like the rest of the brigade, they had a quiet flight across the Channel.

As the first aircraft approached the coast one of the aircrew removed the hatches, and they could see dimly the white waves breaking on the beach, lines like those identity stripes painted around the body of their aircraft. Then from sea, beach, and cliffs to strange silhouettes of woods, and the patterns made by fields and hedges. A red light, then a green one. Go. The parachutes fluttered out and floated down. Only the sign of the wind through the struts. Then the ground interrupted this idyll.

It took until about 0200 hours for the 12th Battalion to muster enough of their number to make a start towards their goal of Le Bas de Ranville. Lieutenant-Colonel A. P. Johnson, commanding them, collected more men who had landed outside the dropping-zone, and together they all advanced on the village.

Then came their first brush with the enemy. Just on the outskirts they were stalking along the edge of the road when they suddenly saw two vehicles bearing down on them.

'Fire!' called an officer.

And an enemy motor-cyclist lurched off his machine before it careered madly on and into a ditch. The other vehicle turned out to be an armoured car, and burst through before being stopped at the approaches to the bridge. A focus of fire sent it streaming off the road, and from it staggered the German officer responsible for the defences of the bridges – a belated arrival. Further investigation into the car revealed the remains of a meal and some rouge and face-powder. Evidently these were intended for a destination other than British paratroops about to enter their first French village.

Meanwhile the 13th Parachute Battalion began their particular piece of the jigsaw – clearing the adjacent village of Ranville and its vital bridges over the Orne. Vital, too, was the task of getting rid of the anti-airborne poles which dotted the ground earmarked for glider landings later in this eventful night.

Those of the 13th who came to earth in the specified area fared well, but many of the rest – nearly half of the battalion strength – came to grief amid the surrounding trees. Desperately, they tried to free themselves in the gloom of the woodlands, but a number were located and killed by enemy fire before they had a chance.

But the majority were able to respond to the brigade's hunting horns, which blared out into the night as if attached to some phantom pack. The enemy garrison in Ranville heard this blood-curdling call with terror, and by 0230 hours they had all been overrun and Ranville had fallen: the first French village to be liberated.

While this historic, if small, action went on the company detailed to clear the landing-fields for the gliders were going about their job thoroughly, and the main glider force of seventy-two machines, with guns, transport, and equipment, prepared to take-off over in England. Their time of landing had been worked out for 0330 hours, to allow them two hours before daybreak in which to complete their mission.

Shortly before 0200 hours the air armada began. The tug planes roared down the runway, their engines racing to take the strain of guiding a glider. Then the tow was taut, the rope quivered into a straight line. Plane and glider gradually moved. The ground slid beneath them; the wheels left it and went on revolving; there was no turning back.

All the troops could see as they crouched in their gliders was rain outside the cockpit, and now and again a glimpse of light from their particular towing aircraft. Guiding them where? Unseen below them, the sea armada sailed on south – some ships 10 miles, others 50 miles, from the D-Day coast. Then as the cloud cleared they caught a momentary glimpse of the ships edging nearer. But back in the cloud again the gliders' wings wobbled in the gusty gale – a wind which sent a shiver through their wooden framework.

0300 hours, and the enemy coast below. Denser cloud now, and no sign of even the tug's rear light. Just as they really needed good visibility the clouds closed in on them. Then the inevitable flak started; a kaleidoscope of colour flashing all around. Seventy-two gliders and as many tugs seemed silhouetted at once. As if they were frozen still in the sky. Sitting targets at 2,500 feet.

One glider was hit just enough to throw it off balance. The trouble was that neither the towing aircraft nor the gliders themselves could manoeuvre much while they were still linked. It was an unpleasant position, to put it mildly. Over on one side another glider got a direct flash of flak, and twenty-six men plus the pilot perished. Then another glider went down.

Over the Channel songs had been sung. Not now.

Beneath them they saw the weaving, watery lines of the Orne and the Canal de Caen threaded through the land. Over the target area now, but *they* were the targets. Below, the beacons and the flak all became inter-mingled in colourful confusion.

Then, one by one, the tows parted. The gliders wavered in the wind before their noses angled down through the flak. One last magic moment of quiet after they had got out of the flak and before scraping the ground. A last dive in the dark, with beacons, lights, roads and churches, and other unidentifiable shapes lurching on each side of them. Any second now. This was how the first assault troops would be feeling a few hours later on the beaches. For airborne troops the moment of truth had already come. Obstacle posts were torn and ripped right out of the ground. The splitting and splintering gliders groaned to a halt, some upright, others upturned, others actually on end with their tails pointing high to heaven. The men clambered into the cornfield which was their airfield, leaving a litter of gliders facing in every direction of the compass, crazily up against hedges or actually touching one another. But however the airborne men had arrived, they were here, that was the important thing: in the proper place at the right time.

While enemy guns still fired into a sky so lately filled with the slow, vulnerable gliders, the men moved quickly through the ripening corn, rustling it as they went. And then came the less soft sounds of equipment being shifted into action stations.

On the perimeter of the field a sentry challenged some one, and the code name response came at once. None of them could take chances.

On the field an alarming panorama presented itself. The whole zone seemed to be full of hopelessly wrecked gliders – each minus a wing or a wheel. And even as the early arrivals glanced at the apparent desolation a late-comer bumped in low over the corn and smashed straight into a house on the perimeter. In fact, however, two out of every three gliders landed safely and accurately. Most of the men and their weapons came to no harm, and ten of the eighteen anti-tank guns were left in working order.

So, as quickly as they could, they moved off towards Ranville church. The only opposition to be seen took the form of a rapidly retreating German military car, and then soon afterwards the British took their first prisoner – a chestnut-brown horse which had been minding its own business on the landing zone! The animal came under the care of Major-General Richard Gale's aide-de-camp, and accompanied them to their temporary headquarters at Ranville. Perhaps he would prove a lucky mascot.

Gale himself, ignoring the occasional punctuation marks of snipers' bullets, took a jeep to survey the state of affairs at the bridges which the British held.

The airborne operation as a whole proved to be far from plain sailing, or flying. One Albemarle tried seven times to find the dropping-zone, but before it could do so it was hit by flak, and had to turn round to head for home. At the actual moment the shell exploded the Brigade Major of the 3rd Parachute Brigade – Major W. A. C. Collingwood – was waiting to jump. The blast blew him through the opening, and his line wound round one of his legs. As the aircraft aimed sadly north once more he actually hung there beneath it for half an hour, with a 60-lb. kitbag weighting his other leg. Eventually the concerted strength of those safely inside the plane succeeded in hoisting him aboard the Albemarle again. The post-script was that the plane got back to England, and Collingwood insisted on joining his brigade, which he did later on D-Day.

The brigade's mission was far-flung, and not made easier by the wild night and inevitably inaccurate dropping. Their task was to destroy the bridges in the Dives valley and seize a ridge between the Dives and the Orne. In fact, the two rivers looked indistinguishable from the air, which constituted another difficulty. Coming into this chaos, the aircraft encountered ack-ack fire, forcing them to undertake urgent evasive manoeuvres, with the result that Brigadier S.J.L. Hill and his men jumped while the planes were travelling too fast, and were consequently carried beyond their goal.

The 1st Canadian Parachute Battalion dropped between 0100 and 0130 hours into an area forty times as large as planned. One aircraft had no choice but to return home to Down Ampney without dropping any of its number of troops, because, as it shuddered at the impact of enemy flak on its fuselage, a parachutist fell into – instead of through – the exit, and wedged it tight till they were minutes and miles past the dropping-zone!

As another aircraft crossed the mouth of the Canal de Caen it was met by a stream of tracer which cracked past only 15 feet to starboard. The plane at once swung violently left, and when the men had sorted them-selves out they found that they had altered course so severely that following pilots probably confused the Orne and Dives rivers. Many of the eighty-six Canadians taken prisoner by the enemy as a result of the scattered drop rejoined their units soon afterwards – a testimony to their ingenuity in any circumstances, foreseen or otherwise.

Several sticks of the 9th and 1st Canadian Parachute Battalions fell into the river Dives or in the flooded, desolate wastelands beside it. Some men were drowned in these swamps – just one tragic way of dying on this day of days.

The 8th Canadian Parachute Battalion, under the renowned and ex-perienced Lieutenant-Colonel Alastair Pearson,[1] dropped in a much more scattered pattern than had ever been intended, and as a result some paratroops were trapped in the tree-tops of the Bois de Bavent. Pearson dropped safely, but he had scarcely shaken himself free of his harness when a bullet him him in the hand. Despite losing blood steadily, he went on with his duty, and rounded up enough men for their job of destroying two bridges.

Four of the five bridges over the Dives were blown up as rehearsed, but the fifth only succumbed due to a daring improvisation. Pearson's

---

[1] Afterwards Colonel Alastair Pearson, O.B.E., D.S.O., M.C.

men met a group of sappers who had landed north of the Bois de Bavent. They explained that they had not enough explosive left, and so the sappers drove their jeep, laden with the necessary charges, straight through the enemy-held town of Troarn. Miraculously, they survived machine-gun fire aimed right down the road at them, and they managed to blow a gaping gap in the bridge.

Like so many other airborne units, the 1st Canadian Battalion suffered a severely scattered drop, and some were cut off from the rest by woods or marshes and taken prisoner. The Germans lined up five of these Canadians and summarily shot them. Four died, but the fifth was only wounded in the leg; somehow he slipped away to make contact with the Resistance, and was soon hobbling off to rejoin his unit. The Canadians, needless to say, succeeded in blowing their bridges over the Dives and at Robehomme.

Captain R. M. E. Kerr of the British 13th Battalion landed right in the river Dives, but managed to struggle free from his harness, stagger ashore, soaked and shivering, and find a farm which four other parachutists had also reached. The French family were pleased to see them, even though it was the middle of the night, and a young French boy offered to take them to their objective of Varaville.

With his help they found the place at about 0330 hours, but violent enemy action warned them not to enter it. They recognized every sort of weapon, and so skirted the village and entered a wood. Quite suddenly a German patrol appeared from nowhere, and through the night air one of them came close enough to hurl a stick grenade, which burst on the boy's head. This was war now . . .

So we come to the main mission of the 3rd Parachute Brigade: to destroy the dangerous enemy battery by the coast near Merville.

Major-General Gale said, 'The Hun thinks that only a bloody fool will go there. That's why we're going!'

To Lieutenant-Colonel T. H. B. Otway, Royal Ulster Rifles, and the 9th Battalion, 3rd Parachute Brigade, fell the duty of destroying the battery: a strong-point with four 150-mm. guns (it was thought), housed in thick concrete, ten machine-guns, mines, and other elaborate defences. He had to be sure to silence the battery by half an hour before first light, so that the invasion fleet could begin the bombardment in the knowledge that the beaches west of the Orne estuary were safe from the fire of the Merville guns, which could conceivably knock out enough of the British invasion forces to endanger the entire operation. The enemy garrison was thought to number about 180 men.

The involved plan included eleven separate parties, each with a specific job. Added to these were to be three troop-carrying gliders, which would crash their way right into the midst of the battery just as the paratroops were due to start their assault.

The glider force and two other parties took off from Brize Norton and

Harwell at about 2330 hours, the rest earlier, at 2310 hours. The first to drop were the reconnaissance party, to mark the dropping-zone and find a route to the battery through the defences. Wearing jumping-socks with the alarming decoration of skull and crossbones marked in luminous paint on the left breast, they dropped quite close to their intended spot.

The next part of the plan, timed for 0030 hours and 0040 hours, went into operation as a hundred Lancaster bombers flew in over the battery to saturate it before the start of the main airborne assault. Unluckily the weather was again against the Allies, and not at all good for highlevel night bombing. A great weight of 4,000 lb. bombs screamed down through the clouds, but exploded half a mile from their target, which, in an attack of this precision, meant that they were virtually wasted. One or two of them actually fell near the airborne reconnaissance group as they groped their way towards the battery; these men were understandably shattered to suffer this extra hazard of bombs from their own air force.

Next came the main drop. Four minutes away from the zone, and already confusing the mouths of the Orne and the Dives in the darkness, the pilots also had to contend with intense flak. Veering violently to evade it, they gave the paratroops a nasty few minutes. Men with 80-lb. loads plus parachutes were flung all over the aircraft as they reeled to escape the searchlights. There was nothing for it but to go ahead with the drop – despite the conditions. The sticks of paratroops groped their way out of lurching aircraft in an order as different from their normal disciplined descents as it was possible to imagine.

Instead of being concentrated into an area roughly a mile long by half a mile wide, the paratroops were spread over 50 square miles. The stick earning the doubtful distinction of landing farthest from the target came down 30 miles away! So much for the weeks of rigorous rehearsal.

This was bad enough, but worse followed, with the loss of the five equipment gliders. The strong squall over the Channel strained and finally snapped the towropes, and the quintet glided helplessly down into the sea, taking their anti-tank guns, jeeps, and much more with them: equipment Otway and his men would need before many more minutes had elapsed.

Meanwhile Otway himself was flung fiercely from his Dakota, which was banking steeply away from the ground fire. It was nasty enough to jump by parachute in the middle of the night from a steady aircraft, but this was the worst way possible of launching the War's most vital operation.

And then, of all places to land, he and two others drifted down into a garden beside the H.Q. of a German unit, some way from Merville. The enemy at once fired on them with Luger pistols, but none were hit. Then one of the other two paratroops, Otway's batman, clambered on to the roof of the greenhouse attached to the house and heaved a brick through the window. The Germans apparently assumed that this must be a grenade, and while they were recovering the trio of British paratroops rushed out of the garden and were gone.

They moved as fast as they could towards the rendezvous, and when they reached it found that practically everything had gone not according to plan. The five-day briefing was discarded at one stroke as soon as Otway realized at 0250 hours that the total strength of the battalion had grown to only 150 men, with twenty lengths of Bangalore torpedo. No 3-inch mortars; no 6-pounder guns; no jeeps; no trailers; no glider stores; no sappers; no field ambulance; no mine detectors. On the credit side: some signals; a machine-gun; half of one sniping party; six medical orderlies, who would be needed before much longer. In one way this simplified the situation. Yet, looked at soberly, it seemed mad to go on.

Otway decided to advance at once.

They could not waste more time looking for guns which might have dropped almost anywhere in Normandy. For they were still a mile and a half from Merville. So they set out – decimated but determined. Walking through high-banked lanes within a mile of Merville seemed unreal, yet here they were.

One part of the plan that happened more of less as anticipated was their meeting with Major G. Smith and the reconnaissance party, already in the environs of the battery. Smith told Otway that he and his men had cut one fence, negotiated a minefield inside it, and spent some time in those early hours trying to place the exact sites of the sentry posts from the sounds of the Germans on guard. One patrol passed precisely two feet from where they were waiting.

Otway and the main force advanced farther and reached the party actually charged with the task of penetrating the minefield. Despite trip-wires and other obstacles, doubly dangerous in the dark, these men had forged a route through the mines and marked it with their heels. And not a single casualty had been caused. This took the main force to the inner wire.

0424 hours: only a few minutes to zero hour, as two of the three gliders bearing the special, almost suicidal, assault teams arrived overhead as planned. The tow-rope of the third parted early on, and the glider had to land in England, instead of right in the teeth of the murderous Merville fortifications.

But two were present and correct, even if everything on the ground was not. Both tugs and gliders received hit after hit as tracer from the ground tore towards them. Despite this inferno, one of the planes circled the battery four times before releasing its glider. But as no star shells could be fired by the paratroops – they had been lost in the drop – the pilot of one glider understandably became confused between the battery and the village of Merville. Just in time he swung the glider clear of the village, but it came down some 4 miles away.

So then there was one. Anti-aircraft fire had hit four of the special troops on this last glider, and, with the machine itself starting to smoulder, the pilot decided to get down without delay. He saw a large field a short way from the battery, but suddenly spotted a *Minen* sign too. By now the wheels were on the grass, yet somehow he managed to hoist the glider clear of what could have been a fatal field, over a hedge and road, and bring it down again in a safer spot. Safer from mines, at any rate. The glider was wingless and burning now, and as the men – whether wounded or fit – plunged out of it they took on the Germans in a useful diversionary action which helped to leave Otway free for the main task.

As the glider came to its halt six enemy machine-guns opened fire on Otway's base from outside the perimeter. Four more inside it brought the total to ten. The lone Vickers gun with the assault force silenced three of its opposing number, while a diversion group did the same over on the right flank.

Now the die was cast. At about 0435 hours Otway ordered the starting-signal – and the first of the twenty lengths of wire-blowing torpedo shot forward over the uneven ground. These Bangalores did their job well, and left the vital gaps in the wire defences.

Working through mines and through craters made by shells and bombs, the assault force (divided into two parties) forced themselves forward in the face of frightening machine-gun fire. The plan was now far simpler than originally. One party went for the gunners themselves and closed them in combat, until the sight of the parachutists' skull sign provoked a German to screech out in terror, whereupon that particular group gave in.

The other assault party raced straight for the big guns. They fought their way across the bomb-scarred ground until they saw that two of the doors of the main emplacements were open. Fingers forced hard on to triggers, the party fired everything they had through those doors – and the Germans inside surrendered out of a panic-stricken desire for self-preservation.

Within minutes the paratroops destroyed three of the main German guns by Gammon bombs. Another one they put out of action success-fully by the expedient of exploding two of its own shells simultaneously through the barrel. (The four guns proved to be 75-mm.'s – not 150-mm.'s, as expected.) Lieutenant M. Dowling was fatally hit during the action, but as his job was to check that the guns had definitely been neutralized he struggled on, somehow, to do this before he collapsed and died.

Only twelve minutes or so since Otway had given his signal to start the final offensive, he was ordering another signal, this time to the naval force assembled off shore, telling them that the Merville mission had been accomplished with time to spare. All through the preceding hours the signals officer had carried a companion in his battledress blouse. Now he tenderly took it out, and a slightly startled pigeon blinked at the scene all around. With a confirmatory message of their victory, the bird was flung high into the smoky air above the battery, and later on D-Day it landed safe and sound at its destination in England!

Then Otway took stock, and found that out of his tiny force of 150 men (far smaller than was originally planned) nearly half were casualties. Eighty still stood on their feet; the rest were killed, wounded, or missing. So a handful of men with one Vickers machine-gun had stormed one of the most fiercely fortified strong-points on the French coast, and captured and destroyed it within fifteen minutes of launching the assault.

Half an hour after it was over H.M.S. *Arethusa* was due to begin the naval bombardment – the starting-signal of the invasion by sea.

But the stage was not yet set from both wings for the final, withering onslaught. While the British paratroops stormed Merville and the bridges around the vital Caen area to the east, away on the west the Americans aimed to do the same sort of thing at Ste Mere-Eglise, behind Utah beach.

In the fiery afterglow of a storm-streaked sunset Eisenhower hurried around seven airfields in southern England to talk to his paratroops – their helmets dotted with camouflage, faces daubed dark. Before he was back at Southwick House the planes were airborne. Briefly, the tasks of these two airborne divisions were as follows:

The 101st U.S. Airborne Division was to ensure safe exits from Utah beach by occupying the causeways inland over the swampy ground. (One regiment had to follow the same pattern as the British followed at the Orne, and blow up the bridges along the Douve.) The 82nd U.S. Airborne Division, dropping near Ste Mere-Eglise, was to see that the seaborne forces would not be hemmed in behind the series of inland inundations.

So much for the theory.

Ahead of the waves of carriers fighters created cover and a clear route for the first paratroops – the pathfinders. These twenty pathfinder aircraft preceded the main force of 432 carriers bearing 6,600 paratroops of the 101st Division. The main force took off at 2215 hours. Despite having to fly in low, and thus render themselves vulnerable to flak, these first planes reached the six dropping-zones, for both divisions, aided by a thick, enveloping cloudbank. But these same clouds made accuracy very difficult for the following aircraft. Formations flew tight until they reached the French coast, but the the flak flew into them. One plane lurched to a hit, its port engines afire. Wheeling round desperately to head for home, it left a sheet of fire – a searing semicircle in the sky as it spiralled downward. Then the seconds passed and a sudden mushroom of flame burst from the ground.

Other aircraft veered violently to escape the flak, so that they were flying too fast and high for accurate jumps. But the men piled out, black shapes slipping from the belly of the planes. Operation Albany was on. Actually the flak fire did comparatively little damage, owing to the cloud conditions, but the human element – so often overlooked – produced an effect not envisaged. For most of the pilots, this was their baptism of battle, and the anti-aircraft fire unleashed against them caused excessive evasive action.

The 101st Division dropped from aircraft desperately trying to shake off the shattering effect of flak-bursts as experienced by men for the first time. This evasive action was natural, and, in fact, coupled with the weather, accounted for the few losses in the air. But it also meant that the men were strewn over a 25-mile length of landscape. They were literally pitchforked from wildly weaving aircraft without any idea as to where they would come down. As the sound of shells and engines throbbed away above, the single, scattered parachutes billowed out unseen, their grey-green khaki colourings invisible in the 0130 hours darkness of D-Day just begun.

Some of the men fell even farther afield, miles from their objectives during the middle of the night, in a foreign land, where the scenery seemed indistinguishable one field from the next. Some one, however, had thought of this, and so the whole division carried clicking snappers, which they sounded to try and find each other.

Typical of the confusion was the case of Lieutenant-Colonel Robert Cole. He landed actually near Ste Mere-Eglise, where he collected thirty men of his own division and a few from the 82nd Division. Backtracking north, they all headed for the two northern exits of the beach, and the group snowballed to 75 men. On the way they met and killed some members of an enemy convoy, and then moved on towards the coast.

The battalions aiming to capture the southern-beach exits also had bad drops; in one instance eighty-one planes were scheduled to drop their troops in Zone C, and actually only ten aircraft found their mark.

The enemy had evidently anticipated a drop in Zone D, for the aircraft ran into concentrated ack-ack fire over this area. An oilsoaked building near the drop-field was set on fire as they actually floated down towards it, and then was heard the familiar deadly chatter of machine-guns and the clonk of mortars. Silhouetted, with all their 'chutes and supports, many of the Americans were riddled in the air before they had a chance to reply.

It was too soon then to count the cost, but, in fact, only about 1,000 of the 6,600 men in the division reached their rendezvous by dawn. And, far more serious, some 1,500 were killed or captured, while more than half of their equipment dropped was lost as the bundles fell futilely into the surrounding swamps or into fields covered by enemy fire.

They needed that lost equipment and ammunition desperately. Captain Charles Shettle came down, and actually walked towards the nearest town, looking for his men. He found fourteen of them, and by the time he had managed to reach a bridge over the river, at about 0430 hours, the number had risen to thirty-three.

Despite fire from the opposite bank, they forced a crossing and occupied the east side. This scratch bridgehead force accounted for a few of the enemy and their machine-guns, but by dawn the fight became unequal as the Americans ran short of ammunition – so much had been dropped in the swamps – and had no hope of friendly forces to reinforce them. They withdrew to the west bank soon afterwards, and held it.

Another objective of the American 101st Division was the lock on the Douve at La Barquette. Again, inaccurate dropping nearly caused the complete failure of this mission right at the outset. Some of the sticks of paratroops bumped down deep in enemy territory, others in swampy bottom lands to the west, and one command's personnel was particularly hard hit. The Commanding officer was killed almost at once, and his executive officer captured. All the other company commanders and staff were missing initially.

In the light of this an accident which partly saved the day could be called doubly providential. As the jump signal flashed in Colonel Johnson's plane a bundle of equipment became tightly wedged in the drop door! There were a furious few seconds while they fought to free it. Then it sailed out. But if Johnson and his men had jumped on the signal they would have found that they had unloaded prematurely and were short of their zone.

Moving south, Johnson collected 150 miscellaneous men and advanced to a junction north of the lock. A force of fifty men reached the lock in a single dramatic dash, and dug in on the soft ground before the enemy could bring it under shellfire.

Then, just in time, fifty-one gliders soared out of the early sky to re-inforce the 101st Division. The bodies of the great gliders churned up the French earth as they scraped in to land accurately beside the main rendezvous. Welcome white-painted stars near their tails cheered up the scattered Americans, who saw them from their various vantage-points.

These fifty-one Waco gliders, carrying command personnel and anti-tank weapons, as well as 150 troops, landed just before dawn. This type of landing had never been attempted before without full daylight, and, although they came in accurately, many of them were wrecked as they hit the small Normandy fields. Men and materials both suffered, and Brigadier-General Don Pratt, assistant commander of the 101st, was killed in landing. The losses remained reasonable, however, and with the extra troops Major-General Taylor, commanding the 101st, secured all the vital exits from the western causeway leading off Utah beach, including the village of Pouppeville. They could not blow the bridges, but succeeded in their main task.

An hour after the main 101st sticks were dropped the 82nd Division followed. The regiment earmarked to take Ste Mere-Eglise fell within two or three miles of the dropping-zone, but this was, in the words of the official account, 'far from good.' Many men found themselves nearer the 101st, and actually fought with elements of the other division for days. But about half the force of 2,200 men landed in the dropping-zone, and most of the others assembled quite quickly. They were fortunate to find themselves in an area almost free of Germans, and they took advantage of their luck. They landed at 0230 hours. By 0330 hours Ste Mere-Eglise was in their hands, and the main road from Carentan to Cherbourg successfully cut.

The planes carrying this regiment ran into fog and flak – a change from cloud – and the chances of a tight drop seemed slim. But some of the planes which had moved out to prevent possible collisions circled back before flashing the green light. The result: the good drop already described.

Colonel Krause learned from a Frenchman that the Germans had recently established themselves along the roads outside the town, so he planned to take the town and erect road blocks before daylight.

'Go directly into the town, without searching buildings,' he told the paratroops, 'and while it's dark use only knives, bayonets, and grenades.' This was so that enemy small-arms fire could be spotted by sight and sound.

The paratroops streamed silently down the straight main road running right through the town; at the same time other paratroops outlined the town's perimeter. Across the fields, the churchyard, and the compact orchards they moved, till they entirely surrounded the town. Then they raised the very same American flag which they had flown over Naples when the Italian city was entered, and within two hours of their arrival they made Ste Mere-Eglise the first town to be taken by the Americans in the invasion.

The success at Ste Mere-Eglise assumed added point as a critical situation developed along the line of the Merderet river, where the well-laid plans of the other two regiments went astray as soon as the sticks started to fall in a pattern very different from that planned.

The regiments flew in on time, between 0230 and 0300 hours, only to see that the preceding pathfinders had not been able to mark the dropping-zones, because the enemy were actually among them. Puzzled by the absence of marker-lights, many pilots overshot the zones, and whole groups of paratroops splashed down in the watery marshes along the Merderet.

Aerial photos showed only a grassy swampland, but in fact the area was one of wide floods, owing to the closure of the La Barquette lock. The grass growing out of this lakeland had sprouted so thickly that from above it looked like a prairie, instead of treacherous water several feet deep. Into this water dozens of heavily laden troops were plunged, and, far from it being an offensive operation, the first task was to rescue as many as possible.

Only one man in twenty-five of these two regiments came to earth near his intended zone, and the whole force had to fight for its life, almost without worrying about destroying bridges over the Douve or the Merderet. Nevertheless, they did fulfil a useful role in occupying the 91st German Infantry Division, a reserve earmarked to tackle any invasion army on the beaches.

With enemy fire building up in one particular place, counter-measures were held up while the Americans tried to retrieve a jeep and an anti-tank gun from the marshes, where they had fallen from heaven.

Men of another battalion, under Colonel Timmes, established a bold bridgehead at one place, but within an hour it was lost. The German artillery countered quickly. Small-arms fire came from the south, and tanks rumbled from the west. So the main force pulled out, leaving the bridgehead in the hands of four officers and eight men. This dozen Americans, with grenades, rifles, and one machine-gun, fought off the enemy – seen now as well as heard – and Gammon grenades shattered two of the leading tanks trundling towards the bridge. But they were not equal to armour, and had to withdraw.

Dawn brought Operation Detroit and fifty-two gliders with weapons and transport intended to equip and reinforce the 82nd Division. But once again inaccuracy proved the stumbling block, and only twenty-two of them got to the landing-zone. Meanwhile swampland and other hazards had multiplied the difficulties and the engagements of the airborne troops. Instead of two or three neat operations, they fought fifteen to twenty separate little battles, often only a few hundred yards away from each other, yet unable to link up or get a clear idea of what was happening or where their services would be needed most. The two American airborne divisions did pave the way for their colleagues landing later, though not as planned.

Through this night, too, the air was alive in a dozen different ways. Aircraft of Bomber Command, 1,136 of them, thundered through the night to drop 5,853 tons on picked positions, such as coastal batteries. Again the silent ships heard the reassuring roar of their engines, both before and after the operations, which finished at dawn.

There were smaller, secret sorties, too, such as Operation Sunflower, covering the drop of Special Air Service reconnaissance parties in six areas.

Already the enemy's Radar stations had been rocked with rockets streaming into unlikely woods, so Leigh-Mallory could report that in the vital period between 0100 and 0400 hours, when the assault armada was nearing the lowering-positions, only nine enemy Radar stations were in operation. And during the whole night the number of stations active in the Neptune area (the entire invasion coastline) only amounted to eighteen out of a normal ninety-two. No station was heard operating at all between Le Havre and Barfleur, the two cape extremities covering the D-Day goal.

The enemy received no Radar warning at all either of the sea forces or the airborne operations. While the first paratroops floated down easily, wondering what awaited them, the *Luftwaffe*'s night fighter force was flying furiously around the Amiens area, where electronics had created for the Allies 'ghost squadrons' of bombers requiring interception. Another scientific miracle that further confused the badly bewildered

Germans on that night was our dummy parachutists, complete with special delay devices to emit cracking sounds like rifle fire! These were duly reported between Le Havre and Rouen, east of the actual invasion front, after aircraft crews had bundled the dummies out of their planes, chuckling at the thought of the Germans' reactions when they discovered their mistake! Even at 0400 hours the precise places of the main attack could not be anticipated by the harassed von Rundstedt. This was a strategic triumph – real paratroops, dummies, diversions, tinfoil dropped to simulate ships, and the rest of the ingenious ideas, and all in the middle of the night! Where was the mass attack going to take place? The answer was not long in coming.

34 *The Pathfinders*

In October 1943 Leonard Cheshire took command of 617 Squadron and opened his fourth operational tour as a Wing Commander. He had relinquished the rank of Group Captain at his own request to take up flying duties again. He was already one of the most decorated men in the Royal Air Force.

He soon began to devise a fresh way of ensuring accuracy against comparatively small targets. It developed as the new marking system by an aircraft flying lower than the rest of the force. Cheshire pioneered this 'master bomber' technique with 617 Squadron, confirming its effect in practice by attacks on the flying bomb sites in the Pas de Calais. The method was later adopted for a series of small specialised raids on targets in France vitally associated with German aircraft production. By the end of March 1944 eleven of these twelve targets had been destroyed or damaged, using the new marker system of attack and a 12,000-pound blast-bomb.

The very first raid with this remarkable bomb was on an aero-engine factory at Limoges on 8 February. Cheshire led twelve Lancasters through cloud to reach the target in moonlight. He then dipped his marker Lancaster down to a mere 200 feet over the factory and dropped a load of incendiaries right in the middle of it. These burst at once, throwing up volumes of smoke. The deputy leader then dropped two red-spot fires from 7,000 feet into the incendiaries, so the rest of the bombers had a perfect aiming point. Four of the five 12,000-pound monsters fell right on the factory, each obtaining direct hits on separate buildings. The damage was therefore quite devastating.

Cheshire soon realised that something more manoeuvrable than a Lancaster was needed for the marker, and so got two Mosquitoes for this low-level task.

The 'master bomber' technique quickly established itself as adaptable to all conditions, where more normal methods would have failed. On 10 March the squadron target was a needle bearing factory comprising an area only 170 by 90 yards. Despite the weather forecast of a full moon and clear visibility, a screen of cloud obscured practically all the moonlight. Cheshire and his deputy tried repeatedly to pick out and mark the target, but decided it was no good using the red-spot fires or green indicators as intended. Improvising immediately Cheshire dropped incendiaries on the eastern and western edges of the target, and then told the force to bomb between these twin glows. Although their success seemed doubtful, later daylight reconnaissance proved that they had succeeded beyond all their expectations, and almost entirely destroyed the vital small factory.

Group Captain Leonard Cheshire and the Pathfinders release their target indicators at the start of the attack on the Gnome and Rhone aero-engine works at Limoges on 8 February 1944

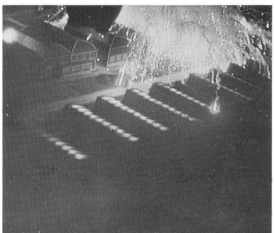

Still operating over France, one of Cheshire's next targets called for bombing on an altogether larger scale: the railway marshalling yards at La Chappelle, just north of Paris. The night of 20/21 April was chosen for the attack, as part of the general pre-invasion softening-up and dis-location of communications in the entire northern France region. Number 617 Squadron was only one of many participating and the plan called for separate attacks on two aiming points within the overall target of the marshalling yards. More than 250 aircraft were due to be employed.

Bombing by now had developed into a highly skilful and scientific operation. First of all, at 0003 hours, six Mosquitoes reached the target area two minutes ahead of the time for the start of the attack. These aircraft dropped 'window' – strips of metal-covered paper – to confuse the enemy's radar-directed air and ground defences.

Aircraft from a Group other than Cheshire's were due to drop green target indicators first of all, but although these devices were released they failed to cascade at once. So Cheshire had little time left to find and mark the exact bombing point. He operated rapidly, however, and located the aiming point – marking it with red-spot fires and telling his deputy to add more fires for a clearer indication. He gave orders for the controller of the force to instruct bombing to begin, but a further delay occurred due to a failure in the VHF radio-telephone between Cheshire and the controller. The latter did not receive the instructions till after the main force of bombers was actually in the La Chappelle area. Despite the delay and congestion, the attack proceeded smoothly from then on, and sub-sequent reconnaissance revealed that the entire zone around the aiming point lay utterly irreparable. This yielded further proof of the efficacy of the marker technique, which had survived even setbacks such as the delay of the first indicators to cascade and the interruption of communi-cation between Cheshire and the attack controller.

Much of the Allied bombing potential was naturally being directed against the invasion areas and the links with it, but Cheshire and his squadron fulfilled a wish to try out the marker technique where it would be most severely tested: against targets in Germany itself. Two raids during April especially proved its worth, the first on Brunswick, the second on Munich.

Cheshire's Group, No. 5, received orders to bomb Brunswick on 22 April with a strong force, which turned out to be 265 aircraft. Two Mosquitoes flew ahead to report on the weather to the twenty Lancasters due to mark the target: the industrial region of Brunswick. But trouble developed with their VHF radio-telephones, so no such reports were returned. The next confusion came when the enemy – wise to the new flare system – began laying their own dummy target indicators. They looked like the genuine article, but unluckily for the Germans, they were the wrong colour. The lack of contact with the two Mosquitoes, however, was one of the things which caused the first of the flare force to drop its flares in the wrong area by about five miles.

The error did not prove too serious, though, for the ever-alert Cheshire made a low-level reconnaissance by the light they had created, and realised the mistake. He did not release his vital markers yet, waiting for another batch of flares to go down. This shot was much more on the mark, and by their light the aiming point could be assessed as accurately as necessary.

With the right region marked by the familiar red-spot fires, Cheshire authorised the attack to begin. But all did not go smoothly, because of the difficulty in the VHF communications. The interference on the radio-telephone resulted in orders being partly misinterpreted, so that some of the crews bombed the dummy green target indicators instead of the accurately placed red-spot fires. Cheshire had to report that only half the bombs of the main force fell in the target area, the rest exploding in the wrong area that had been illuminated by the green indicators. Nevertheless, a railway equipment works, an artillery tractor plant and other industrial objectives were struck by at least fifty per cent of the 741 tons dropped during the operation. Only three of the 265 aircraft were lost – a remarkably low proportion for a raid so deep into the German heartland.

Directly after Brunswick followed the famous Munich raid. Munich was selected for this attack so that the method of marking at low level could be tested against a heavily defended target, again in the heart of the *Reich*. Munich had particularly fierce anti-aircraft and searchlight defences. The number of guns in the immediate area of the city was thought to be about 200: nearly one for each aircraft.

It was only two nights after the Brunswick bombing, on 24 April, that exactly the same number of aircraft aimed for the city so dear to Hitler and the Nazi movement. All aircraft except ten actually attacked. The scientific approach reached one sophisticated stage further with the inclusion of a feint raid on Milan by half-a-dozen Lancasters of 617 Squadron to lure enemy fighters from Munich itself.

The main force flew via south-west France to avoid some defences. But four Mosquitoes carrying out the marking flew direct. From Augsburg to Munich they endured continuous and never-jangling ack-ack fire, yet they reached Munich precisely on scheduled time. Cheshire's aircraft was caught in a cone of searchlights and every gun within range opened fire on it. He dived to 700 feet; identified the aiming point; and dropped his red-spot fires at 0141 hours. The other three marker Mosquitoes did likewise.

The main force then flew in to the attack. Cheshire continued to fly over the city at a mere 1,000 feet as the bombs were falling. Shell fragments hit his aircraft, but he went on with his control of the operation. Searchlights so blinded him at one stage that he nearly lost control. Still at only the height of the Empire State Building, he stayed till he was sure he could do no more. But extricating himself to head for home proved worse than flying in. He had to suffer withering fire for twelve minutes before he finally got clear. But he did. Out of the 265 aircraft taking off, nine were lost – a proportion of three-and-a-half per cent or one in thirty. Typical odds of survival.

Group Captain Leonard Cheshire as commanding officer of the celebrated 617 Squadron

The damage done was out of all scale to the size of the force, and much of Munich seemed affected, including Nazi buildings.

To Leonard Cheshire the final weeks before the invasion meant more operations with his marker method. During his fourth tour of duty, he led 617 Squadron on every occasion. One such operation early in May 1944 was against the large military depot and tank park at Mailly-le-Camp, where thousands of enemy troops were believed to be located. Cheshire's Mosquito hummed over the area in dazzlingly clear moonlight, but despite the fact that this was the only operation of the night, he managed to mark the target correctly. All enemy fighters could be made available against the raid but it made no difference. The attack went ahead as planned, but because of the bright moonlight and quantity of fighters against them, forty-two bombers were lost out of the 338 that set out from England.

As his contribution to D-Day, Cheshire led Operation Taxable. This was designed to mislead the enemy radar defences between Dover and Cap d'Antifer into thinking that an armada was approaching that part of the coast. Sixteen Lancasters and eighteen small ships were chosen to create this illusion. Some of the ships towed balloons with reflectors attached, to simulate the sort of radar echoes emitted by large ships. The

Lancasters had the more unusual job, though. They had to stooge around at precise points in flattened ellipses and release 'window'.

Cheshire said:

'The tactics were to use two formations of aircraft with the rear formation seven miles behind the leaders, each aircraft being separated laterally by two miles. Individual aircraft flew a straight course of seven miles, turned round, and flew on the reciprocal course one mile away. On completion of the second leg, it returned to its former course and repeated the procedure over again, advancing far enough to keep in line with the convoy's speed of seven knots.'

An average of two bundles of 'window' were jettisoned on each circuit. The operation started soon after dusk on D-1 and went on steadily until the D-Day landings along the Normandy coast. It played a valuable part in helping to achieve surprise for the greatest invasion in history.

So D-Day came and went. And with it came a new weapon for 617 Squadron, even bigger than the blast-bomb. This was the terrifying Tallboy, a 14,000-pounder which reached the ground at a speed faster than that of sound – so no warning preceded its arrival. It was developed for targets where the deepest penetration was needed, and extreme accuracy would be essential.

Tallboy made its debut on 8 June, when 617 Squadron attacked the Saumur railway tunnel, which ran north-east to the Normandy front. Four Lancasters of another squadron were detailed to drop flares, so that Cheshire could lead the assault by marking the target. This small flare force encountered difficulty, yet although many flares dropped wide, Cheshire could make out his whereabouts just sufficiently to release his familiar red-spot fires into the cutting leading to the tunnel, only forty yards from the actual mouth. Nineteen Lancasters made the attack with Tallboys after several dummy runs to be sure they were in the precise position. Here they had to be exact, but it could hardly be expected that many of their giant bombs would drop in so small an area.

In fact, one fell on the roof of the tunnel, the crater caused by this being 100 feet wide, and three exploded in the deep cutting approaching the tunnel, blocking the whole line with craters still wider than the one on the roof. And the main line stayed blocked until the Allied armies occupied the area. So the operation succeeded in its purpose, even if the actual entrance to the Saumur was not definitely blocked. The railway was the object, after all.

Jubilant at the dramatically devastating impact of these bombs, 617 Squadron looked forward to the chance of using them again. This came within a week. On 14 June Cheshire led a small section of Lancasters from 617 to attack the E-boat pens at Le Havre. The aim was to try and stop the activities of these small vessels against the supply line of the Normandy beachhead. They carried Tallboy bombs to penetrate the thick concrete roofs designed to protect the pens from the air. Needless to say, the marker for the mission was once more Cheshire.

He was as determined as ever to leave an accurate mark for the following bombers, so he dived well below the altitude range of the anti-aircraft guns, which peppered the aircraft. Their barrage geared up to a great crescendo as he descended. They actually hit his aeroplane repeatedly, but he still dived lower and lower, in daylight and with no cloud cover. He only released his markers when he felt sure the devices would do their job. The aircraft was blazing by now, but somehow Cheshire got out of that holocaust of Le Havre – and made England again. The force following scored several direct hits on the E-boat pens, and one of the Tallboy bombs pierced the roof, destroying part of the wall. Leonard Cheshire survived the war to become even more celebrated in peace. But that is another story . . .

35 *George Bush and the Flying Casket*

Autumn 1943: United States Navy pilot Ensign George Bush was training for future action in torpedo-bombers. After finishing his flight training, Bush was posted (or in the States 'assigned') to the USS *San Jacinto*, a light aircraft carrier. Now it was Spring 1944 as the *San Jacinto* sped west over the watery vastnesses of the Pacific. Bush would be piloting a TBM Avenger, designed to carry and drop a 2,000-pound torpedo or similar bomb-load. It was called 'low and slow' by some of the pilots, and 'flying casket' by other people. But Bush rather fancied the idea of diving almost to water-level and then gliding along to release his torpedo.

Bush's first sight of fatalities came one day after he himself had landed safely on the carrier. Another pilot crashed into one of the ship's gun positions. George saw all four of the gun crew killed before him. Some of the Avenger's early assignments were shielding land forces as they fought from island to island. Or the Avengers glide-bombed specific enemy strong points on land. On still other occasions, they searched for submarines and in this role they carried depth-charges ready to be dropped.

Bush was one of the pilots providing low-altitude screening for the Americans when they hit Guam and Saipan, often flying through frightening ack-ack counter-attack. He said later: 'We could see the troops going ashore and the big guns from the battleships firing over them. All I could do was count my blessings that I was up there instead of down below.'

In Europe, D-Day came and went. Mid-June now in the Pacific, as the enemy instigated air attacks on the US ships grouped off Guam, Saipan, and other Mariana Islands. The *San Jacinto* inevitably formed one of the prime aims for the 300-strong air armada. The carrier's fighters took off first to counter the threat, but the order went for the Avengers to fly off, too, to avoid any danger of their being bombed while on their own flight deck.

Actually as George Bush was about to be catapulted into the air, he suddenly saw that the Avenger had oil-pressure trouble in its engine. The launch went ahead, but the engine faltered in only a minute or two. George was carrying his normal crew complement of two others – and a weapon-load weighing 2,000 pounds. Bush guided, coaxed, the Avenger over the wave-tops; hauled the nose upwards; and then the tail just grazed the sea. The nose went forward almost gracefully and the crew of three moved rapidly from wing to raft. They began quite a frantic paddle motion, thinking of the depth-charges still aboard the sinking Avenger. At a predetermined depth, the weapons went off – without harming any

George Bush flew fifty-eight missions as a USN pilot. When he and the other two crew had to abandon their Avenger in the Pacific, Bush was the only survivor

of the trio. They were saved by a US destroyer and duly returned to their carrier. Just a microcosm in the whole sea war.

Through midsummer months, the same pattern of operations followed: either attacking enemy land-targets on the islands, or seeking Japanese submarines. June, July, August. On 1 September 1944, Bush and the rest of his Avenger squadron had as their target an enemy radio communications post on one of the Bonin Islands. They were getting nearer to Japan itself now – only five or six hundred miles. Ack-ack opposition interfered with the attack, which was only partially successful. The Avenger pilots learned that the enemy radios still transmitted, so it proved no surprise when they received word that they would be resuming their attack on the following day.

George Bush had Jack Delaney as his radioman/gunner. And a pal of Bush's, gunnery officer Ted White, asked if he could accompany them on the raid. White received permission from their commanding officer and the three of them catapulted off promptly on time. The Avenger was one of four from the carrier, escorted by a squadron force of protective fighters. The Avengers had their full complement of bombs for the attack – four Avengers each with four bombs adding up to 2,000 pounds per plane. A dangerous load to be carrying as they flew slowly into really shaking shellfire from the ground.

The opening pair of Avengers included the one flown by the squadron commander. They dropped their loads through the ground firing, and observed strikes on a transmitting tower as well as hitting other adjacent targets. Then George Bush and the fourth Avenger prepared to go in. Bush commenced the dive preparatory to dropping, but almost at once received an alarming physical impact. An ack-ack shell tore at the Avenger's engine. Fire threatened the wings of the bomber and the usual acrid smoke thickened around the cockpit. Bush continued the course of the dive; the four bombs were released and scored hits on the radio station; and then they pulled away – fast.

Bush swung around in the direction of open waters, as he knew the Avenger was doomed. Over the bomber's intercom. he told Ted White and Jack Delaney: 'Bale out. Bale out.'

Bush did not get an answer, so he put the bomber on as level a heading as he could, and baled out himself. But in so doing, he pulled the cord of his parachute before he was fully free of the plane. The parachute became enmeshed in the tail of the Avenger and Bush hit his head on the tail. By some stroke of fortune, the parachute wrenched itself free under the wind pressure and took Bush with it. The descent was too quick but did not injure him. Bush shook the harness of the parachute off him and managed to strike out towards the life-raft. Once aboard the raft, he looked all round the 360 degrees of seascape engulfing the small craft – but he could not see either of the other two aircrew. He paddled strongly to try to keep the raft away from the island they had been attacking. He did not want to end up as a prisoner-of-war in Japanese hands.

Bush had hit his head badly on the plane's tail and it was still bleeding after an hour or more. He went on paddling by instinct and after a couple of hours he felt really ill. Head hurting, arms aching, sick after swallowing seawater. 'It seemed just the end of the world,' he said later. At that stage, he did not know if there was going to be any 'later'.

George Bush needed a minor miracle. It appeared in the form of a moving dot that increased in size by the second. The other Avenger crews in the attack had in fact spotted his raft and radioed his position back to base. The message reached the US Submarine *Finback*. The dot that Bush was watching turned out to be the periscope of *Finback*. Like some revelation, he watched while the conning tower of the submarine heaved onto the surface, and soon the whole mammal-like bulk dripped itself glossily dry. It only took a few minutes for the *Finback* crew to get Bush on board, before the craft vanished once more below the surface.

Only one of the crew of two were spotted baling out of Bush's Avenger, but the man's parachute failed to deploy properly. The second man must have gone down with the plane. He may have been killed or injured but in either case he was never seen again. The loss of his two aircrew has always been a shadow over George Bush's survival.

That was not quite the end of the story. *Finback* had picked up three other USN aircrew from the sea and the four fliers had to remain submerged in *Finback* for about a month. They even experienced being depth-charged by an enemy bomber. Bush said later: 'That depth-charging got to me. It just shook the boat, and those guys would say, "Oh, that wasn't close".'

It was actually almost two months before Bush got back to *San Jacinto*. The date: end-October. United States assault troops were landing on Leyte. George Bush now had a new Avenger aircraft, which he flew on further air strikes aimed at shore installations in the Philippines, as well as enemy shipping off the coast. He went on flying until nearly Christmas, when he was sent home. His flying log read as follows: '1,228 hours airborne; 126 carrier landings; 58 combat missions.' Less than a fortnight after Christmas, George Bush married Barbara Pierce on 6 January 1945. Neither of them knew that one day they would be living in The White House, Washington . . .

36 *It Should Have Been a Milk Run . . .*

Gene A. Pfister remembers:

'It was to have been a milk run . . . The story started in the autumn of 1944. A foggy, wet and drippy evening that never happens in America. The road had got slippery with wet leaves. The lights from the pub across the road blinked briefly through the blackout and the damp, misty haze. Globules of water clung to my clothing as I crossed the road toward the American Red Cross recreation room. I was to wait here for the liberty truck that would take me back to the airfield.

'I opened the door and stepped into an atmosphere that reeked of cigarettes mellowed somewhat with the aroma of coffee and doughnuts that was about standard for all these places. The room was a temporary refuge for the usual collection of American night-roamers. Mostly they were Air Corps and Engineers. Some were aglow with the last pint of bitter that had been hastily drained as the landlord had called "Time, gentlemen, please".

'There was a riffle of cards at the tables where a never-ending game of blackjack was in progress. The door was flung back and a group of fly-boys lurched in, singing with drink-sodden voices: "Coming in on a wing and a prayer." They made up in volume what they lacked in harmony. Over the radio a woman's voice was telling the recipe for the morrow, which I gathered was Woolton Pie. It sounded revolting to an American palate.

'The BBC news came on. We mostly didn't listen, because its content was really designed for the British ear. But towards the end we crewmen caught a flash that made our ears prick up: "Royal Air Force bombers last night raided Leipzig. Large sections of the city were left in flames with considerable damage to the railway yards . . ." Then in the crisp British accent: "Seventy-nine of our aircraft are missing."

'"Jesus H. Christ" said somebody. "I didn't know they had that many." There hadn't been losses like that since sixty Fortresses went down over and along the route home from Schweinfurt one day in 1943. I closed my eyes and in my mind I could still see those beautiful ships curling over and drifting earthward, with smoking engines. The 'chutes tumbling and twisting on the wind like so many thistly seeds borne on the summer breeze. Other ships went on, ghost airplanes, crewless and burning. Yet others went down slowly in a flattened dive that told of a pilot, with a desperately wounded crew, trying to put the ship down without further hurt.

'But seventy-nine aircraft down at night. I thought of 'chutes opening in the darkness, swinging and twisting and circling in the Stygian blackness over blacked-out Germany. Of the long streamers of flame that marked the death plunge of yet another crew. Four hundred 'chutes spewing out, flak and flames all around, captivity below . . . Hell in microcosm. I wondered what it must be like to land alongside a burning street in Leipzig with the bombs still falling. I thought of the fear that would grip these men as they struggled with the 'chute shrouds to avoid falling into the flames. There would be no ritual waving of fists and cursing here – it would be for real. The Krauts would display no curiosity. And no *hausfrau* would bring hot tea and biscuits.

Lucky the ones that fell into the hands of the police. Unluckier the ones who would be found swinging from the girders of the rail station the following day, hanged by the angry mob. In the fury of the moment, no ambulancemen would show them kindness.

'I knew fear myself at that moment. Soon I would be winging my way across that same country which would be holding the survivors of that Leipzig raid. I wondered how long I would survive them.

'Maybe I was cracking up. Perhaps I should ask for some leave, maybe a flak farm. I opened my eyes. The radio was now playing dance music. The atmosphere still combined smoke and the aroma of coffee. Nothing had changed. An enormous red-faced infantry Sergeant lay snoring on a leather sofa. The fly-boys were regaling each other with lies about their sexploits. A hard-faced canteen assistant called time on the coffee bar. Latecomers raced across the room before the shutters snapped down.

'Outside, the liberty trucks trundled up to take us back to camp. The drivers revved their engines to add a note of urgency to the routine of the occasion. A songstress on the radio sang, "I'll be seeing you in all the old familiar places". There was much drunken laughter as inert bodies were thrust aboard the trucks. One truck stayed for latecomers still queuing at the fish and chip bar. As we rolled out of town, the fingers of the chill, clammy fog cooled my face and soothed my spirits. "Life such as it is goes on", I thought, "except for the poor bastards who just died over Leipzig".

'It was now December 1944.

'The war was as good as won – they said. They kept on saying it and we believed it. There was a sense of destiny in the air – that soon all would be changed. This livin' breathin' cow of a war would soon be part of our past and we could all go home. If we were still alive . . .

'It was a sparkling day with all the portent of Christmas. The public address system crackled its message: "All crews report to the briefing room immediately." Profanities filled the air as the news spread from hut to hut. "Twice today and time for one more . . ." "A sunshine alert." Well, it made a change from take-offs in peasoupers.

'The briefing officer had more surprises. Didn't he always! We were going to bomb Caen. That meant crossing the Channel at its broadest part. The trip would be some 250 miles, and even allowing for the climb to 26,000 feet, we would still get back in time for five o'clock chow. Somebody mumbled, "Bloody milk run".

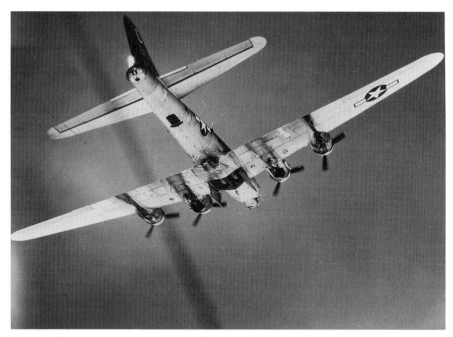

For their B-17, it should have been a milk run. This shows the defensive armament – chin, ball and tail turrets with twin .5 in guns and a waist gunner on each side

'The briefer's pointer traced our course, showing us the German flak batteries we already knew so well. He etched our evasion course, which he knew none of us would take because of the increased flying time. "Oh yes," he feigned an afterthought because *he* knew that *we* knew what was coming next in this daily ritual. "Watch out for the yellow bellies". They flew Fw 190s, specially armoured against the guns of the B-17s. Well, it might turn out to be an interesting afternoon after all.

'It would be especially interesting to our pilot, who had twenty-four raids under his belt, because if he made it back to base with this one, he had also bought his ticket Stateside. He would go home. He would become an instructor and train pilots coming to Britain. Or he could stay in Britain and train them when they got here – it was his option. His girl-friend, an English nurse, would be waiting by the control tower when he got back. A little melodramatic maybe, but that's the way it was then . . .

'Take-off went well, with no incidents and nobody going out. The climb to the rendezvous seemed especially endless but we crossed the French coast without any trouble, apart from some accurate flak. Somebody said: "Should be accurate – they get enough f . . . ing practice."

'The flak persisted. A clear indication that they were under group control and firing perhaps thirty or forty guns at a time. We had no place to run or hide. These were the German 88 mm guns that could reach an altitude of 30,000 feet. They could be fired in devastating shotgun

B-17s just below contrail height. The fighters trailing above are flying in typical loose pair battle formation

salvoes, and fifty guns operated in this way could put up what seemed like an impenetrable barrier. The flak was inexorable. As we flew toward it and through it, one was assailed with the smell of it and the feel of it and occasionally the sound of it – as the shrapnel raked the bombers, as if searching out the frightened flesh that huddled within them. Suddenly, no flak. That meant instead, fighters.

'The fleet of ships flew rock steady, ploughing our aerial furrow onward toward Caen. Out of the blue dead ahead – twelve o'clock high – a swarm of gnats levelled off, aiming straight into the noses of the bomber formation. They came on . . . swelling in seconds from gnats into birds into fighters. Cannon fire flashed from their wings, like the sparks from a king-size welding torch. Front gunner screamed obscenities. We trembled involuntarily for a few seconds as the adrenalin pumped around. Away to my left, a bomber stumbled through the air, like the poor dead thing it already was. No 'chutes . . . We thought of the panic going on as survivors struggled to remove wounded and bodies from the exit.

'Suddenly we were falling out of formation, spiralling slowly as if the pilot were taking his part in some gigantic aerial ballet. In truth, he was slumped forward, a headless horseman with blood and brains and broken plexiglass all over the cockpit. Maps and charts and oxygen bottles swirled around to join him in a dance of death.

'The co-pilot fought to regain control, screaming down the interphone for the navigator to come forward and help him. But the navigator could not come, because he was braced against his table. And against the pull of gravity, too. The engineer in the top turret hung on tight to his guns as the big bird slowly levelled off and the G forces no longer nailed us to the floor.

'Minutes later, the navigator and the engineer, bloody and sick, were wrapping the remains of the pilot in his parachute and stuffing the hole in the gaping plexiglass. We were all alone in the sky. The squadron had gone on, leaving the sky overcast with its contrails. We were low now, low enough to see the waves breaking. There was little chatter on the interphone as we raced toward the welcoming British shore. The direction-finding stations peeped and squawked their courses. The radioman phoned them to the shaken navigator. By landfall the co-pilot had the heading for the home base.

'The rest of the squadron had already landed. We had been reported by many of them as having "gone down and no 'chutes seen" over France. But in the squadron it was "never say die". Scores of eyes had been scanning the afternoon sky for the straggler. "Remember Cowboy McKay", they said. "He came zooming in an hour and a half late with his rudder shot to hell."

'The English nurse kept calm. She stared through the control tower windows; and later for a while through a borrowed pair of sunglasses, standing on the roof. Then we were a glint of sunlight low in the south. There sounded the voice of 427 crackling through the ether and played out over the public address.

'In ten minutes we were landing – with our red flare arching high over the field to announce we had dead and wounded aboard. The ambulance rolled to a stop exactly as we did. The doctor scrambled aboard. His haste proved unnecessary. He peered under the blood-encrusted folds of the 'chute and motioned the ambulance crew aboard.

'"Tell the driver take it slowly," he said. "The guy is dead."

'We heard later that the nurse and our pilot had become engaged the night before – after his twenty-fourth operation. This one was to have been a milk run . . .'

37 *Even the Birds Walk*

On the morning of 17 December 1944 with the Ninth United States Air Force in Belgium, Major Hohn Motzenbecker was piloting his Thunderbolt fighter-bomber – covering the quiescent Monschauduen area with his squadron of P-47s. It was a routine mission. Two of the planes were carrying leaflets. Others were supposed to attack any ground targets requested by the 78th Division, which the P-47s were supporting.

The major was slightly bored. It was too damned quiet.

The 78th ground controller cut in on the radio. 'We have no targets for you today,' he said, sounding a bit sleepy.

'That means we've got an hour to kill,' the major replied.

'Well,' said the ground controller, 'we think there may be a counter-attack coming somewhere. If you want to, you can have a look around and see what you can find'.

'Roger.'

The major told his squadron to follow him down. Below them they

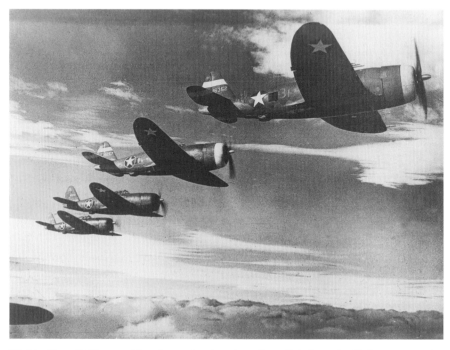

Flight of four P-47s, capable of escorting bombers from Britain to the Ruhr

A good view of the P-47 wing, the trailing edge of which resembles the Spitfire

could see a river that looked pretty and peaceful as it wound among the white snow and green firs.

'There's a main road down there,' said the major. 'Give me some top cover and I'll go down and have a look.'

He dropped in lazy circles down to the road, and had a look. What he saw made his head bounce back against the canopy. The road was clogged with German tanks, halftracks and motor transport. They were heading directly into Allied lines south of Monschau. There were at least 150 vehicles in this one convoy and it stretched for four and a half miles. All the side roads were crammed with transport. The major had not seen anything like this since the headlong flight of the Germans across the Seine in August.

Ground guns began firing at him. A piece of flak ripped through his wing. That shocked him out of his stupor, and he fought to gain altitude to reform his squadron for the attack.

That was the beginning of Von Runstedt's counter-offensive. It was the first time anyone had seen the magnitude of the German operation. It was also the start of what has been called the first decisive battle in which the air faced the ground force alone in a running engagement very similar to the big air-sea battles of the Pacific War.

In three minutes the major had his flight and then his squadron back together again. He called fighter control back at Ninth TAC. 'There is a hell of a big convoy heading into our lines just south of Monschau. They fired at me. Could that be us or is it the enemy?'

'That is the enemy,' said fighter control.

'Then,' said the major, 'send some reinforcements. We are going down on them.'

He split the squadron into four flights of four planes each, then took them onto the deck. By the time they got there the big enemy column had dispersed into the woods and bushes, and light ack-ack fired at them from the foliage. About fifty of the Tauger trucks were still on the road and the Thunderbolts made a sweeping pass at them from the side. This meant 128 fifty-calibre machine guns were firing at the trucks simultaneously. The squadron came back again. And again. Then they were finished with the trucks. Every vehicle that had been on the road was burning fiercely or had been thrown into the ditch by the blast of the firing. The squadron moved down the side roads.

They found a concentration of tanks in the woods and dropped their 500-pound bombs directly in the middle of it. Tanks disappeared in smoke, and the guns stopped firing. Then the Thunderbolts ranged up and down the side roads strafing everything they saw. The trucks lay cock-eyed on the roads, some turned over and smoking. Flak came up in streams from both sides of the road, crossing overhead to form a canopy. One of the Thunderbolts ran into this canopy, blew up and crashed fifty yards ahead. The pilot didn't have a chance to get out. Fires burned in the woods. Everywhere drivers scrambled out of trucks and dashed into the woods. P-47s strafed the woods over and over again.

At 1508 hours another squadron arrived to take over, but what was left of the great convoy was now split up into little groups of four and five vehicles.

The first phase of the great land-air battle was over. Air claims, later verified by the ground, were 107 enemy vehicles destroyed, twenty probably destroyed, and forty-five damaged. Fifteen 88 mm guns were knocked out.

On the night of 17 December bad weather set in over the battle area. It was the forty-first anniversary of the Wright Brothers' first flight. At the major's base the pilots fretted. In the morning, fog was still there. Everyone looked out of the windows and one sergeant recounted an old gag, 'On a day like this even the birds walk'. It was used a total of twenty-one times in a three-hour period.

At noon the phone rang in the group CO's office. The group CO was Colonel R.S. Stecker, a great all-American halfback at West Point thirteen years earlier. The phone call was from Colonel Gil Meyers, operations officer at the Ninth TAC Headquarters, and it came there instead of to any of the other group COs for one principal reason. During the

Formidable array of P-47s provide cover for US bombers

campaign in Sicily, Stecker had been operations officer for the desert air force. At that time this forerunner of the present Ninth Air Force was supporting Montgomery's Eighth Army in their drive from Mt Etna to Messina. One day the British had come to Stecker and said, 'The Germans move at night. During the day they camouflage their vehicles and hide on the dense olive groves. It's up to you to find them and shoot them up'.

So Stecker had figured out a way of finding the Germans and sneaking in on them at treetop level without getting murdered by flak. And now he was known as a specialist at that sort of thing.

Colonel Meyers knew Stecker from away back. 'That Jerry column you hit the other day,' he said, 'has been reinforced and has broken through our lines to Stavelot. In fact, there is now nothing between it and the English Channel but service troops and cooks and bakers,' said Meyers.

'The weather,' said Stecker.

'I know,' said Meyers, 'the weather is down on the deck, and it probably will be suicide, but God damn it, the army says we've got to get something in there or the bastards will be in Liège. If you can just send a four-plane flight, it might help.'

'I'll see what we can do', said Stecker. He hung up. He called in the squadron that had been standing by since daybreak. This squadron was commanded by Major George Brooking, of Livingston, Montana.

'Men,' said Colonel Stecker, 'this is going to be rough, but the Krauts have just given us a hell of a kick in the pants at the front.' He explained the situation to them. Then he briefed them on what they were supposed to do.

At 1305 hours the first flight of four planes, headed by Brooking, took off into the fog. Other flights were to follow at twenty-minute intervals. Each plane carried two 500-pound delayed action bombs.

Brooking led his flight to the battle area. He had been there the day before. The Belgian mountains and woods were covered with fog. The German column had penetrated into them. The P-47 pilots couldn't see a thing except a solid white floor. For half an hour they cruised around waiting for a break in the clouds. But none came. The next two flights showed up, but there was nothing for them to do, so Brooking sent them home.

Finally, Brooking said, 'I'm going down there to poke around by myself. There must be a break somewhere in those mountains'.

'You're crazy,' said his wingman, Lt Bob Thoman, of Rochester, NY. But Brooking set out anyway. He pushed down through the clouds, just narrowly missing mountain ridges as they loomed up in front of him.

Firemen dowsing the long-range belly tank of a P-47 after a crash landing on a tactical airfield

The mountains in that area were 2,000 feet high. Brooking zoomed around among them, and at last found what he was looking for.

At the floor of one of the valleys, there was an opening of about fifty feet from the ground to the clouds. Brooking headed for the opening. There was just enough room for the Thunderbolt to squeeze in above the treetops, but he made it. He went up the length of the valley, made a sharp turn and came back again. The valley roads were empty. There was no enemy there.

Brooking figured out that since valleys usually run parallel to each other, there must be another one just over the ridge to his right. He put the Thunderbolt's nose up into the clouds again and crossed the ridge blind. He dropped down through the murk. He might have hit another mountain. But his hunch was right. There was another valley down there. He dropped down but still there was no sign of an opening as in the other valley. He expected to feel the crash of his plane against the ground at any moment.

But, suddenly, he broke through the clouds.

He wasn't more than twenty feet above the biggest concentration of German tanks and armoured vehicles he had ever seen in his life. They were rolling serenely along the road as if the German weatherman had said to them, 'Don't worry your little heads at all about enemy aircraft today. Nothing can fly in weather like this'. The Germans looked at Brooking – and Brooking looked at the Germans. The surprise was so mutual that not a single shot was fired.

Brooking scooted up the valley and called his flight down. Gingerly, other P-47s came down through the clouds. 'Follow me, boys,' said Brooking. And in a single file they roared up the valley just a few feet above the ground and a few feet beneath the clouds. As they reached the enemy column, a tremendous concentration of flak came up to meet them. But they crashed through and dropped their bombs.

Captain Jim Wells, of Houston, Texas, dropped his two bombs right in the middle of eight German tanks travelling a foot or so apart. At this point the German column was on a road running on the top of a hill. Two of the tanks disappeared altogether. The other six were literally thrown off the road. They lay on their sides at the bottom of the hill with their lone 88s twisted at crazy angles. There were two big craters blocking the road. The rest of the flight had the same luck with their bombs. Then they split up to strafe. They made three passes apiece and many fires began to burn on the road beneath them.

After that Brooking tried to reform the flight. But Lt Wayne Price, of Sunnyside, California, said, 'I've been hit too badly, Brook. I'll have to try to belly-land somewhere'. Price disappeared, flames streaming from his P-47. He showed up at the base the next day . . .

Meanwhile:

'They've got me, too,' said Wells.

'Badly?' asked Brooking.

'No, I think I can make it home', he said.

'Okay', said Brooking. 'You escort him home, Thoman. I'll stay here alone and direct traffic.'

Brooking called fighter control at Ninth TAC and told them to send every available fighter-bomber in the area. 'When they get here', said Brooking, 'tell them to call in to me and I'll put them on the target. There's plenty for all.'

While he waited for the first flight to show up, he investigated two other valleys heading west and found them teeming with tanks and armoured vehicles. Every time he found an enemy column, Brooking strafed the lead vehicle from the rear, setting it on fire and blocking the road. Since the roads generally ran along defile hills in the mountain terrain, this would stop the column. As soon as a column got underway again, Brooking came back to block it off.

Flights of Thunderbolts began to arrive from all over France and Belgium. As they hit the area they checked in with Brooking who located them and led them through to the target. If they couldn't find the target, Brooking would go down through the clouds, strafing, to show them where the enemy tanks were. Now the horrible weather was an advantage. Thunderbolts played hide and seek in a fifty-foot opening and the German ack-ack couldn't spot them before they disappeared into the clouds. Some of the flights had tremendous luck. Major Arlo Henry of East Dearborn, Michigan, found a genuine hole in the clouds and dive-bombed deliberately. His flight accounted for forty enemy vehicles. Captain Neale Worley, of Emporia, Kansas, found the same hole and accounted for forty more. Colonel Stecker led the last flight just before dark closed in to end the battle of Stavelot.

The next day a high-ranking officer at First Army phoned Major General Hoyts Vandenburg, who commanded the Ninth Air Force. 'Thank God,' he said, 'for your men yesterday.'

The day after that, a teletype came in from First Army. 'It is now established,' the teletype said, 'that the fighter-bomber attack on the column heading westward from Stavelot inflicted damage which caused it to change its direction to the south.'

The day after that, the First Army units advancing into the valleys where the battle had taken place reported that damage done to the advancing German column had greatly exceeded the Ninth Air Force claims of 107 vehicles destroyed.

Later on, Colonel Stecker wrote official recommendations for both Major Motzenbecker and Major Brooking, which, he said, would probably be ignored because someone would look at the recommendations and remark, 'Why, they didn't shoot down a single enemy aircraft'.

38 *The Skies of Iwo Jima*

Leyte Gulf, Luzon, Iwo Jima, Okinawa – the United States Navy's fliers were in all these epic Pacific battles and shot down literally hundreds and hundreds of enemy planes. This chronicle cannot cover every one of these events, of course. But the brief adventures of a single ship, the USS *Lunga Point*, summed up the whole drama of one of these four famous fights – Iwo Jima. It was February 1945 when the escort carrier had its narrowest escape, actually during the Iwo Jima operation. All hands seemed to have a premonition that they were about to undergo a severe attack. Tenseness was tangible throughout the ship.

Then just at dusk, a group of Kamikaze bombers launched an aerial torpedo attack. The planes could not even be seen until within range of *Lunga Point*'s guns. They shot the first down and he fell in flames to the starboard quarter, about 200 feet from the ship. The second was hit but turned and flew low over the carrier's stern and out of sight. It probably ended up in the sea.

US Marines plant the Stars and Stripes on summit of Mount Suribachi after the capture of Iwo Jima

More than fifty Japanese ships lie sunk, or shattered at Manila Bay in the Philippines as a result of attacks by USN carrier-based 'planes. 9 January 1945

A white plume of water hurled skyward by a bomb from a land-based Japanese bomber, covers the stern of a USN aircraft carrier (background) just as the carrier's anti-aircraft guns trap the enemy 'plane with their fire. The 'plane, now lost behind a cloud, plummeted to the sea a few moments later. Crewmen of the American carrier in the foreground, on whose deck a Hellcat fighter-bomber is spotted, are also firing their guns furiously at attacking 'planes. The action took place on 24 October 1944 during the historic second Battle of the Philippine Seas

Surface units of a USN task force: nine aircraft carriers, twelve battleships and a large number of cruisers, destroyers and supply ships, ride at anchor in the waters of an atoll lagoon in the Marshall Islands of the Central Pacific. They represent only a part of the powerful task force whose combined aerial and surface power hammered into submission heavily fortified Japanese strongholds in the Marshalls

Crew members and airmen walk cautiously over the sloping deck of the crippled USS *Yorktown*, examining the damage done by Japanese air raiders in the Battle of Midway. The three-day air and sea fight off Midway Island 5/6 July 1942, resulted in Japanese losses of four aircraft carriers sunk, three battleships damaged, two heavy cruisers sunk, three heavy cruisers damaged, one light cruiser damaged, three destroyers sunk and several damaged with heavy losses in lighter craft and aircraft. US losses, which were light, included the aircraft carrier *Yorktown* and the destroyer *Hammann*

They hardly had time to reload their guns when the third and fourth torpedo bombers came straight toward them in suicide attacks. They made easy targets for the baby flattop's guns, which shot them down quickly. One burst into a frightening mushroom of fire as it struck the sea 300 feet off. The fourth bounded blazing across the flight-deck, after shearing off his starboard wing and landing wheel as he hit the afterpart of the bridge. The plane sprayed gasoline all over the deck, actually setting fire to it before it bounced into the water and exploded on the port beam. Several sailors in the port gun batteries were burned by the plane's scorching fuselage. Fire parties quickly extinguished the flight deck, and first aid treated the men's burns. Meanwhile the bombers had gone but had dropped three torpedoes which, while all this went on, whistled by *Lunga Point* with only a few gallons of water between them and the bows.

The significance of these misses was brought home to everyone on board as they watched their sister ship *Bismarck Sea* go down from an exactly similar bomber attack just 2,000 yards on the starboard quarter.

Iwo Jima created chances for heroism among the navy fliers on Lunga. Lieutenant 'Bud' Foster had accompanied other planes on a direct support hop over Iwo Jima in his Wildcat fighter; and a part of his mission was to drop napalm fire bomb on his target. When he got there, however, he found that the bomb release proved faulty and he could not get rid of the bomb.

After completing the rest of his mission, Foster returned to their operating area and called the captain to tell him of the situation. Should he bale out or try to land on *Lunga Point?* The skipper told Lieutenant (jg) 'Max' Palena, the aviation ordnance officer, to report to the bridge, where they went into a detailed discussion of the release system of the bomb racks. They decided to help Foster to get rid of the stubborn bomb. To do so, they put him through almost every conceivable manoeuvre, including 'Flying on his back,' but even fifteen minutes of this failed to shake off the bomb.

The captain then called Admiral Durgin over the TBS (Transmission between ships), and asked him for advice. It was an awkward decision. If Foster baled out, he would probably be picked up unharmed but they would have lost a precious plane. If they brought him in, Foster – and many others – might die as a result. Even the ship itself might be sunk.

Admiral Burgin left it up to the captain, saying, 'Do what you think best. Good luck, CAT'.

The captain and Palena then went into the possibility of the bomb's fuse being armed and the chances of the bomb being released by the impact of a landing. To check whether or not the bomb was armed, the captain got one of the torpedo bomber pilots to fly wing-on to Foster, as close as possible, to see if the arming wire was still secured to the rack. The pilot's reply was 'Affirmative'.

'Do you want to try to land aboard?' the captain asked Foster by radio.

'If you think it advisable, I'll land aboard, captain', Foster radioed.

Catalina flying boats patrol US invasion fleet entering Lingayen Gulf during the Philippines campaign of January-June 1945

Foster knew his life was at stake. For ten more minutes he tried to shake off the bomb by manoeuvring, but it was no good. Foster came into the landing circle. All planes were taken below to the hangar deck except two for which no room could be found. All fire parties manned their stations and everyone took a long breath or two. Foster first made a pass at the ship, flying close to the bridge, so that the captain and Palena could see that the bomb was still secure. Then the captain advised Foster to land.

Commander Eastwold and Lieutenant (jg) Palena were the only ones on the flight deck when Foster came in with a very good landing. No one breathed at all now. The Wildcat touched down. For a fleeting instant the bomb remained intact on the plane. Then the impact of the arresting gear loosened it. The bomb bounded down the deck toward the parked planes. If it hit them, it might go off, throwing liquid fire all over the ship. Even sink her.

Palena was standing near the bridge block, and as the bomb slid beneath the third barrier, he jumped out after it and caught it between the barrier and one of the planes. He straddled the bomb and yelled,

'Somebody give me a wrench!'

A big pipe wrench appeared out of nowhere, but it was too big.

Seconds later, Aomz Glup, one of Palena's ordnance men, ran across the flight deck with a small wrench for him to use in removing the fuse. As Palena was working on it, the executive officer stood beside the fire parties who had their hoses trained on the bomb and Palena. All the while, Palena knew of the chance that it might go up. Seconds seemed like hours as he withdrew the fuse. Then suddenly out it came. They threw the bomb over the side and all was well. After Iwo Jima came Okinawa and eventual victory.

39 *Assault on the Rhine*

Crossing the Rhine marked the start of the first phase in the assault against Germany. The enemy was being driven back in Northern Italy, and the Riviera 7th Army Forces had long since linked up with the Allies advancing eastward further north.

Now on a day in March 1945 the greatest airborne offensive of the war was about to be launched: more than 40,000 troops landed right in the *Reich*. Typical of all these airborne forces were the 45th Troop Carrier Group, First Allied Airborne Army.

One of their gliders was carrying a howitzer team. As the men loaded their equipment, some were silent and serious while others joked. They had been slated to take off at 0749 hours, but this was put back half an hour to 0819 hours. As they accelerated along the runway, with the tow ropes tautening, they used every foot of the field before becoming airborne. From the astrodome, or miniature sun-porch, in the towplane, they could get a good bird's-eye view of the formation. The towplanes and gliders all looked a pretty sight in the sun – until the first glider fell. It broke loose from the towplane and immediately began circling frantically for an emergency landing. But as it hovered birdlike about 200 feet above the ground, the wings buckled and it dived nose-first into the ground. No one got out of it.

Staff Sergeant Ernest Collins was sitting in the radio operator's seat when the glider fell. He lit a cigarette and said: 'Anyone got a pencil? I want to check my bomber code.'

1000 hours: ahead of them, the first parachutists to drop in Germany itself were falling from their planes. As well as the largest mission in troop-carrying history, this was also to be the largest in distance – nearly 600 miles.

Mike Maciocia, T/Sgt, had a picture of Betty stuck up in the plane. And a brightly coloured scarf of heroes hung from one of the overhead spars for luck.

They were nearing their objective now and trying to identify all the different aircraft that the USAAF had flung around them. Snub-nosed P-47s; P-38s lazing and zooming; British Spitfires on the hunt for the enemy; and A-26 medium bombers on patrol, passing them as if they were standing still.

Near the Rhine they could pick out the cratered areas on both sides of the river. Far below, two P-47s lay smoking on the ground after emergency landings. Time getting short now. They flashed the ten-minute signal to the two gliders behind them. First Lieutenant George Bewel

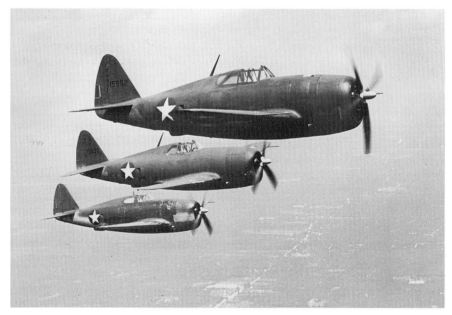

Three P-47s in stepped down echelon

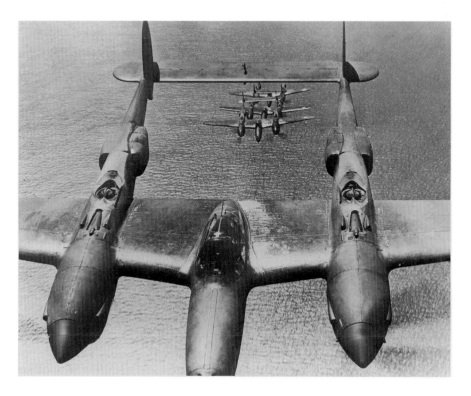

P-38s in line astern

came back to put on his chest parachute and flak-suit. The rest of them did the same.

They were waiting for the first ack-ack and the crew passed the moments arguing about which would be the safest place in the plane if it were hit. The pilot said he was glad to be up front in his cabin with its flak-pad upholstery, and told the rest of them to crowd up forward if they felt like it.

Mike Maciocia took a look at Betty and patted the gas tank he was sitting on. 'I'm staying right on this gas tank. If they hit the tank we've had it anyway. So I'm staying right here.'

Three minutes away from their gliders' landing zone, they were no longer just anticipating flak – they were getting it. Air-bursts banged in the sky and tracers curved courses towards them. A C-47 went down blazing at five o'clock: direction not time.

They passed over the parachute dropping zone, where thousands of white patches broke the brown terrain, indicating that the paratroops were already fighting it out below.

At long last, over their own landing zone, covered by a haze of artificial fog, Sgt Collins grabbed the Aldis lamp and signalled hurriedly through the astrodome for their gliders to cut loose. They seemed to drop right away from the towplane, and become mislaid in the chaos of burning planes and flak.

Two other gliders glittered into flame and fell fast. A towplane flying to the rear of the howitzer team's aircraft took a flak shot square in its nose. The plane dipped, emitted three parachutes, and then as someone fought for control, it pulled into a steep climb. But the aircraft was doomed. A moment later it stalled, nosed over, and described a straight line into the ground.

The team's aircraft was down to 700 feet, low enough to hear a rifle crack. But now, with their load lightened, the motors roared and the pilot steered his plane through a black-and-white polka dotted sky. They were sweating somewhat. After all, this might well have been their last sortie in Europe and none of them wanted to get it at that stage.

It was not until they passed the Rhine on the way back that the crew relaxed, though they realised that on this occasion they had the easiest job. Down there on the ground the howitzer team were already in action. Down there . . .

In the landing zone, the paratroops had been down for two hours and were advancing when the gliders appeared. They came in orderly pairs, bouncing before a 100 mph wind from the propwashes of the towplanes. Then a sudden slowing as the towlines fell, followed by the crack-crack of bullets through cloth wings.

That was when they heard flak instead of simply seeing it as harmless balls of smoke in the mid-distance. That was when they realised how slow and ungainly a glider really was. That was when the ground still seemed so far away. As the gliders glided down.

Gliders on the ground after the airborne landing near the Rhine: 25 March 1945

Not all of them found their landing zones. The 20-miles-square area of the drop lay in a smoke-shroud: artillery smoke, the smoke from burning buildings, and the smoke of their own smoke-shells marking the landing zone for the pilots. Two divisions of men being dropped by parachute and glider into enemy terrain.

The area of the drop was much-wooded and interspersed with small farms, their fields forming the dropping and landing zones. The paratroops preceding the gliders landed roughly as planned, and moved out to their goals.

But many of the gliders made landfall in fields some way from their intended zone. Many, too, splintered into matchwood or plywood and hung limply from trees. One struck an obstacle with its tail while landing, causing it to bounce into the air and circle. Then its nose struck something and it looped for a second time. The whole crew were killed.

The last aerial photographs of the area were taken on the afternoon before the jump. At that time, the photos showed the chosen fields as clear, but in the few hours since then the Germans had somehow made several changes.

Two gliders loaded with medics landed in a field where three machine-guns formed a defensive triangle around a searchlight. As the gliders sailed in, the guns opened fire, raking them from both flanks. The medics tumbled out complete in their newly painted Red Cross helmets. They were unarmed. They were shot in a crossfire from a range of 20 yards. One of the medics was a young Harvard Medical School graduate who had just finished his training at the Mayo Hospital in Rochester, Minnesota, before entering the army. He was among the first to die.

A paratroop captain was landing near one of the zones, a field that adjoined a double-track railway intersected by a road at a grade-crossing. Around the crossing hung some trees and a clump of woods shaped itself darkly north of the railroad. The captain apparently saw the woods and jerked the shroud lines of his parachute to slip past them. But he did not see the trees around the grade-crossing until it was too late. His 'chute was fouled by the top of one of them, and there he hung in plain view of some Germans in the woods beyond the tracks. The captain swung his body like a pendulum in desperate throes to break the parachute loose. He was swinging downward from the peak point of one arc when a machine-gun got him.

Wherever the troops went, they stopped to look for friends they had not been able to trace. They went from parachute to parachute, lifting the silk to glance at a face, then dropping it. If they recognised someone across a field, they frequently dashed through fire to get to him. They never knew when they picked up a parachute whether or not they would find a body beneath it.

Almost all the opposition came from ack-ack. The German crews had billets in little farmhouses dotting the landing zones. Each of these houses became a separate small fortress, which had to be reduced by 75 mm pack artillery or cleaned out at closer quarters.

This nasty work was going on when the Liberators boomed overhead, following the glider trains with additional supplies dropped by 'chute. Their pilots took no chances of error. Coming in low in front of the fierce flak, they swept across their targets at a mere 100 feet to toss the supplies exactly where they were intended to go.

As one plane came over, some of the soldiers on the ground saw a man in its doorway struggling with a heavy load. The bundle broke loose, and toppled the man out as well. He pulled his 'chute ring frantically, but it scarcely had time to trail out in a loose stream before he was bounced along the ground, end over end – like the core of an apple thrown from a moving car. They never knew if he survived or not. It seemed unlikely.

That night, between bursts of artillery and one strafing plane, the Yanks had a few moments to rest and relax. They had fallen from the sky on to enemy soil.

As a direct result of the Rhine crossings, the Allies encircled the vital Ruhr area of Germany, and then while they reduced this at their leisure, other units raced eastward toward Berlin and the Russians advancing westward. By 7 May 1945 it was all over in Europe.

40 *The Atomic Bomb and Victory*

While the US Third Fleet and British Task Force 37 were striking at the very heart of Japan – Tokyo's airfields – the cruiser *Indianapolis* set sail from San Francisco on a crucial and top-secret mission.

By 24 July 1945, the Allied fleets were in virtual command of all the waters washing the quickly diminishing Japanese Empire. The fliers of the Third Fleet found some of the remnants of the enemy navy at anchor in Kure harbour. Around the clock, USN planes pulverised them with bombs, bullets and rockets. Hit after hit wrecked the Japanese warships, trapped in the harbour below. Then night fighters and torpedo planes intensified the attack.

In two days the Third Fleet sank or damaged a quarter of a million tons of enemy warships and got 130 planes while losing only 32 of their own. Some of these pilots were saved, however. Ensign Herb Law, flying from the ship *Belleau Wood*, was one.

He was badly hit in the left leg while attacking an airfield, and his plane started smoking. He was too low to bale out, and somehow landed and escaped from the agonised aircraft. As he tried to bandage his bleeding leg, a woman ran out of the bushes and fired at him from ten yards, but missed. She ran off for help, and the enemy soon found him.

They took off his clothes, bound him, and gave him no food or water for three days. He was beaten with clubs, fists, leather straps and, in general, used as a judo guinea pig. But he survived to tell his story.

On 28 July, the navy fliers returned to the scene of the shambles at Kure and finished off all the ships they could see there. An air of expectant inevitability surrounded the events of those last few days of July. Throughout 28 July, too, navy planes focused their fire on the battleship *Haruna*, which stayed afloat for a few hours, but at last gave up and sank in shallow water. The crowning disgrace to the enemy was to see her turrets still sticking above the level of the water as it lapped around them. By nightfall the Japanese navy no longer existed as a serious fighting force. Only a few stray submarines and other small craft still survived in the open seas.

That night, more planes pitched into the important port of Hamamatsu. Another scene was designed for the climax to the whole war.

To tell it, we return to *Indianapolis*, which had left San Francisco the day the Third Fleet planes were raiding Tokyo. The ship sailed under the Golden Gate at 0836 hours – with a big box on board.

This wooden box contained the main nuclear parts of the first atomic

B-29 Superfortress similar to those used to drop the atomic bombs, seen here unloading conventional bombs. The extensive bomb-bay and defensive armament are clearly visible

bomb. Tests of the bomb had just been completed at the time of the Potsdam peace conference, then in progress in Europe, and President Truman got news of its success while he was actually there. The Allies agreed to use it only if the Japanese refused to give in.

The wake of *Indianapolis* spread quickly westward from San Francisco to Pearl Harbor. After refuelling, she surged on again, this time to Tinian, anchoring in the harbour there about 1100 hours on 26 July. The vital section of the bomb was unloaded, and two days later the rest of the nuclear parts for both the Hiroshima and Nagasaki bombs arrived by air.

On 29 July, with her part played, *Indianapolis* sailed unescorted out of Tinian on her way from Leyte to Guam. The famous cruiser made the usual zigzag course during the day until darkness fell. Then she straightened up for a normal night. But by one of those million-to-one chances, a solitary submarine of the shattered Japanese fleet happened to be lying on the surface actually at right angles to the course which *Indianapolis* was plying – and at exactly the right range for firing torpedoes. The captain of the submarine waited in the gloom of those first few minutes of 30 July, until the cruiser sailed unaware into the trap.

The Japanese captain aimed forward and hit the bow area twice.

The great cruiser began to settle by the bow. With all her complex communication gear struck, it was hard to give orders. Soon afterwards, Captain Charles B. McVay III, was forced to give the order, 'Abandon ship.'

In the nightmare of that night, no SOS signal went out from her radio. And it was four days later when the pilot of a Ventura reconnaissance plane chanced to see the oil slick from the sunken ship – and the dots of many men's heads kept afloat by their life jackets. Eventually, 316 men were rescued from *Indianapolis* . . .

At 0245 hours on 6 August 1945 the crews of the three B-29s scheduled to drop the first atomic bomb went aboard their aircraft after a tropical rainstorm. The bomb-carrying plane took off first and went up to 4,000 feet. It was commanded by Colonel Paul Tibbetts.

The bomb commander assembled the nuclear weapon slowly, with infinite care. Then they all ate breakfast, while the B-29 throbbed on toward Iwo. At dawn they met the other two aircraft and together the trio climbed to 10,000 feet, where the weather was better.

They had been in the clouds most of the time till then, and the rain had spattered the screens. But otherwise it still seemed to them all a quiet flight. Except that they carried the means of ending the war in a single flash of fission. They did not talk much now.

Before climbing they had armed the bomb. Now the bombers gained altitude. Navigation was right – to the minute and the mile.

They saw Hiroshima huddled below, far below. The weather had become clear, yet with a slight haze. One of the two escorting B-29s circled to come in some miles behind the bomb-dropper to take pictures. The other one stayed on their beam.

Only about four minutes more. Then three. Then two. The bombardier gazed through his periscope, motionless – if not emotionless. One and a half minutes. After that he did not touch the bombsight once.

They were coming in high and fast now. The second hands of their watches crept around to zero and a hush radiated through the plane. The sky seemed still, horizons muted. Then the bomb fell, within fifteen seconds of the exact moment that had been planned six months earlier.

The B-29 turned sharply to try to get as clear as possible of the stupendous shock which would soon be arising. They lived through a strange ninety seconds more, while the bomb dropped.

A flash in the firmament. The bomb burst vividly, vehemently. A ball of fire from the flashpoint, growing each semi-second. The historic mushroom-shaped cloud pumped up bigger and bigger. The plane was banking at about that moment, and snapped like a tin roof. The crew looked at one another. Then they heard the noise. A sharp crack and crash followed by a long roll like thunder.

They circled around only a mile or so above the holocaust, taking pictures of the cloud that was boiling before their eyes. Black smoke, and

After Hiroshima, the second atomic bomb was dropped on Nagasaki. The plume rose to 20,000 feet – nearly four miles high. Then the Japanese surrendered. The fight for the air was finally won

orange, blue, grey. That was all they saw, for the dust hid the whole city. They could not speak, only watch hypnotised.

Suddenly it was over for them, as the breeze caught the ball, breaking it into a raging, ragged, billowing cloud. They headed for home. The flight meant a long seven-hour haul and most of them slept some of the time, for they had been awake for a day and a half.

By mid-afternoon the three B-29s buzzed down at 300 mph, lost height and landed. The Japanese had refused to surrender. Now 70,000 of them were killed by the bomb, and as many injured.

Everything up to a mile from the flashpoint was destroyed, except for a small number of reinforced concrete buildings designed to withstand earthquake shock. Even multi-storey brick buildings had been demolished. Beyond that range, roof tiles had been bubbled or melted by the flash heat. And there were many other eccentricities. People scorched to walls in grotesque silhouette. Some 60,000 of the 90,000 buildings in the city were either destroyed or severely damaged: two in every three structures. The atomic age had been born.

Three days later, it all began again. The nightmare of Nagasaki started at 1102 hours on the morning of 9 August. And it was only because of bad weather that Nagasaki was the target at all for the second atomic bomb.

The town lay at the head of a long bay, forming the best natural harbour on the southern Japanese home island of Kyushu. The main commercial and residential area of the city was on a small plain near the end of the bay. Two rivers split by a mountain spur formed the two valleys in which the city lay. This spur and the irregular layout of the land reduced the area of destruction after the bomb, so that at first glance Nagasaki appeared to have been less devastated than Hiroshima. The heavily built-up area was confined to less than four square miles out of a total of some thirty-five square miles of the whole city.

Nagasaki had been one of the largest seaports in southern Japan and was very important for its varied industries, such as ordnance, ships, military equipment and other war materials. In contrast to many modern aspects of Nagasaki, the dwellings were without exception flimsy wood or wood-frame buildings, with wooden walls, perhaps plaster, and tile roofs. Many of the smaller industries and businesses were also in this kind of wooden building or flimsily-mounted masonry erections.

Nagasaki had never been subjected to large-scale bombing before the atomic bomb. But on 1 August 1945, some high explosives had actually been dropped on the city. A few of these bombs had hit the shipyards and dock areas in the south-west part. Several of the bombs had struck the Mitsubishi Steel and Arms Works, and half a dozen had landed at the Nagasaki Medical School and Hospital, with three direct hits on buildings there.

While the damage from these bombs had been relatively small, it had created considerable concern, and quite a number of people – principally school children – had been evacuated to rural areas for safety, so reducing the population actually in the city at the time of the atomic attack.

The morning of 9 August: an air raid alarm echoed through Nagasaki at about 0750 hours local time, but the all-clear followed forty minutes later. When only two B-29 Super-Fortresses were sighted at 1053 hours, the Japanese apparently assumed that they were only on reconnaissance. No further air raid alarm was deemed necessary.

Dead on 1100 hours, the observation B-29 dropped instruments attached to three parachutes, and at 1102 hours the other aircraft released the atomic bomb. Commander F.L. Ashworth, United States Navy, was in technical command of the bomb, charged with the task of assuring that it was successfully dropped at the proper place and time. This second atomic mission was much more eventful for the crews than the first had been. Again, the men had been specially selected and trained. But then bad weather introduced some momentous complications.

Commander Ashworth described the whole operation like this:

'The night of our take-off was one of tropical rain squalls, and flashes of lightning stabbed into the darkness with disconcerting regularity. The weather forecast told us of storms all the way from the Marianas to the "Empire".

'Our rendezvous was to be off the south-east coast of Kyushu, and 1,500 miles away. There we were to join with our two companion observation B-29s that took off a few minutes behind us. Skilful piloting and expert navigation brought us to the rendezvous without incident.

'About five minutes after our arrival, we were joined by the first of our B-29s. The second, however, failed to arrive, having apparently been thrown off its course by storms during the night. We waited thirty minutes and then proceeded without the second plane toward the target area.

'During the approach to the target, the special instruments installed in the plane told us that the bomb was ready to function. We were prepared to drop the second atomic bomb on Japan.

'But fate was against us, for the target was completely obscured by smoke and haze. Three times we attempted bombing runs, but without success. Then with anti-aircraft fire bursting around us and with a number of enemy fighters coming up after us, we headed for our secondary target – Nagasaki.

'The bomb burst with a blinding flash, and a huge column of black smoke swirled up toward us.

'Out of this column of smoke there boiled a great swirling mushroom of grey smoke – luminous with red, flashing flame – that reached to 40,000 feet in less than eight minutes. Below through the clouds we could see the pall of black smoke ringed with fire that covered what had been the industrial area of Nagasaki.

'By this time our fuel supply was dangerously low, so after one quick circle of Nagasaki, we headed direct for Okinawa for an emergency landing and refuelling.'

The bomb actually exploded high over the industrial valley of Nagasaki, almost midway between the Mitsubishi Works in the south and the Mitsubishi-Urakami Ordnance Works (for torpedoes) in the north, the two main targets of the city.

Nearly everything within half a mile of the flashpoint vanished – including heavy structures. And including people. All Japanese homes were destroyed up to three times this distance – one-and-a-half miles. Within a radius of as much as three-quarters of a mile, both people and animals died almost instantaneously.

So to the summary of damage at Nagasaki: 14,000 dwellings were destroyed and 5,400 half-destroyed. This destruction was limited by the layout of the city. And the casualties: the source which recorded the Hiroshima figures as 66,000 dead and 69,000 injured, gives the equivalent Nagasaki totals as 39,000 dead and 25,000 injured.

The war was over within a week.

Annex A *Boeing B-17 Flying Fortress*

Surprising as it may seem, the Flying Fortress was conceived as far back as 1934 in response to a United States Army Air Corps competitive specification. At that time the bomber that became a byword for the American attacks on Europe was really thought of more in defensive than offensive air war terms. The time sequence of early development was as follows:

First flight on 28 July 1935, averaged in excess of 250 mph during a trans-America trip soon afterwards, and began to be delivered to the USAAC from the spring of 1937. The Flying Fortress had the designation B-17. In January 1939 the earliest example of a B-17 with turbo-supercharged engines underwent favourable flying tests and thereafter went into production.

Of course the great revolution of the Flying Fortress in the pre-war days of the 1930s was a four-engine conception – a revolution in its era. Added to this power unit, the overall aeroplane design gave an advanced, clean,

B-17Gs bombing somewhere in Europe

low-slung appearance for a bomber. So the initial 39 Flying Fortresses were B-17Bs powered by four 1,000 hp Wright R-1820-51 engines incorporating the successful exhaust-driven superchargers. First deliveries reached the Army in June 1939 but only one-third of the ninety ordered reached delivery stage as war broke out in Europe.

The Flying Fortress had metal midwing cantilever monoplane wings giving the look more of actual low-slinging. The fuselage was a semi-monocoque structure, very tough in flying operations, while the bomber tapered to a cantilever monoplane tail with aluminium-alloy frame. Its four engines were fitted in the undersides of their respective nacelles. Six to ten aircrew were required by the Flying Fortress. Two pilots sat side by side just ahead of the leading edge; vulnerably placed in the nose was the bomb-aimer; the radio operator sat centrally in the body of the bomber; just behind and above the pilots' cockpit was an upper twin-gun turret; another twin-gun turret protruded below the fuselage, bulbous and uncomfortable; while a final gun position sprouted towards the tail. The bomber besported six .50 in machine guns and could carry some 6,000 lb of bomb-load.

The B-17C was powered by four 1,200 hp Wright R-01820-65 engines and some of these represented the earliest Fortresses to achieve actual air combat, with the RAF during a daylight raid on the French port of Brest in July 1941. This was followed by high-altitude day raids on Germany in the same year. As a result of experience thus acquired, B-17D and B-17E went into production. B-17E represented what has been termed major re-thinking of some of the important aspects and details. So when this type received the go-ahead on a massive scale, it included gun turrets driven by power plus the tail gun position. By now the total of machine guns had grown to eleven. B-17F added practical improvements like extra fuel tanks on the wings, while provision was also contrived for as heavy a bomb complement as two 4,000-pounders. Then came the B-17G with R-01820-97 engines and some armament modifications, such as a remote-controlled chin turret instead of nose guns controlled by hand. Other versions were a photographic reconnaissance B-17F Fortress as a special VIP transport.

By the time the B-17E had gone into large-scale output, the Flying Fortress was really powerful in attack and in defence, with the tail turret and ball turret among its additions. Both in Europe and the Pacific air theatres, the Flying Fortress with its bristling guns and bombs went to war. As many as 3,400 B-17Fs were built, and when a particular B-17G joined the USAAF, it represented the 5,000th Flying Fortress built by Boeing – the occasion being marked by the signatures of employees covering the entire exterior surface! Eventually, over 12,500 Flying Fortresses were constructed, including four for the USN for anti-submarine and coastguard duties. Apart from Boeing, Fortresses were built by Douglas and Vega.

The B-17E arrived in Java as early as February 1942 and undertook the majority of the air bombing in the Pacific theatre for the rest of that year. Although in 1943 they were being replaced for the further flying Liberator. After a 17 August 1942 raid against the Germans, Flying Fortresses participated in the 1943 precision bombing offensive against the Nazis and their occupied countries. Huge tonnage of bombs were dropped, but despite the damage caused the raids on Ploesti and Schweinfurt in successive months of August and September 1943 involved heavy bomber losses at the hands of *Luftwaffe* fighters. The Flying Fortresses executed their duty. So did their aircrews. But at a price in precious life.

The Specification of the B17-G was as follows:

Engines	Four 1,200 hp Wright R-1820-97
Span	103 ft 9 in
Length	74 ft 4 in
Height	19 ft 1 in
Weight empty	32,720 lb
Weight loaded	60,000 lb
Crew number	Ten
Maximum speed	287 mph
Service ceiling	35,000 ft
Normal range	2,000 miles
Armament	Thirteen .50 in machine guns; up to 17,600 lb for short distances

Annex B   *Grumman Hellcat*

From the Wildcat was evolved the Hellcat single-seat carrier-borne naval fighter. This turned out to be a more powerful fighter conception by the same manufacturers and an even faster one, too. The Hellcat was really born during 1941, about the time that the Wildcat went into production for the USN. So speedy was its development that the actual design dated from early 1942 and the experimental prototype left the ground in the summer of '42. There seems to be a slight disagreement as to exactly which month it did in fact first fly! Anyway whenever the date, the Hellcat F6F-3 was a resounding triumph and went into full-scale manufacture late in 1942 – when it succeeded the Wildcat at the Grumman assembly plant, the latter transferring to General Motors. The initial service models started to reach their USN destinations very early in 1943, while the actual primary war action involving Hellcats dated from September that year – the fighters being flown off a carrier task force during an assault against the Pacific target of Marcus Island. Continuing the production story to the end of the war, over 12,000 Hellcats had been made by late

A pilot exits rapidly from burning Hellcat

A Hellcat receiving 'fire treatment' on crash landing after battle damage

1945, including 4,000 of the F6F-3 and 6,000+ of the F6F-5.

The Hellcat F6F was basically a mid-wing cantilever monoplane, and had that comparable slightly bloated body of the Wildcat. There was a retractable tail-wheel and an arrester-hook for aircraft-carrier use. It was powered by a Pratt and Whitney 2000 hp R-2800-10W Double Wasp engine and had an enclosed cockpit over the wing, again similar to the Wildcat from the same stable and thus the same design team. The pilot was well protected by armour. Three .50 in machine guns were placed in each wing.

The F6F-5 was slightly different from the F6F-3. The F6F-5 incorporated a restyled cowling, fresh ailerons, better armour for the pilot, and stronger tail surfaces. It was also arranged to take a couple of 1,000 lb bombs below the centre. Alternatively drop tanks could be selected instead of bombs when longer flights might be required, while the fighter could also carry rockets. The F6F-5 was known as the Hellcat II.

The British Fleet Air Arm received some 250 Hellcat Is under Lend-Lease, these being dubbed Gannets for some time. The FAA later on got Hellcat IIs to a total of nearly 1,000. Some of these were adapted to take wing-mounted radar, like the USN F6F-5Ns – the N designation signifying night fighter. The British codification was Hellcat FMk II meaning fighter and NF Mk II meaning night fighter. So the Hellcat served successfully with both the USN and the FAA, a sophisticated fighter emerging from a considerable lineage of such naval combat designs. Swifter and more streamlined than the Wildcat, the Hellcat took over where the former left off. Together they more or less won the naval fighter war – all 20,000 of the combined output of these two famous fighters.

The specification of the Hellcat F6F was:

Engine	One 2,000 hp Pratt and Whitney R-2800-IOW Double Wasp
Span	42 ft 10 in
Length	33 ft 7 in
Height	13 ft 1 in
Weight empty	9,042 lb
Weight loaded	11,381 lb
Crew number	One
Maximum speed	375 mph at 17,300 ft
Service ceiling	37,800 ft
Normal range	1,090 miles
Armament	Six .50 in machine guns; two 1,000 lb bombs or rocket projectiles

Annex C   *Boeing B-29 Superfortress*

The 99-feet-long Superfortress has gone down into aviation history as the aircraft entrusted with dropping the two atomic bombs on Japan in 1945. The *Enola Gay* was the bomber making the attack against Hiroshima on 6 August and then another Superfortress released the second atomic bomb over Nagasaki on 9 August. The long-range heavy bomber has the designation of B-29 and was developed to supersede the B-17 Flying Fortress. Its ultimate achievements turned out to be far more than only the atomic attacks.

The actual aeronautical studies for such a bomber began towards the end of the 1930s and the original specification from the American War Department emanated in January/February 1940, with war in Europe already a reality. The official terminology for the bomber was a Hemisphere Defense Weapon. Boeing designed Model 341 originally, later modified into Model 345 to accommodate additional requirements. This latter model was one of four submissions to the USAAF, which gave Boeing the go-ahead on 24 August 1940 to produce three prototypes. The first of these flew on 21 September 1942, and the second on

Early Superfortresses

A formation of B-29 Superfortresses unloading their bombs

28 December. Even before the maiden flight the B-29 had been ordered in bulk, and by the end of 1942 the figure stood in excess of 1,500. Boeing could not possibly cope with such a vast total and so the Superfortress was also made by Bell and by Martin. Four plants including the two Boeing works were thus involved in the project. The date quoted for the first Boeing Wichita plant B-29 was 15 April 1943; and the first one flew from the Renton production plant of Boeing at the end of that year.

By the middle of 1943, however, the initial Superfortress unit had already been formed. The first pre-production B-29 flew on 26 June and the unit began to receive deliveries the following month. Within a year, the Superfortresses were in operation. It had been agreed that the B-29 would be restricted to use against targets in the Pacific was and not be considered for Europe. So on 5 June 1944, as Eisenhower's forces were actually preparing or sailing for Normandy, the Superfortress went into action. Initially using bases in India and China, the B-29s successfully bombed enemy-held railyards at Bangkok in Siam. Then ten days later came the start of pulverising raids on Japan itself launched from China bases.

The build-up of bombers and all their attendant equipment began about the same stage, the Mariana Islands providing no fewer than five bases for the great aircraft. When it is borne in mind that each one of these Mariana airfield complexes were conceived to cope with 180 Superfortresses, the scale of the forthcoming operations against the

Japanese mainland can quickly be gauged. From the Marianas and also from Guam, the Superfortresses began the series of remorseless raids – often employing up to 500 B-29s in one attack. The first raid on Tokyo came as early as June 1944 and then after eight or nine months of day attacks the B-29s started to operate at night as well. When victory in Europe was won, the Americans had already built over 3½ thousand B-29s. Then came the historic date of 6 August 1945 when Colonel Paul Tibbetts commanded the Superfortress attacking Hiroshima. The total B-29 production reached nearly 4,000, including a version modified for photographic reconnaissance.

The Superfortress was a success story from start to finish. Powered by four 2,200 hp Wright R-3350-23 engines, this ultra-heavy bomber was a mid-wing cantilever monoplane, and also with cantilever monoplane tail having single fin and rudder. The four-blade propellers measured 16 ft 7 in. The crew varied from ten to fourteen. A normal complement would comprise two pilots, navigator, engineer, bombardier, radio-operator and a quartet of gun-control operators. In the far forward crew compartment right up to the nose were housed the pilots side by side, and the bombardier. Then immediately rear of the first pilot sat the navigator, while the engineer was behind the second pilot and facing to the stern. The radio operator brought up the rear of this aircrew group. A 'crawl-tunnel' across bomb bays took the crew to another pressurised compartment with a trio of transparent 'blisters' housing gun-sighting positions. The tail gunner sat in isolation, also fully pressurised. So slight was enemy opposition to the B-29 that in the late stages of the war a substantial batch of the bombers were built with only tail guns.

B-29 Specification:

Engines	Four 2,200 hp Wright R-3350-23
Span	141 ft 3 in
Length	99 ft
Height	29 ft 7 in
Weight empty	74,500 lb
Weight loaded	135,000 lb
Crew number	10 – 14
Maximum speed	358 mph
Service ceiling	31,850 ft
Normal range	3,250 miles (longest 4,100 miles)
Armament	12 .50 in machine guns and one 20 mm cannon. 12,000 – 20,000 lb bombs

Index